Challenges and Reforms in Gulf Higher Education

This edited volume explores the educational reforms and challenges in higher education in the Gulf countries during the COVID-19 pandemic.

Featuring a truly global spread of contributors and perspectives from countries such as Bahrain, India, Georgia, Malaysia, Oman, Pakistan, and Saudi Arabia, the book navigates experience-based and practice-linked research spectrum of the ramifications of the COVID-19 pandemic on higher education. It targets key challenges such as the move to online and distance learning, the impact of job-related stress, and the preparedness of institutional risk management. Using qualitative research, autoethnographic accounts, and case study findings, the book makes recommendations for reform implementation within higher education as well as discusses the wider socio-cultural and political landscape left by the pandemic in the Gulf region.

Highlighting current trends and challenges based on the empirical works of the authors, the book will be of interest to scholars, researchers, and academics in the field of higher education, international and comparative education, and leadership strategy more specifically. Those involved with educational technology, education policy, and middle-eastern studies will also find the book of value.

Reynaldo Gacho Segumpan is Professor and Dean, City Graduate School, City University Malaysia and Fellow, Higher Education Academy, UK.

John McAlaney is Chartered Psychologist and Professor in Psychology, Bournemouth University, UK.

Educational Policy and Leadership in the Middle East and North Africa

Series editor: Khalid Arar

Series co-editors: Selahattin Turan, Sedat Gümüş, and Julia Mahfouz

This timely series addresses the need for up-to-date, current literature on educational policy, leadership, and scholarship in the Middle East and North Africa (MENA) region to support the work of researchers from developing areas and give a voice to perspectives rarely heard in the West. The series will offer important insights into the dynamics governing the interplay between global market and education forces in each local context, and will therefore further examine important political, societal, and cultural barriers that continue to hinder the development of education systems in the MENA region. Books in the series will give a critical analysis of the research undertaken and support a global understanding of the scope, scale, and complexity of educational policy, politics, and leadership in MENA countries.

Books in the series include:

Higher Education and Scientific Research in the Arabian Gulf States
Opportunities, Aspirations, and Challenges
Khalid Arar, Abdellatif Sellami, and Rania Swalhi

Demystifying Educational Leadership and Administration in the Middle East and North Africa
Challenges and Prospects
Edited by Khalid Arar, Selahattin Turan, Sedat Gümüş, Abdellatif Sellami, and Julia Mahfouz

Challenges and Reforms in Gulf Higher Education
Confronting the COVID-19 Pandemic and Assessing Future Implications
Edited by Reynaldo Gacho Segumpan and John McAlaney

For more information about the series, please visit https://www.routledge.com/Educational-Policy-and-Leadership-in-the-Middle-East-and-North-Africa/book-series/EPLMENA

Challenges and Reforms in Gulf Higher Education

Confronting the COVID-19 Pandemic and Assessing Future Implications

Edited by Reynaldo Gacho Segumpan and John McAlaney

First published 2024
by Routledge
4 Park Square, Milton Park, Abingdon, Oxon OX14 4RN

and by Routledge
605 Third Avenue, New York, NY 10158

Routledge is an imprint of the Taylor & Francis Group, an informa business

© 2024 selection and editorial matter, The Gulf Research Centre Cambridge, Reynaldo Gacho Segumpan and John McAlaney; individual chapters, the contributors

The right of The Gulf Research Centre Cambridge, Reynaldo Gacho Segumpan and John McAlaney to be identified as the authors of the editorial material, and of the authors for their individual chapters, has been asserted in accordance with sections
77 and 78 of the Copyright, Designs and Patents Act 1988.

All rights reserved. No part of this book may be reprinted or reproduced or utilised in any form or by any electronic, mechanical, or other means, now known or hereafter invented, including photocopying and recording, or in any information storage or retrieval system, without permission in writing from the publishers.

Trademark notice: Product or corporate names may be trademarks or registered trademarks, and are used only for identification and explanation without intent to infringe.

British Library Cataloguing-in-Publication Data
A catalogue record for this book is available from the British Library

Library of Congress Cataloging-in-Publication Data
Names: Segumpan, Reynaldo Gacho, editor. | McAlaney, John, 1979- editor.
Title: Challenges and reforms in Gulf higher education : confronting the Covid-19 pandemic and assessing future implications / edited by Reynaldo Gacho Segumpan and John McAlaney.
Description: Abingdon, Oxon ; New York, NY : Routledge, 2023. | Series: Educational policy and leadership in the Middle East and North Africa | Includes bibliographical references and index. |
Identifiers: LCCN 2023035788 (print) | LCCN 2023035789 (ebook) | ISBN 9781032588223 (hardback) | ISBN 9781032600420 (paperback) | ISBN 9781003457299 (ebook)
Subjects: LCSH: Education, Higher--Persian Gulf Region. | Educational change--Persian Gulf Region. | COVID-19 Pandemic, 2020---Influence.
Classification: LCC LA1431.4 .C53 2023 (print) | LCC LA1431.4 (ebook) | DDC 378.53--dc23/eng/20230809
LC record available at https://lccn.loc.gov/2023035788
LC ebook record available at https://lccn.loc.gov/2023035789

ISBN: 978-1-032-58822-3 (hbk)
ISBN: 978-1-032-60042-0 (pbk)
ISBN: 978-1-003-45729-9 (ebk)

DOI: 10.4324/9781003457299

Typeset in Galliard
by KnowledgeWorks Global Ltd.

Contents

List of Figures	viii
List of Tables	x
About the Editors	xii
List of Contributors	xiv
Preface	xxii
Acknowledgements	xxiv

Introduction   1

PART I
Understanding Regional Higher Education Reforms in a COVID-19 Context   5

1 **Potential Reforms in the GCC Higher Education Post COVID-19**   7
HAJAR MAHFOODH AND RABAB ISA SALEH ALMUQAHWI

2 **Pandemic Upsurge: Insights from Higher Education Reforms in the Gulf**   26
MUHAMMAD REHAN SHAUKAT AND ABDUL SAMI

3 **Towards a Self-Sustainable Higher Education Quality Assurance System: The NFCFFE Model for Gulf and South Asian Nations**   41
RADHA KRISHAN SHARMA

4 **Pandemic Challenges of Higher Education: Reconsidering Core Values**   60
MARIAM ORKODASHVILI

vi *Contents*

5 **Higher Education in the COVID-19 Environment: ICT-Based Perspective for GCC Countries** 74

UMARA NOREEN, ATTAYAH SHAFIQUE, AND BELLO MUSA YAKUBU

6 **Application of Risk Management on COVID-19 by Universities in the Gulf Cooperation Council (GCC)** 89

WAN NORHAYATE WAN DAUD, FAKHRUL ANWAR ZAINOL, REYNALDO GACHO SEGUMPAN, AND JOANNA SORAYA ABU ZAHARI

7 **Directions in Gulf Higher Education: Conclusion** 101

JOHN MCALANEY AND REYNALDO GACHO SEGUMPAN

PART II
Reframing Higher Education Reforms 105

8 **An Empirical Analysis of Oman's Public and Private HEIs Student's Behavioural Intention (BI) in Using E-Learning during COVID-19** 107

MOHIT KUKRETI, AMITABH MISHRA, AND VISHAL JAIN

9 **Transforming Online Teaching of a First-year Business Course: An Autoethnographic Reflection of Managing Teaching and Learning Amidst the Pandemic in the Gulf Region** 124

MARY PRECY P. AGUILAR AND REYNALDO GACHO SEGUMPAN

10 **University of Buraimi in Oman: Pandemic Lessons and Initiatives for Education Reform from Instructors' Perspectives** 137

IBRAHIM RASHID AL SHAMSI AND BOUMEDYEN SHANNAQ

11 **The Role of Internal Crisis Communication on Faculty Members Implementation of Blended Learning Practices in the Gulf** 157

RIDWAN ADETUNJI RAJI AND BAHTIAR MOHAMAD

12 **Impact of Job-related Stress on Professional and Personal Life During Coronavirus Pandemic** 174

VISHAL JAIN, AMITABH MISHRA, AND MOHIT KUKRETI

Contents vii

**13 COVID-19 and the New Normal: Re-imagining the
Future of Higher Education** 191

KHURAM SHAHZAD, MUHAMMAD REHAN SHAUKAT, AND SYEEDA
SHAFIYA

**14 Gulf Higher Education Reforms vis-à-vis the Pandemic:
Conclusion** 209

REYNALDO GACHO SEGUMPAN AND JOHN MCALANEY

Index *212*

Figures

1.1	Questions 1 and 2, round	13
1.2	Impact/Effort model	18
1.3	UDL paradigms	19
1.4	Paradigm one: Representation	20
1.5	Paradigm two: Action and expression	21
1.6	Paradigm three: Engagement	21
3.1	Layer 1 – QIA Need: PCPGDR Model	51
3.2	Layer 2 – QIA Focus: FOM Model	52
3.3	QIA Culture: OTR Model	53
3.4	QIA Framework: RII Model	54
3.5	QIA Feedback: CAFU Model	55
3.6	QIA Essentials: 4D Model	56
3.7	NFCFFE Model	57
8.1	TAM model	111
8.2	Structural model	117
10.1	Secondary data (attributes and instances number)	142
10.2	Secondary data distribution (semester based)	143
10.3	Survey results for technology effect	145
10.4	Survey results for delivery of course contents	145
10.5	Experience of using e-learning tools	146
10.6	Statistical results from Fall 2017–2018 to Fall 2021–2022	147
10.7	Position of use new technologies	148
10.8	Comprehensive strategic and operational plan	152
10.9	National and Gulf region initiatives in the form of strategic and operational plans based on instructor perspectives	153
11.1	Proposed theoretical model	160
12.1	Conceptual model	178
12.2	Structural model	184
13.1	Gender distribution of participants	199
13.2	HEI sector of participants	199
13.3	Age categories of participants	200
13.4	Educational level of participants	200

Figures ix

13.5 The teaching staff was able to tailor the academic activities into an online mode 201
13.6 The transition from the traditional to online education reduced my learning efficacy 201
13.7 My college/university opted effective measures to convert the educational process in an online mode during COVID-19 202
13.8 I was able to access the essential equipment or tools (like laptop, desktop, internet connection) for continuing education through online 202
13.9 The stress due to COVID-19 concerns impacted my learning ability 203
13.10 I am satisfied with the digital (IT) resources my HEI provided during the COVID-19 203
13.11 I found it easier to study individually in an online mode as compared to the face-to-face classroom teaching 204
13.12 The teaching staff was approachable and connected in the virtual learning settings during COVID-19 pandemic 204
13.13 I was able to arrange a quiet place at home to attend the lectures online 205
13.14 Moving forward, what mode of study would you prefer; attending classes physically, online or hybrid (mix of physical and online)? 205
13.15 After the resumption of on-campus education, I feel more comfortable to concentrate on my studies 206

Tables

1.1	Thematic analysis of Delphi Protocol open-ended questions	16
1.2	HMW model	17
4.1	Summary of the suggested policy introduction-implementation models	69
5.1	Descriptive statistics of faculty's demographics	80
5.2	Descriptive statistics of faculty teaching experience and computer literacy	80
5.3	ANOVA analysis of achieving pedagogical and curricular aspects	81
5.4	ANOVA analysis of student's involvement and technical skills	81
5.5	ANOVA analysis of accessing ICT	82
5.6	Descriptive statistics of challenges faced by faculty by using ICT	82
5.7	Ranking of challenges by using ICT tools	83
5.8	Descriptive statistics of student demographics	84
5.9	Descriptive statistics of dependent and independent variables	84
5.10	Correlation analysis	84
5.11	Regression analysis	85
5.12	Descriptive statistics of challenges faced by students in using ICT	85
5.13	Ranking of challenges faced by students by using ICT tools	86
8.1	Rotated component matrix	112
8.2	Demographic profile by gender	114
8.3	Students' cohort	114
8.4	Respondents' programme and specialisation	114
8.5	Location of public and private HEIs	115
8.6	Source of internet	115
8.7	KMO and Bartlett's test	115
8.8	Total variance	116
8.9	Model reliability and fit measures	116
8.10	Regression analysis for hypothesis testing	117
10.1	Demographic information about the participants	142
10.2	Reliability of the research tool	144
10.3	Survey stability coefficients	144

Tables xi

11.1	The results indicating the Cronbach alpha and composite reliability	166
11.2	The results show the Q^2 values	167
11.3	The results show the R^2 values	167
11.4	Hypotheses testing	168
12.1	Factors and symptoms of stress	176
12.2	Demographic profile	181
12.3	Health condition affected during Coronavirus pandemic	182
12.4	Factor loading and descriptive statistics	182
12.5	Total variance explained	183
12.6	Descriptive statistics, reliability coefficients, and inter-construct correlations	183
12.7	One-way ANOVA for demographics and health condition differences	184
12.8	Standardised regression weights	185
13.1	Number of affected male and female learners in GCC	196

About the Editors

Prof. Reynaldo Gacho Segumpan is a Professor and the Dean of the City Graduate School, City University Malaysia, Petaling Jaya, Malaysia. He is a Chartered Manager and Chartered Fellow (CMgr FCMI), Chartered Management Institute, UK; Chartered Scientist (CSci), Science Council, UK; Fellow, Institute of Science and Technology (FIScT), UK; and Fellow, Higher Education Academy (FHEA), UK. He is also a Certified Human Resource Professional having passed the Professional in Human Resources – International (PHRi) examination conducted by the HR Certification Institute (HRCI) based in Alexandria, Virginia, USA. He holds a PhD and a Doctor of Communication (Chancellor's List), three Master's degrees, and a Bachelor's degree (*Magna Cum Laude*).

Professor Segumpan has edited books, presented papers, delivered keynote speeches, and published researches on higher education, communication and social media, human resource management, qualitative inquiry, business, and social sciences in various occasions in the UK, USA, Europe (e.g., Italy and Switzerland), Gulf Region (e.g., Oman and United Arab Emirates), and Australasia (e.g., Australia, Brunei Darussalam, India, Indonesia, Malaysia, Mongolia, Philippines, Singapore, South Korea, and Thailand). He attended HPAIR 2018 in Harvard University, USA and GRM 2018, 2019, and 2022 in the University of Cambridge, UK. Prof. Segumpan, who taught in Oman for 16 years, also completed a training on qualitative methods (January–March 2022) conducted by the ProQual Institute for Research Methods, University of Georgia, USA.

Prof. John McAlaney is a Professor, Chartered Psychologist and Chartered Scientist in the Faculty of Science and Technology at Bournemouth University, United Kingdom, with an interest in the interaction between humans and technology. Professor John McAlaney teaches psychological principles of behaviour change to students from several disciplinary backgrounds, including psychology and computing, and informatics. He has previously acted as the Head of Education for the Department of Psychology and as Programme Leader for the British Psychological Society accredited BSc Cyberpsychology degree. He has served as an external examiner for

About the Editors xiii

Manchester Metropolitan University, the University of Westminster, and the Institute of Art, Design and Technology in Dún Laoghaire, Ireland.

In his funded research projects, Professor John McAlaney has explored the role of technology in relation to cybersecurity behaviours, online gambling, and digital addiction. He has also conducted work and supervised doctoral students completing research on the topics of organisational cybersecurity culture, education, and training in the military. He has published extensively in these areas in journals and has also edited books on cybersecurity, social media use, and quality drivers of higher education in the Gulf. Outside of Bournemouth University, Professor McAlaney acts as a Trustee for the Gordon Moody Association, which provides residential treatment and other services for people experiencing gambling harms.

Contributors

Joanna Soraya Abu Zahari, a senior academic and researcher, has an Honours Degree in Accountancy and a Master of Business Administration from *Universiti Teknologi MARA*, Selangor, Malaysia. She worked in Johor Capital Holdings and Johor Investment Ltd. before her role as a Research Officer at Universiti Utara Malaysia. Some of her works were published in European Journal of Social and Human Sciences, International Journal of Business and Behavioral Sciences, and Asian Journal of University Education. Her most recent edited book, *Mixed Methods Perspectives on Communication and Social Media Research* (co-edited with Reynaldo Gacho Segumpan) was published (2023) by Routledge/Taylor & Francis, United Kingdom. She was previously with the Ministry of Higher Education, Sultanate of Oman, and was assigned to teach business and management courses at the Colleges of Applied Sciences in Salalah and in Sohar and Rustaq College of Education. Joanna Soraya was with University of Technology and Applied Sciences in Ibri, Oman before engaging in private consultancy work.

Mary Precy P. Aguilar, PhD, has been involved in international higher education for more than 28 years and has taught in Thailand, Vietnam, and the United Arab Emirates. She has been involved in curriculum development in programmes such as Tourism Management, Human Resource Management, Accounting, and Business Management. She was awarded the RMIT University Teaching Award High Commendation in 2007. Dr. Aguilar was among the 40 Doctoral students around the world mentored by renowned International Business scholars during the Academy of International Business and Sheth Foundation Doctoral Student Consortium in 2017. Her research interests include business education, international higher education, IntELS (internationally educated local staff), international human resource management, organisational commitment, and First Year Higher Education (FYHE). She has a PhD in Management from the Royal Melbourne Institute of Technology (RMIT), Australia and holds a Graduate Certificate in Tertiary Teaching and Learning from RMIT, Australia.

Contributors xv

Rabab Isa Saleh Almuqahwi, EdD, holds PGDip, UCert-Ed, UCertLang, MBA, EDipHR, CertLang, PGDipEd, and BA and is an English Lecturer and the Arabic Language Programme Coordinator at the Royal College of Surgeons in Ireland- Medical University of Bahrain (RCSI-Bahrain). She graduated from the University of Liverpool, UK with a Doctorate Degree in Higher Education, specialising in Professional Education and Curriculum Development. Dr. Rabab is a Research Lead in her work Language and Culture Unit and has published research papers on language communication and teaching languages for specific professional purposes. Recently, she presented a paper at the Forum for Open Access Research in MENA 2022 in New Cairo, Egypt. Dr. Rabab won several awards and honours, such as the FELTA Teaching Assistance programme at Wellesley College of Arts in Boston, USA in 2006 and was also nominated for the RCSI-Bahrain Dean's Award in 2015. She is actively engaged in some collaborative research projects with local, regional, and international higher education institutions.

Ibrahim Rashid Al Shamsi, PhD, is an Associate Professor and Dean in College of Business, University of Buraimi, Sultanate of Oman. His areas of specialisation include business, human resource management, and other management-related subjects. He obtained his Master in Business Administration from UK and PhD in Business Administration from Malaysia. He also serves as a reviewer in indexed journals and is involved in various academic and research roles. Before joining the academia, he worked for 20 years with Directorate General of Health Services, Al Buraimi Governorate, Ministry of Health where he held important positions as Head of Administration Department, Director of Administration and Finance, and Director of Planning and Studies. He has appeared in national media for his expert views on entrepreneurship and business management. Dr. Ibrahim has been in academics since 2006 and is an active researcher as the main author and co-author of many publications in indexed journals.

Vishal Jain, PhD, is an Assistant Professor and served as Head of Major (Business) at the University of Technology and Applied Sciences (UTAS), Ibri, Sultanate of Oman. Previously, he worked as a Dean at BBDNITM, Lucknow, India. He holds a PhD, MBA, PGDCA and has 25 years of rich experience in industry and academia. His main areas of expertise include Business Management, Marketing, International Marketing, Entrepreneurship, Operations Management, Operations Research, and Research Methods, to name a few. He has received research grants from The Research Council, Oman for 2019–2021 and 2022–2023. His main citations comprise a 3D model of attitude; survival skills of business management graduates; paradigm shift of Indian retailing; financial inclusion; selection behaviour of elective courses; and a journey towards a cashless society. Dr. Vishal has presented some of his scholarly papers at MTMI International Conference, Dubai, UAE; Gulf Research Meeting, University of Cambridge, UK; ITTD xvi *Contributors*

Congress, Ankara, Turkey; IFIP 8.6 Conference, IIM, Tiruchirappalli, India; and ISDSI-Global Conference, IIM, Nagpur, India.

Mohit Kukreti, PhD, has worked as a Department Head in Nepal, Ethiopia, Sultanate of Oman and as a Program Director of the IBA Program me with the Directorate General of 6 CAS campuses at the Ministry of Higher Education, Sultanate of Oman. At present, he is at the University of Technology and Applied Sciences (College of Economics and Business Administration). Dr. Mohit has a PhD in human resource development (HRD) with more than 26 years of international experience in higher education administration, academic quality assurance, and higher education institution (HEI) strategic planning. He has contributed several articles and chapters in peer-reviewed international journals and books as well as participated and presented papers at conferences in Nepal, Turkey, and University of Cambridge, UK. His research areas are HRD, business management, higher education strategy development and quality assurance, entrepreneurship, tourism development planning, and luxury tourism, to name a few.

Hajar Mahfoodh, PhD, is a prolific author on global poetry traditions, language teaching, culture, and sustainability, and teaches English at the University of Bahrain. She obtained her PhD at the University of Surrey on Concepts of Home and Exile in Modern Arabic Poetry and MA in Cultural Studies from Bowling Green State University, Ohio, USA. An assistant professor, Dr. Hajar publishes regularly on Higher Education and Sustainability; she has also served as a chair in several conferences at the University of Bahrain, including the annual International Conference on Resilience and Sustainability, Beyond 6 Characteristics: EDI for the Modern University at the University of Lancaster, and the Annual PGR Conference at the University of Surrey. She has been involved in many scientific committees, peer reviews, and editorial posts, and recently published *Politicising World Literature: Egypt, Between Pedagogy and the Public* for the Journal of Post-colonial Writing.

Amitabh Mishra, PhD, has more than 20 years of experience in international higher education. He is currently associated with the College of Economics and Business Administration at the University of Technology and Applied Sciences in the Sultanate of Oman. He holds a PhD and Master's degrees in Tourism Management and Business Management. He has diverse expertise in Tourism, Hospitality, and Business Administration and has contributed significantly to the academic community, publishing over 20 research papers and articles in various peer-reviewed and Scopus-indexed publications. Dr. Amitabh has also authored three books in his area of specialisation, further highlighting his expertise in the field; furthermore, he has reviewed many research papers, book chapters, and conference papers, demonstrating his commitment to the academic community. He has supervised more than 25 undergraduate and Master's degree dissertation students. Dr. Amitabh has been invited as a resource person, keynote speaker, session chair, and guest of honour at a number of international conferences in Oman and abroad.

Bahtiar Mohamad, PhD, is an Associate Professor of Corporate Communication and Strategy at Othman Yeop Abdullah Graduate School of Business (OYAGSB), Universiti Utara Malaysia (UUM). With a Bachelor's degree from National University of Malaysia, a Master of Science from *Universiti Putra Malaysia*, and a PhD from Brunel University London, United Kingdom, Bahtiar has been serving UUM for approximately 19 years. His research and publications are in the areas of corporate identity, corporate image, crisis communication, and corporate branding from the point of view of public relations and corporate communication. Dr. Bahtiar has published over 100 research papers in reputed journals and conferences and has authored, co-authored, and edited 8 textbooks. He is a Member of Institute of Public Relations Malaysia, European Communication Research and Education Association, World Communication Association, and Pacific & Asia Communication Association. Associate Professor Bahtiar is currently a Visiting Scholar at the Faculty of Business, Curtin University, *Universitas Pendidikan Indonesia*, and Asian Institute of Cambodia and also the Academic Advisor for *Universiti Sultan Zainal Abidin*, SEGi University, and Kolej Universiti Poly-Tech MARA.

Umara Noreen, PhD, is an Assistant Professor at the Finance Department, Prince Sultan University in Riyadh, Saudi Arabia. She obtained her PhD from Foundation University Islamabad, Pakistan. Dr. Umara has 24 years of extensive teaching experience at the undergraduate, graduate, and postgraduate levels and has published 26 refereed and indexed Journals, 15 conference proceedings, and a book. She is a professional ISO-certified trainer for the USAID program me with Asia Foundation, Islamabad, Pakistan. She has also developed training manuals for non-profit organisations under The Asia Foundation USAID project at CIIT where she delivered intensive training to executives and senior level managers under this program me as well as to the executives of Riyadh Bank, Saudi Arabia and training under Elite Monsha't PSU program me to entrepreneurs held at Prince Sultan University, Saudi Arabia.

Mariam Orkodashvili has been affiliated with Pennsylvania University; UC Berkley; California State University; Peabody College of Education, Vanderbilt University, USA; Tbilisi State University, Georgia; Georgian American University; The Parliament of Georgia; Max Planck Institute for Social Anthropology, Halle-Saale, Germany; Education Research Institute in Washington, DC; and Edinburgh University, Scotland, UK. Mariam's publications have appeared in SAGE Encyclopedia of Theory (SAGE publications); Oxford Studies in Comparative Education; International Perspectives on Higher Education Institutions (Peter Lang Publishers); Sociology of Education (SAGE publication); European Education: Issues

xviii *Contributors*

and Studies (Taylor & Francis); Comparative and International Education (Sense Publishers); International Perspectives on Education and Society (Emerald Publishers, UK); and Peabody Journal of Education (Routledge/Taylor & Francis). At present, she is an associate professor at Georgian-American University.

Ridwan Adetunji Raji, PhD, is an Assistant Professor of Integrated Strategic Communication at the College of Communication and Media Sciences, Zayed University, Abu Dhabi, United Arab Emirates where he teaches Media Planning and Management, Media, Communication and Society and Communication Research Methodology. He earned a PhD in Media Management from Universiti Utara Malaysia. Dr. Ridwan has won international research grants and presented at international conferences on issues revolving around Sustainability Image Development and Sustainable Consumption among Youth, Green City Identity, Social Innovation, and Corporate Identity. The findings from his previous studies have been published in refereed journals such as Journal of Marketing Communication, Journal of Promotion Management, Journal of Research in Interactive Marketing, and Malaysian Journal of Communication. Prior to joining Zayed University, Ridwan was a Visiting Senior Lecturer at Universiti Utara Malaysia.

Abdul Sami, PhD, is an Assistant Professor and Head, Department of Management Sciences at the University of Jhang, Pakistan. He also serves as an editor of University of Jhang's research journal, *Pakistan Journal of Multidisciplinary Research,* and the Editor-in-Chief of the *Journal of Public Value and Administrative Insight.* He has 32 research publications in renowned journals, is a founding member of Research Organization Connecting ASIA Sdn. Bhd., and has organised research training workshops and worked as an editorial member for several international conferences. He obtained his PhD from *Universiti Teknologi Malaysia* (research on Public Value and Leadership), Master of Public Administration from the University of the Punjab, Lahore, Pakistan, and BSc from Government College University, Lahore. His current research centres around leadership, public administration, human resource management, organisational behaviour, organisational culture, and sustainability.

Attayah Shafique, PhD, is an Assistant Professor in the Department of Communication and Management Sciences at the Pakistan Institute of Engineering and Applied Sciences, Islamabad, Pakistan. She completed her PhD in Management Sciences (major in Finance) from COMSATS University Islamabad, Pakistan in 2020. Her areas of interest are Behavioural Finance, Corporate Finance, Portfolio Management, Asset Pricing, and Financial Modelling, among others. Dr. Attayah has publications in Scopus-indexed journals, among others.

Syeeda Shafiya is currently Deputy Head of the Business and Accounting Department at Muscat College, Sultanate of Oman. She obtained her Master of Commerce from Osmania University, Hyderabad; has more than 15 years of proactive teaching experience at national and international levels; an Associate Fellow of the Higher Education Academy, UK; and an approved Finance and Accounting faculty for the University of Stirling programmes. She also has broad experience of teaching professional courses such as FIA and ACCA and has expertise in Intellectual Capital, Corporate Governance, Corporate Social Responsibility and International Accounting standards as well as Accounting software, course advising, and career counselling. She has co-authored book chapters and journals and also participated in numerous international conferences.

Khuram Shahzad is a Lecturer in Consultancy Skills/Project Management at the Lancashire School of Business and Enterprise, University of Central Lancashire, UK. He has been a reviewer of Gomal University Journal of Research since 2021. His research is situated in the field of project management, with a special focus on green building practices in construction projects, quality in higher education, and sustainable procurement. He did his master's in project management in 2014 and MBA in 2009 from COMSATS University Islamabad, Pakistan. During his 13 years of experience in the higher education institutes of the UK, Oman, and Pakistan, Khuram has taught several modules on the knowledge areas of project management at the undergraduate and graduate levels. He is a certified Project Management Professional (PMP) of the Project Management Institute (PMI), USA, and holds the Fellowship (FHEA) of Advance Higher Education, UK.

Boumedyen Shannaq, PhD, is an associate professor in the Department of Information Systems and information systems expert in MRMWR (Ministry), Sultanate of Oman. His researches focus primarily on information management, data sciences (data mining), knowledge management, and web programming. He develops many smart systems oriented to improve the education systems (e-learning and visual learning) and workplace productivities in industrial and academic domains. Recently, Dr. Boumedyen developed new e-management modules based on artificial intelligence (AI) algorithms as information system applications to manage the Education process.

Radha Krishan Sharma, PhD, is Professor (MBA) and Associate Dean (Internal Quality Assurance), KL Business School, Koneru Lakshmaiah University, Vaddeswaram – 522502, Guntur District, Andhra Pradesh, India. He is a versatile professional with over 30 years of real-life experience as well as a consultant on higher education quality assurance and accreditation. His research interests are in finance, accounting, fintech, and higher education quality, and he has published in reputed journals and presented at national and international conferences at the University of Cambridge, UK, JNU (India), and AMU (India), among others. Dr. Sharma is an international

xx *Contributors*

expert for PhD Exam Board/Panel; a member of many professional societies; and serves as a member of Board of Studies of different universities. He has earned over 20 awards and accolades including *Outstanding Contribution to Education Community* and *Best Accounting Professor of the Year*.

Muhammad Rehan Shaukat served as a System-Wide Coordinator in the Department of Business Administration at the College of Applied Sciences-Ibri of the University of Technology and Applied Sciences (UTAS), Sultanate of Oman. He has degrees in computer science, electronic commerce, and business administration and has decades of teaching and research experience and extensive experience working with people from a variety of ethnic backgrounds. His areas of research interest are electronic business, innovation, gamification, SMEs, smart cities, artificial intelligence, and higher education. He has published a chapter on Quality Prospects in Higher Education: A Case of Oman in an edited volume of *Higher Education in the Gulf: Quality Drivers* published by Routledge/Taylor & Francis in 2021. Currently, he is the Head of Major (Business) at the College of Economics and Business Administration at UTAS-Ibri, Sultanate of Oman.

Wan Norhayate Binti Wan Daud, PhD, is a Professor from the School of Finance and Banking, Faculty of Business and Management (FBM), Universiti Sultan Zainal Abidin, Malaysia. She teaches Enterprise Risk Management, Risk Management, Strategic Management, Takaful/Insurance, and Entrepreneurship, among other management subjects. Her research on Poverty in Brunei received funding of MYR8.5 million (USD1 = MYR4.6) from the Ministry of Culture, Youth, and Sports, Brunei Darussalam. She also received a grant from the Islamic Research & Training Institute (IRTI), Jeddah amounting to USD15,000 to lead a research that measured the quality of leaders among takaful/insurance operators in Malaysia. In 2020, she led another research on Cybersecurity Risk Management for Public Universities in Malaysia which was funded amounting to MYR100,000.00. Dr. Wan Norhayate also serves as Assistant Vice-Chancellor and Director for the Centre for Talent & Training Management at Universiti Sultan Zainal Abidin. She is also one of the active panel assessors appointed by the Malaysia Qualification Agency (MQA) to assess new programmes for all universities in Malaysia at the national level.

Bello Musa Yakubu, PhD, is currently doing postdoctoral work at Chulalongkorn University, Bangkok, Thailand. He obtained his PhD in Computer Science from COMSATS University Islamabad, Pakistan, and MTech in Computer Science and Engineering from Sharda University, India. Dr. Bello has worked with the Kano State Agricultural and Rural Development Authority (KNARDA) and as a visiting faculty in many tertiary institutions in Kano State, Nigeria. His areas of interest include network and cyber security, trust management in networked environments, cryptosystems, mobile ad-hoc network security, and data/information security. He has published his research work in national and international impact-factor journals.

Fakhrul Anwar Zainol, PhD, is a professional business coach for SME owners and managers, helping them grow and develop their enterprises. He had years of experience in development banking before becoming an academician. Dr. Fakhrul has a Degree in Accountancy (B.Acc.) and Master of Business Administration (MBA) from *Universiti Teknologi MARA* (UiTM) and completed his Doctorate in Business Administration (DBA) at the University of Newcastle, Australia. He also holds a Postgraduate Diploma in Entrepreneurship (PDE) from Judge Business School, University of Cambridge, UK. He received his formal entrepreneurship training/coaching in Australia and became an Accredited MAUS Coaching Partner, Sydney, Australia, and has been appointed as the 1st President of the Institute of Advisors (Malaysian Chapter). Currently, he serves as the Director, Centre for Income Generation, Investment and Industrial Linkages as well as Associate Professor at the Faculty of Business and Management, Universiti Sultan Zainal Abidin (UniSZA), Terengganu, Malaysia. His areas of expertise and research include entrepreneurship, strategic management, business strategies, corporate strategies, and SMEs management.

Preface

This book comprises of empirical, research-based papers that have quantitative as well as qualitative frameworks within the realms of higher education reforms, the COVID-19 pandemic, and Gulf affairs. It is unique compared to existing references because it weaves the multi-disciplinary perspectives of understanding how COVID-19 has impacted, is transforming, and will continue to shape higher education in the Gulf. The authors provide not only theoretical and methodical perspectives on the interface between higher education reforms and the pandemic but also explicate the practical approaches on how higher education institutions in the Gulf have dealt, and are dealing, with the issues and challenges brought about by the pandemic.

As a proactive response to understand better how the pandemic has transformed higher education institutions (HEIs) in the Gulf region, the editors and authors of this book have synergised in order to systematically problematise the notion of educational reforms in the higher education milieu during the COVID-19 pandemic. Thus, this volume is a modest contribution to contemporary theory-building as well as valuable practice-oriented reference material that is tailored to researchers, scholars, and policymakers in HEIs in the Gulf. It reflects real-world scenarios on how HEIs in the Gulf grappled with the pandemic and how the latter has redrawn instructional, pedagogical, managerial, curricular, assessment, and related spheres of the higher educational landscape.

The other special features of this edition include the scholarship diversity and global pool of contributors. The latter have expertise across diverse-yet-allied areas of higher education, such as higher education management, curriculum development, organisational and cross-cultural communication, language education, business and management, policy making, tourism and hospitality, to name a few. The authors are also cultural diverse; they are not only from the Gulf but also from neighbouring and other regional institutions based in Bahrain, India, Georgia, Malaysia, Oman, Pakistan, Saudi Arabia, Thailand, United Arab Emirates, and United Kingdom. This diversity of scholarship and cultural backgrounds infuses new spectrum of ideas, unique insights, and intellectual perspectives reflecting higher education reforms within the COVID-19 framework and blend of quantitative and qualitative research inquiries.

Preface xxiii

There is a dearth of reading materials that provide unique viewpoints on higher education reforms that are specific to the Gulf Region, in particular, Bahrain, Kuwait, Oman, Qatar, Saudi Arabia, and United Arab Emirates. In addition, there are existing books on COVID-19 and higher education but this volume is distinctively regional in focus (i.e., Gulf) as well as global in outlook because it projects corollaries of the pandemic and how HEIs are projecting the uncertain future and mitigating the impact of the pandemic among the academic community in the Gulf. The "next normal" or any impending pandemic may demand the reframing of HEI efforts and initiatives that impinge on the teaching-learning processes, among others. The bottom line is that this volume will be a significant contribution to knowledge and understanding of the Gulf region in terms of the reforms and programmes that have been in place during this critical milestone in higher education.

The authors of this special edition are highly experienced academics and seasoned researchers whose empirical works were selected in conjunction with the Gulf Research Meeting 2022 at the University of Cambridge, United Kingdom. The convergence of these researchers provided the impetus, the synergy, and the framework for this contemporary volume.

The Editors
Reynaldo Gacho Segumpan, PhD, DComm
City University Malaysia, Petaling Jaya,
Malaysia
John McAlaney, PhD
Bournemouth University
United Kingdom

Acknowledgements

The scholarly space in this volume would not have been filled, shaped, and transformed without the valuable guidance, support, and efforts of the following institutions and individuals:

- Gulf Research Centre (GRC)
- Gulf Research Centre Cambridge (GRCC)
- Dr. Abdulaziz Sager, Founder and Chairman of GRC
- Dr. Oskar Ziemeles, Director of Cooperation, GRCC
- AnnaMary Goodall, Editor for Education, Psychology & Mental Health Research, Routledge/Taylor & Francis Group
- Kanishka Jangir, Editorial Assistant, Routledge/Taylor & Francis Group
- Anonymous reviewers of our book proposal and the peer reviewers of the revised manuscript

We also acknowledge the inspiration and strength from our family members and "significant others", most especially the contributors who provided meaning and substance to this book.

The Editors
Reynaldo Gacho Segumpan, PhD, DComm
John McAlaney, PhD

Introduction

The COVID-19 pandemic is often discussed in terms of the social changes it brought to the world. It could be argued that many of these changes were already underway, fuelled by the continual developments in technology. This is particularly the case with technologies that relate to how we communicate with one another, including how we share ideas and provide education. As has been the case throughout human history, however, new technologies are not always accepted when they first emerge. The COVID-19 pandemic created a situation where the use of many online platforms became a requirement rather than a choice, including within educational settings. In this case, necessity became not only the mother of all invention, but also the adoption of technologies that had already been invented.

The demographics of students in higher education (HE) are changing across the world (Statista, 2023). The stereotype of the traditional student of a young adult from a privileged background is being increasingly challenged, in part due to technologies that lessen some of the economic barriers to engagement with education. It is known that demographic factors can impact how students engage with and progress (Stoet & Geary, 2020). This illustrates the requirement for HE to continue to evolve to serve the needs of these shifting demographics. Nevertheless, in many cases, those attending university or college for the first time are young people who are in the transitional phase between adolescence and adulthood. This life phase has been identified as important in the development of an individual's health, well-being, and future career success, and as such is also a key point in which to target people with prevention and intervention strategies that will empower them to make positive life choices (Faria et al., 2021). This period can also coincide with the first time in which the student has lived away from the parental home, or at least a time in their life when they may be under less direct parental supervision. Coupled with the changes in technologies and the COVID-19 pandemic this means that current generations of students and young people are completing their education in a time of great change, both socially and in their own personal lives. This may create many barriers but also opportunities, as is explored in the chapters throughout this book.

DOI: 10.4324/9781003457299-1

2 Introduction

There is extensive pedagogical research into how and why students engage with education, which has identified a range of individual factors that can influence academic achievement (Radford & Holdstock, 1995). In the past, there could be limited opportunities to adapt HE education to serve the individual needs and characteristics of HE students, primarily due to the practical challenges of doing so in traditional education settings. As highlighted during the COVID-19 pandemic, online technologies can remove some of these barriers and allow greater flexibility and personalisation in programme delivery. Of course, the availability of technology does not mean that it should be used in HE. Another impact of COVID-19 was to stress test HE systems across the world, highlighting areas of resilience and innovation, alongside areas of vulnerability and risk. There can be a temptation to apply a new technological system to challenges in HE without fully understanding the capacities and consequences of that technology. It is important that we do not lose sight of the core values and proven pedagogical techniques that have been successful in HE, regardless of the changes that have been brought about by the COVID-19 pandemic. There is a track record of quality HE education in the Gulf region that it is important to preserve and build upon (Segumpan & McAlaney, 2021).

An increasingly globalised world means increasing competition for graduates when they come to enter employment. This places an expectation on HE institutions to ensure that students are trained in the skills that employers place value on and that students develop skills such as entrepreneurship that will empower them to create their businesses. Central to this is that HE institutions are able to prove that their students have been adequately tested, especially in the case of professionally accredited programmes. During the COVID-19 pandemic, there was a move towards online assessment, including online exams. Some institutions have returned to in-person assessments, whereas others have retained online assessment for some components of the programme. This is becoming further complicated by the rise of artificial intelligence, and concerns about how this may be used by students for academic misconduct. Overall, these changes to assessment have implications for how teaching must be delivered at HE institutions – as Biggs and Tang (2007) observe, how students learn depends to a major extent on how they think they will be assessed.

This book is divided into two sections. The first section, *Understanding Regional HE Reforms*, consists of six chapters that explore how HE has and should be changed in GCC countries. The second section, *Reframing Higher Education Reforms*, consists of a further six chapters that discuss a range of topics that informed how reforms were implemented during the pandemic, including e-learning, job related stress, and the perspectives of educators. Consideration is also given to the future, and how HE in the Gulf can and will continue to develop in the new normal. In doing so this book aims to help equip educators, HE managers, and all of those with a stake in HE in continuing to provide quality education to HE students.

Introduction 3

References

Biggs, J., & Tang, C. (2007). *Teaching for quality learning at university* (3rd ed.). Open University Press.

Faria, M. G. A., Fernandes, R. C., Gallasch, C. H., & Alves, L. V. V. (2021). Contributions of the health-promoting universities' movement: An integrative literature review. *Journal of Education and Health Promotion, 10*, 114. https://doi.org/10.4103/jehp.jehp_24_21

Radford, J., & Holdstock, L. (1995). Gender differences in higher education aims between computing and psychology students. *Research in Science & Technological Education, 13*(2), 163–176. https://doi.org/10.1080/0263514950130206

Segumpan, R. G., & McAlaney, J. (2021). *Higher education in the gulf: Quality drivers.* Routledge.

Statista. (2023). Education worldwide - statistics & facts. https://www.statista.com/topics/7785/education-worldwide/#topicOverview

Stoet, G., & Geary, D. (2020). Gender differences in the pathways to higher education. *Proceedings of the National Academy of Sciences of the United States of America, 117*, 202002861. https://doi.org/10.1073/pnas.2002861117

Part I

Understanding Regional Higher Education Reforms in a COVID-19 Context

1 Potential Reforms in the GCC Higher Education Post COVID-19

Hajar Mahfoodh and Rabab Isa Saleh Almuqahwi

Introduction

The COVID-19 pandemic has created a dynamic space that allows higher education (HE) bodies and institutions to revise their educational policies and pedagogical practices. Although most academic faculty members have experimented with remote education through trial and error and coping strategies during this pandemic, most have developed various reflections on educational policies, assessments, and practices (Pokhrel & Chhetri, 2021). Despite resistance to this change, most educators had to employ remote education, including the Gulf Cooperation Council (GCC) states (Bensaid & Brahimi, 2020). The pandemic has exposed that the traditional modes used in HE are far behind the progress of the digitalised world and the ongoing technological changes in the marketplace (Alshakhi, 2021). HE institutions and bodies lack awareness and competencies in remote education as the major mode of learning and teaching

In the GCC, the HE bodies and sectors follow the regulations and policies of the official authorities, leaving little room for further experimentation and innovation in teaching and learning practices and policies. Consequently, academic faculty members must adhere to restrictions that prevent them from exploring alternative educational solutions and practices. This chapter aims to promote awareness in HE from a top-bottom perspective (e.g. from HE policymakers and senior management to academic and admin staff) towards taking advantage of the lessons learned through COVID-19 by turning the challenges into feasible future opportunities in the various HE institutions in the GCC. The chapter further analyses the readiness plans used in the GCC HE institutions in facing the various changes caused by the sudden pandemic to bring the balance back to teaching and learning processes. It also explores potential plans for crisis management and the scenarios of implementing the Universal Design for Teaching and Learning (UDL) in HE as a sustainable education framework in the GCC. This framework promotes an inclusive culture that accommodates a diverse segment of students, regardless of their differences, based on abilities, culture, and place of residence, and it allows addressing learning needs creatively beyond traditional analysis since it focuses on the

DOI: 10.4324/9781003457299-3

8 *Hajar Mahfoodh and Rabab Isa Saleh Almuqahwi*

fields we do not know or tend to avoid exploring in pedagogy (Chita-Tegmark et al., 2012). It also aims to call GCC HE policymakers to formulate unified policies to accredit hybrid teaching and learning as a sustainable approach in HE institutions. Hence, hybrid learning could be introduced to the GCC educational systems with constructive restrictions and regulations to minimise costs in HE institutions.

Ramifications of COVID-19

With the sudden outbreak of COVID-19 and the emergence of remote education as the only available option, many HE sectors and institutes are exploring remote education by reflecting on their pedagogical experiences, policies, and practices during the pandemic. However, online learning used to be overlooked as a reliable mode of learning in the various HE sectors in the GCC states; most did not accredit remote education for postgraduate degrees (Hashlamoun & Nafeth, 2021). Despite its remarkable impact on educators and students, remote education is often labelled unreliable and deficient compared to face-to-face learning (Schultz & DeMers, 2020). In addition, many academic faculty members prefer traditional modes of education, mainly through the so-called "real classroom," which they consider ideal for providing a communicative and engaging environment (Hrastinski, 2008). This reluctance to remote education is supported by the challenging conditions of the virtual classroom, especially students' assessment and engagement (Palvia et al., 2018). Both online assessment and engagement require adopting alternative methods and tools to generate student participation, inside or outside the classroom, despite the accessibility of digital platforms and tools designed for remote education (Dhawan, 2020). Besides, some students prefer traditional classrooms, considering remote education inconvenient for various reasons, including lack of ICT literacy, reliable internet connection, and financial support (Chakraborty et al., 2021). Instead, they consider eLearning highly frustrating and unsatisfactory, expressing concerns about unclear teaching and inadequate evaluations, which sometimes could lead the student to drop the course (Alqahtani & Rajkhan, 2020; Krishnapatria, 2020). Thus, some students and educators do not prefer remote education due to the malpractices that could sometimes be dysfunctional regarding intended learning outcomes, participation, and students' assessment.

While the pandemic has created a situation where online learning is mandatory as the only option for the various HE bodies, some serious factors need further investigation. Online education is a pedagogical field with distinctive characteristics, differing substantially from remote learning in times of disaster experienced by most HE sectors during the pandemic (Hodges et al., 2020). According to Zimmerman (2020), online learning, or eLearning, is a carefully-planned educational approach of "deep virtual learning experiences with no physical interaction in a physical classroom environment, which indicates a design phase potentially lasting several months in advance of offering the course." Remote education involves a specified amount of time for course design and development before delivering the course to the end-users, the students. However, the abrupt outbreak of COVID-19 did not spare the luxury of time. Therefore, HE faculty members had to rely on improvisations and quick solutions to maintain the continuity of knowledge delivery (Habes et al., 2021). Although the courses continued, the HE online learning experience lacked the time required for an online course plan and design conveniently and professionally. Consequently, remote education during COVID-19 is not a professional example of online education.

Based on the above, online education differs from the current practices labelled as online learning emblematic of COVID-19. Instead, eLearning is an autonomous mode of learning that entails substantially independent work and learning by the students who should respond to various online education methods, including inquiry-based and problem-centred approaches (Alqahtani & Rajkhan, 2020). The educator is more of a facilitator, given that students are substantially in charge of their progress during the course. Online education also needs an articulate understanding of the interactive mode of online courses since they require various forms of interdependent interactions, including student-content, student-student, student-course, and student-class environment (Zimmerman, 2020). Because these characteristics are not found in the current practices of HE bodies and sectors, online learning during COVID-19 tends to be Emergency Remote Education, not online education in its accurate definitions.

COVID-19 has caused many changes to the HE institutions in the GCC. Most universities had to close their campus activities, resorting to online education as a reliable means that sustains knowledge delivery through various platforms and tools (Ahmed, 2020). They also adopted alternative grading systems and e-library services, increasing access ratios through live chat and helpdesk options (Bensaid & Brahimi, 2020). The various international and regional organisations and local authorities adopted various digital initiatives to effectively promote remote education in the GCC, not to mention the close collaboration between the UN educational offices and ministries of education (World Bank, 2021). This trend was also accompanied by the prolific investment in adopting various online professional development programmes, including online conferences, presentations, and desktop sharing through different digital platforms and the learning management systems (LMSs), such as Google Classroom, Adobe Connect, and Zoom (Pace et al., 2020). Such initiatives have contributed to a smooth transition to online learning and a public understanding of remote education during the pandemic in the GCC.

Most HE institutions in the GCC states are well-equipped with different LMSs, which led them to respond quickly but efficiently with fast and flexible administrative policies and initiatives and governmental support regarding finance and equipment to HE bodies (Bensaid & Brahimi, 2020). Exploring the lessons learned from the pandemic in HE bodies, Ayoub et al. (2021) argue that HE academic faculty need further training on innovative education methods by integrating ICT and eLearning in curricula beyond COVID-19. Bensaid and Brahimi (2020) underscore the significance of further collaboration in research, focusing on hybrid and remote modes of education. Mahfoodh and Hashim (2021) also recommend sustaining online involvement in the classroom, including social media platforms and online assessment tools, as an educational asset that prepares students for the real-world marketplace. Other suggestions include adopting hybrid and blended learning as a sustainable education mode through various governmental policies, including procedures that accredit online learning (Hashlamoun & Nafeth, 2021). While the GCC states have successfully managed to adopt online learning to solve the problem of social distancing, reflections on HE policies and practices can be explored to improve HE outcomes, curricula, and policies, creating a sustainable education that does not get disrupted by crises.

Further, the GCC states had the chance to investigate education for sustainability and sustainable development. "Sustainable Development" was introduced to the academic world in the early 1980s, at a time when the international scene was promoting the significance of the link between economic and social development with environmental discussions (Agbedahin, 2019). Although different countries worldwide have witnessed an ongoing interest in sustainable development, the term remains blurred and subject to individual interpretations according to the national interest of each country, region, or bloc (Agbedahin, 2019), such as "it is the development that meets the needs of the present without compromising the ability of future generations to meet their own needs" (United Nations, 1987). In the GCC, the HE bodies explored various ways to embed sustainable development and education for sustainability in their curricula. Most HE bodies had to explore online learning as a sustainable mode of education, encouraging them to explore further collaboration with the UN's Sustainable Development Goals in the HE curricula (Mahfoodh & AlAtawi, 2021). Still, research indicates that understanding sustainability during the pandemic is deficient, leading to a misunderstanding of online education and education for sustainable development (Mahfoodh, 2021). However, the emergence of critiquing and investigating sustainability is still invaluable because it provokes shaping and reshaping HE policies in the region.

Objectives of the Chapter
1 Highlight the lack of sustainability in the GCC teaching and learning in HE policies
2 Use the lessons learned through the pandemic to design HE plans for unifying sustainable teaching and learning approaches in the GCC
3 Create unified GCC accreditation procedures for HE hybrid teaching and learning as a sustainable method
4 Call the HE policymakers in the GCC to set clear sustainable policies in accrediting both hybrid and online teaching to cope with the international HE competitive market

Potential Reforms in the GCC Higher Education Post COVID-19 11

In particular, this chapter will explore the following issues:

- What HE areas lack sustainability in GCC teaching and learning?
- How can HE policies in the GCC use the lessons learned through the pandemic to design a plan for unified, sustainable teaching and learning approaches?
- What means would create a unified GCC accreditation procedure for hybrid teaching and learning as a sustainable method?
- How can the HE authorities collaborate to develop a unified GCC accreditation procedure that allows switching to online teaching and learning (100%) in a crisis?
- Which HE policies could be set in the GCC to accredit both hybrid and online teaching to cope with the international HE competitive market?

Delphi Protocol, Design Thinking Model, and Participants

This chapter combines qualitative and quantitative approaches, blending the Delphi Protocol and the design thinking (DT) model. It adopts DT as the main method since it is human-centred, creating solutions that we face in real life (Plattner, 2013). This model includes five stages: empathising, defining, ideating, prototyping, and testing. Each stage uses a different matrix to process collected data to pinpoint the focal issues, including the Impact/Cost matrix and the HMW (How Might We Solve the Problem) Model. The Delphi Protocol supports and analyses the findings and validates the recommendations. It is embedded in the first stage of the DT model, specifically in "empathising." The Delphi Protocol conducts two rounds due to time limitations.

HE participants from both undergraduate students and educators from various GCC states are involved in investigating the feasibility of creating national policies that regulate hybrid learning as a sustainable education model, including a resilience plan of switching to online education in times of crisis. Only the undergraduate students were selected to ensure a fair experiment because the postgraduate and graduate students usually present reflections based on their work experience. In addition, the course loads, assessments, and knowledge delivery are not the same, and hence, the researchers wanted to create a fair and equal setting for the participants.

In the stage of empathising, two panels were created to investigate the pitfalls of online education in the GCC and possible policies and approaches they would recommend. The first panel comprises ten undergraduate students, and the second panel has the same number of educators. Both panels had to answer ten questions; eight are closed, and two are open-ended questions; after the first round, the feedback of both panels was analysed and summarised in mini-reports. Before the second round, each panel had the chance to see the report of the other panel, and upon reading these reports, the second round was processed with the same set of questions. Once the feedback from both panels becomes consistent, the researchers ended the Delphi Protocol for this phase.

12   *Hajar Mahfoodh and Rabab Isa Saleh Almuqahwi*

In the testing stage, the same participants reflected on the proposed models and plans for hybrid learning policies in the GCC to refine the recommended framework of UDL.

In the next section, the gathered data and literature review are processed through the DT model, accompanied by a Delphi protocol in the empathising stage; the results of the protocol are processed through a comparative analysis and a thematic analysis, as discussed by Braun and Clarke (2006). In the final phase, a virtual round-table discussion that includes all participants is conducted to reflect on the HE policies in the GCC.

Empathising

In this phase, the researchers implemented two rounds of the Delphi Protocol to validate the responses of students and educators. Two panels, each consisting of ten participants, provided feedback on eight closed questions using the Likert scale (i.e. 1 = Strongly Disagree, 2 = Disagree, 3 = Neutral, 4 = Agree, and 5 = Strongly Agree) and three open-ended questions. The e-questionnaire was constructed through Microsoft Forms and sent to university students/ alumni and academic faculty members from various public and private HE institutions across different disciplines in the GCC.

Delphi Protocol: Round One

In this round, students and academic faculty members had to answer eight questions using a five-rate Likert scale. Most responses reflect a great gap between students' opinions and the faculty members. For instance, around 50% of faculty members agree or strongly agree that HE curricula are renewable and updated in the GCC, while 50% of students disagree or strongly disagree, as illustrated in Figure 1.1. Similarly, 50% of students agree that the HE curricula are flexible to be used for both hybrid and online teaching and learning approaches, while 60% of faculty members disagree, as illustrated in Figure 1.1.

This response variation stresses a gap between online education awareness among students and the academic faculty members, who have presented opposite responses to the same questions. However, in most questions, a substantial range of faculty members and students preferred to answer neutral, reflecting a lack of reflection and self-assessment of the online educational experiment during COVID-19. The open-ended questions also reflect a gap between the two end-users in the educational process, the faculty member and the students, although they all acknowledged the HE bodies' efforts and successful transformation to digital education. Students reflected on the dynamic approaches that changed the rigid policies of HE bodies in the GCC. For instance, they mentioned some HE initiatives to cope with the change in educational mode due to the pandemic lockdown in the GCC, including social media usage, shifting to online classes, and using effective and dynamic online platforms. Students also stressed the feasibility of creating national policies in

Potential Reforms in the GCC Higher Education Post COVID-19 13

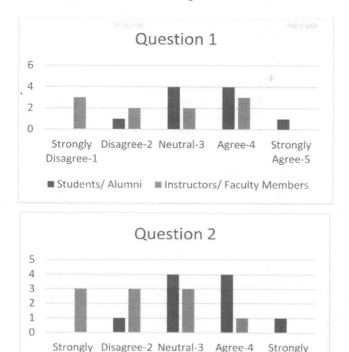

Figure 1.1 Questions 1 and 2, round (1) The statement for these questions included (1) GCC HE curricula are renewable and up to date and (2) GCC HE curricula are flexible to be used for both hybrid and online teaching and learning approaches.

the GCC to impose hybrid learning as a sustainable education model, including a resilience plan for remote education in times of crisis. However, the faculty members focused on the mechanism of digital transformation to online learning. For instance, they underscored the significance of improving digital infrastructure in no time during the pandemic, accompanied by intensive training for academic faculty members on online platform usage.

Another gap appears in the participants' articulations of how to improve the flexibility and readiness of HE in shifting to virtual/online education in the GCC. Students stressed the need to increase the flexibility of HE, such as exploring alternative digital platforms with advanced learners' interaction and examining the feasibility projects for assessment. However, some students acknowledged individual differences in coping with digital educational systems, confirming that online education needs further reflection to create policies that accommodate student differences. They also suggested online education as a necessary component of the curricula, with policies and measures regulating the feasible time for tests and student interaction as part of the course assessment. However, faculty members stressed that improvements include developing curriculum and assessment according to the rules and framework of eLearning. Like students, academic faculty also confirmed the need to explore alternative digital platforms with better interaction tools, but they stressed the need to modify Quality Assurance policies to include a hybrid approach that blends online and face-to-face learning. They also underscored the necessity of creating clear policies that legitimise online education since it is still not credited in most GCC accreditation and attestation bodies.

Students also reflected on some suggestions for developing HE policies to accredit hybrid and online teaching and learning in the GCC, aligning with the international HE markets. They suggested "a democratic method of education:" the student has the right to choose the education process, hybrid or face-to-face. They also indicated replacing traditional assessments, exams, and tests with projects and presentations, adding more flexibility to testing. Some students stressed that the number of enrolled students needs to be minimised for better student-educator interaction. Most importantly, students confirmed the significance of cooperation between the ministries of education and other educational entities to effectively secure the quality of the overall learning experience. However, faculty members expressed fewer suggestions, such as conducting customised accreditation policies according to the recent educational experiment of remote learning during the pandemic. In other words, educators suggested that the procedures that make remote learning acceptable are unclear in the GCC policies, thereby revealing the urgent need to develop new regulations and procedures accordingly.

Delphi Protocol: Round Two

When conducting the second round of the same study questionnaire, the results of the close-ended questions were slightly similar to the first round, indicating that the participants were not ready to change their answers and reflecting the lack of willingness to accept the other end-users' opinion. Thus, the results reflect the gap in accepting online education between students and educators. However, students and educators contributed with deeper input for the three open-ended questions, revealing some willingness to exchange reflection and perspectives after exposing them to the full cohort answers stated in the first round.

Students elaborated further on the HE initiatives to cope with educational changes due to COVID-19 in the GCC. They acknowledged the employment of social media applications as a means of communication between educators and students, and they underscored improving the digital infrastructure, such as updating university applications, streaming lessons on national television channels, and using various digital platforms for assessment.

Potential Reforms in the GCC Higher Education Post COVID-19 15

Students also referred to flexible changes in the HE assessment systems, including grading options at the beginning of the pandemic, an increase in course materials accessibility, and flexibility in choosing the path of the final examinations. Similarly, faculty members acknowledged the variety of digital platforms employed to assure the continuity of education delivery. Their focus, however, is more concerned with the substantial training they received to ensure a smooth transition to digital education, which involved preparing educators for digital communication and students' interaction in the digital-class environment.

Students also suggested the areas that require improvement to increase the HE bodies' flexibility and readiness in shifting to virtual/online education in the GCC. They indicated increasing flexibility regarding hours of attendance and exams. Instead, more reports, projects, and live presentations could replace these assessment methods because they entail more student preparation, thereby, more interaction with the course. Students also signalled that online courses should be legalised as a sustainable component of curricula beyond the pandemic. In addition, they underscored a need to increase access to online resources and libraries. However, faculty members desired more training to explore alternative digital platforms for knowledge delivery and assessment since their online education experience is insufficient. Educators stressed the significance of exploring alternative approaches to sustain interactive and innovative sessions using digital settings for a sustainable education model, especially reliable software and digital methods that secure examinations and assessments. Alternatives include open-test exams, assessments relying on critical thinking, and increased focus group sessions.

Further, students and educators presented more suggestions to create HE policies that accredit hybrid and online teaching and learning in the GCC to align with the international HE markets. They both suggested that the GCC states need to explore their previous policies on accrediting online degrees after resorting to remote education during the pandemic. However, students and educators underscored the need to re-evaluate the assessment process and methods in HE bodies, which have not changed significantly to cope with the marketplace or align with the international HE sectors in the last decade. In addition, students suggested a unified system of examination, where online and face-to-face testing is the same, to provide an equal opportunity to all students, and they called for incorporating students' voices when creating national HE policies. Comparatively, HE educators called for policies defining the measures accrediting online programmes, attendance, grading system, and fees. They also suggested creating HE policies regarding teacher training and continuous professional development to incentives and motivations. Finally, some educators insisted that laws should be created to sustain a defined portion delivered and assessed online as the first step towards digitalising education in cooperation with the Quality Assurance bodies.

Thematic Analysis of the Delphi Protocol Results

After processing the Delphi Protocol results in both rounds through the thematic method of Braun and Clarke (2006), the following themes have emerged (Table 1.1).

Table 1.1 Thematic analysis of Delphi Protocol open-ended questions: Questions 9, 10, and 11 were open-ended

Question 9	Question 10	Question 11
What are the GCC HE initiatives to cope with the change in educational mode due to the pandemic and lockdown?	*How would you develop/ improve the flexibility and readiness of the GCC HE in shifting to virtual/online education?*	*In your opinion, what sort of HE policies could be set in the GCC to accredit both hybrid and online teaching and learning to align with the international HE markets?*
Learning and training	Online and face-2-face (hybrid model)	Learning experience
Online education became acceptable, online courses/ lockdown browsers – online lecturers	Online classes and online classrooms	Learning acceptable
Remote education learning, shifting to online platforms	Student and faculty training on online teaching and learning skills	Students' needs
Staff and teachers education	Online assessments/ quizzes	Learning styles
Resilience plan	Better online education in quality	Impairments and needs
Hybrid learning/virtual learning	Preparation for students, online lectures	Hybrid learning
Safe Protocols	Staff and instructors	Policies regarding the courses
Education Model	Online Technologies	Remote learning/virtual learning
GCC HE Policies	HE Policies	Ministries of Education
Students and Teachers	Student online choice/ Online resources	Hybrid vs. face-to-face
Online learning/online/ remote education/online session	Lots of students	Students do projects
Zoom/online platforms and tools	Blended learning	Hybrid teaching – teaching and learning
Online examinations	Group sessions	
GCC pandemic	Informative online cooperation	

The researchers explored the responses of the participants and grouped the themes according to the questions, as explained in this table.

Potential Reforms in the GCC Higher Education Post COVID-19   17

Recurrent themes include online and hybrid education, assessment, and policies, suggesting the main three concerns or reflections for educators and students. However, all themes need to be included when addressing the problem before moving to the next step in the DT model. Still, the main paradigms shaping the problem to be addressed include online/hybrid education, policies, and assessment. Consequently, the researchers formulated the following problem: How can the GCC states create HE policies incorporating online education as a sustainable model within the various HE curricula?

After addressing the main problem, the research can proceed to the next stage in the DT model.

Defining

In this stage, the previous themes and the addressed problem were processed in the point of view model, transforming them into more tangible challenges using the How Might We Solve method (HMW), as shown in Table 1.2. The result has become a focused question: How might we create HE policies that clearly define and accredit online education through a standard framework?

In this phase, the two panels were asked to share their suggestions on framing HE policies in the GCC to integrate the lesson learned from COVID-19 in a one-hour virtual panel. The suggestions can be summarised as follows:

1 Create new policies for remote education
2 Reform HE accreditation procedures
3 Benchmark with HE regional and international standards of online education
4 Create a framework that would shape HE policies
5 Integrate UDL as a framework that sustains HE in the GCC
6 Impose clear regulations that oblige HE bodies to use eLearning curricula
7 Abandon online learning because it is not reliable

Table 1.2 HMW model: This model creates a scenario after exploring the situation as a problem narrated through a plot, which is investigated as a case that needs a solution through the question "HMW: How might we solve this issue?"

User	Need	Because	HMW
Students and educators used online learning during the pandemic, but this experience was not acknowledged outside the pandemic borders.	Students and educators need clear policies to regulate online learning regarding policies, standards, and accreditations in the GCC.	Online learning is the future of education in a growing digital marketplace.	How might we create HE policies that define and accredit online education through a standard framework?

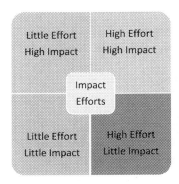

Figure 1.2 Impact/Effort model: This model is also called the "Effort/Impact matrix." It explores the various possible solutions and shows the "quick-fix" answers through the "Low effort/High impact" possibilities, the mid- and long-term projects through the "High effort/High impact" potentials, and eliminate the unfeasible solutions through the "High effort/Low impact" solutions.

Ideating

In order to reach feasible solutions, the previous seven suggestions were processed through the Impact/Effort model (Figure 1.2). The results included four categories:

1 **High Impact/Low Effort:**
   These options are quick gains because their administrative and financial efforts are low, but their impact is high:

   a Create new policies for remote education
   b Integrate UDL as a framework that sustains HE in the GCC
   c Impose clear regulations that oblige HE bodies to use eLearning curricula

2 **High Impact/High Effort:**
   These options can be set as mid- to long-term projects for the HE policymakers as they require feasibility studies to assess their potential success/failure:

   a Reform HE accreditation procedures
   b Benchmark with HE regional and international standards of online education
   c Create a framework that would shape HE policies

3 **Low Impact/High Effort:**
   The option is not feasible as it might be costly in its administration and funding requirements. The researchers did not find any suggestion under this criterion.

Potential Reforms in the GCC Higher Education Post COVID-19 19

4 **Low Impact/Low Effort:**
These options cannot be implemented because they are not feasible and have no substantial impact:

a Abandon online learning because it is not reliable

According to the above, the recommended solutions include creating new policies for remote education, integrating UDL as a framework that sustains HE in the GCC, and imposing clear regulations that oblige HE bodies to use it in curricula. These three points can be summarised as "creating HE policies based on the UDL as a sustainable framework."

Prototyping

Based on the "ideating" recommendations, this research suggests customising the UDL in HE (UDL) as a framework that manages HE policies in the GCC (CAST, 2023). This framework can produce sustainable and flexible teaching and learning policies both inside and outside crisis, potentially improving HE risk management. By adopting the UDL as a framework, the HE systems and bodies will be able to accommodate the sustainable teaching and learning needs of local students and faculty members in the region. They will also be inclusive of international learners and educators who are considered important parts of the region's HE public and private institutions.

UDL is an educational approach based on the learning sciences with three primary principles – multiple means of representation of information, multiple means of student action and expression, and multiple means of student engagement (Figure 1.3). It is distinguished by efforts "to create universal, barrier-free access to education for all students, including students with and without disabilities" (Scott, 2018). This framework is adequate for managing HE policies because it inspires blended and online learning by adopting various LMSs and alternative digital platforms to create an inclusive environment accommodating students' differences (Ferguson et al., 2019). It also

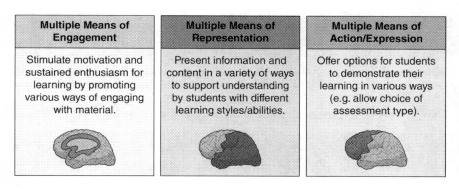

Figure 1.3 UDL paradigms.

encourages student engagement with the course material because the course and the curriculum are developed and improved according to students' feedback. Therefore, UDL can be customised to manage HE policies regarding administration, management, teaching faculty, and support services. Research indicates several barriers to implementing UDL, such as technology, training in digital teaching, and financial concerns (Scott, 2018). However, HE policies can overcome such barriers once they are addressed and investigated.

The proposed framework utilises the three paradigms of the UDL framework to manage HE policies, considering the HE experiment of COVID-19. The suggested model that manages HE policies is summarised as follows.

Paradigm One: Multiple Means of Representation

This paradigm allows HE policies to create sustainable and alternative means to display information and knowledge, creating an inclusive environment for students, including disabilities, personal conditions, and international students. It mainly stimulates the individual student to be interested and motivated in learning (Figure 1.4), and it can include the following set of HE policies and regulations:

1. Develop a variety of knowledge-delivery instruments, tools, and methods
2. Partial implementation of online/digital education in curricula
3. Develop inclusive environments in HE classrooms
4. Provide various options to sustain student comprehension
5. Implement digital platforms with various options for language, mathematical expressions, and symbols
6. Collaborate with the various HE bodies and students to refine HE policies through seminars and conferences
7. Revise procedures of degree attestation and accreditation through benchmarking
8. Integrate student engagement in the curricula and assessment

Paradigm Two: Multiple Means of Action and Expression

This paradigm allows HE educators to offer students various ways of sharing their work and reflecting on their learning, which potentially helps to solve individual differences. It also defines how learners interpret, understand, and

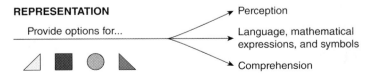

Figure 1.4 Paradigm one: Representation.

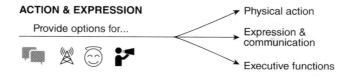

Figure 1.5 Paradigm two: Action and expression.

digest the information presented (Figure 1.5). HE policies should maintain the educators' roles in three significant points: provide students with options for physical activity, expression and communication, and executive functions (Rose et al., 2006). These policies must ensure that HE educators provide and display knowledge and course content in many forms to increase how learners associate the content with real-world experience (Scott, 2018). Therefore, the suggested HE policies under this paradigm include the following:

1 Deliver courses physically and virtually as a policy, not an option
2 Reform HE curricula to blend online and face-to-face assessment and interaction
3 Customise various digital platforms and applications to increase course accessibility
4 Assess and benchmark communication between HE faculty, policymakers, and students
5 Assess communication between HE decision-makers and international HE bodies and organisations
6 Define acceptable measures for remote education by defining the acceptable means and platforms for digital learning

Paradigm Three: Multiple Means of Engagement

The third paradigm motivates HE educators to increase their students' learning engagement and interaction. It entails different methods enabling the learners to navigate their learning environment and articulate what they have learned (UDL, 2014). This paradigm also requires considering the students' and educators' abilities to communicate and access communication tools: cultural background, neurology, personal relevance, and prior knowledge. In addition, policies under this paradigm should consider the educator's role, which includes providing options for recruiting interests, sustaining effort and persistence, and self-regulation (Figure 1.6). This paradigm is closely related to

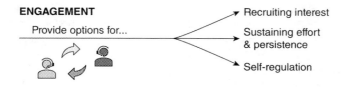

Figure 1.6 Paradigm three: Engagement.

providing inclusive environments because they significantly increase students' engagement (Katz, 2013).

Under this paradigm, the following points can be customised to define the framework for the HE policies in the GCC:

1 Define the measures and segments of students' engagement in HE
2 Implement digital communication as an integral part of student engagement
3 Promote digital communication via curricula and course designs
4 Assess student engagement with the course and educators every two years
5 Create action plans to improve student engagement with educators and course
6 Link the assessment of student engagement to the quality reports and action plans
7 Create collaborative projects that engage students and educators to improve student engagement in HE

Testing

In this phase, the suggested UDL framework was shared with the same Delphi Protocol educators' panel since they have more knowledge in the fields of education and GCC policies. The panels acknowledged the advantages of employing UDL as a framework for creating HE policies, and they mentioned the following advantages:

1 Empowers educators and learners
2 Allows students to express what they know of knowledge through different ways
3 Motivates students to show more interest and engagement
4 Enables educators to revise and improve taught materials and assessments
5 Creates space for various teaching tools

However, the panel also had the following reflections to improve the suggested UDL model:

1 Although the UDL is a universal design that will help the HE authorities establish new educational policies to support the diversity and internationalisation of the HE institutions, culture is a sensitive issue in this region. Most GCC states are composed of Arab Muslim communities with a conservative culture committed to their history, beliefs, and norms, which must be considered when defining "the inclusive environment."
2 The UDL still cannot prepare students to achieve the required level for success in standardised international assessments, which indicates that implementing such standards might be costly in time and finance.
3 The framework needs a SMART framework that ensures policy implementation by breaking it into steps or phases with feasible time and objectives.
4 All paradigms should go through a by-annual self-assessment to measure the success and feasibility of policy implementation.

Potential Reforms in the GCC Higher Education Post COVID-19 23

The researchers suggest adding the participants' feedback as notes to be attached to the suggested UDL framework to make it more flexible and able to accommodate further reforms whenever necessary.

Conclusion

This chapter has explored some reflections on sustaining HE policies in the GCC through the five phases of the DT model, two rounds of Delphi Protocol, and two round-table virtual discussions. Its analytical frame reflects a substantial awareness among educators and students of the necessary reforms to be implemented in the HE policies and practices, namely customising the HE experiences during the pandemic in the GCC to reform policies. These results also revealed that HE policies require some reforms and revisions to align with the shift in the mode of education and the newly adopted learning styles during the pandemic. Policies that provide clear procedures and regulations regarding remote education are highly significant, especially regarding pedagogical practices, accreditation, and curricula. These policies should also be standardised, leading HE in the GCC towards more internationalisation, advanced education quality, and sustainability. Therefore, the following points are recommended:

1 To implement a customised version of UDL as a national framework that manages HE policies and reform procedures, focusing on the emerging modes of hybrid, blended, and remote education
2 To explore the feasibility of educational reforms, including accrediting procedures and policies that regulate attestation procedures of online degrees, especially for students obtaining postgraduate degrees from foreign universities
3 To create a framework that clearly states conditions managing sustainable HE policies based on the pandemic experience
4 To create a clear and feasible timeline to implement the framework effectively
5 To assess and develop the framework periodically

While these recommendations could help reform education policies, more research to explore implementing the paradigms through a SMART action plan is recommended before implementing UDL in HE bodies of the GCC. Hence, this chapter opens the road for further investigation into effective ways to reform educational policies in the GCC.

References

Agbedahin, A. V. (2019). Sustainable development, education for sustainable development, and the 2030 agenda for sustainable development: Emergence, efficacy, eminence, and future. *Sustainable Development, 27*(4), 669–680.
Ahmed, A. (2020). COVID-19: University students in the UAE exempted from academic warnings and dismissals. https://gulfnews.com/uae/covid-19-university-students-in-the-uae-exempted-from-academic-warnings-and-dismissals-1.71090887

Alqahtani, A., & Rajkhan, A. (2020). E-learning critical success factors during the covid-19 pandemic: A comprehensive analysis of e-learning managerial perspectives. *Education Sciences, 10*(9), 216.

Alshakhi, A. (2021). EFL teachers' assessment practices of students' interactions in online classes: An activity theory lens. *TESOL International Journal, 16*(2), 148–176.

Ayoub, A. E. A. H., Almahamid, S. M., & Al Salah, S. F. (2021). Innovative work behaviour scale: Development and validation of psychometric properties in higher education in the GCC countries. *European Journal of Innovation Management, 26*(1), 119–133.

Bensaid, B., & Brahimi, T. (2020). Coping with COVID-19: Higher education in the GCC countries. In A. Visvizi, M. D. Lytras, & N. R. Aljohani (Eds.), *The international research & innovation forum* (pp. 137–153). Springer.

Braun, V., & Clarke, V. (2006). Using thematic analysis in psychology. *Qualitative Research in Psychology, 3*(2), 77–101.

CAST (2023). *About universal design for learning.* Retrieved September 3, 2023, https://www.cast.org/impact/universal-design-for-learning-udl.

Chakraborty, P., Mittal, P., & Gupta, M. S., & Yadav, S., & A. Arora. (2021). Opinion of students on online education during the COVID-19 pandemic. *Human Behaviour and Emerging Technologies, 3*(3), 357–365.

Chita-Tegmark, M., Gravel, J. W., De Lourdes, M., Serpa, B., Domings, Y., & Rose, D. H. (2012). Using the universal design for learning framework to support culturally diverse learners. *Journal of Education, 192*(1), 17–22.

Dhawan, S. (2020). Online learning: A panacea in the time of COVID-19 crisis. *Journal of Educational Technology Systems, 49*(1), 5–22.

Ferguson, B. T., McKenzie, J., & Dalton, E. M., & Lyner-Cleophas, M. (2019). Inclusion, universal design and universal design for learning in higher education: South Africa and the United States. *African Journal of Disability, 8*(1), 1–7.

Habes, M., Ali, S., & Khalid, A., Haykal, H. A., Elareshi, M., Khan, T., Ziani, A. (2021). E-Learning acceptance during the Covid-19 outbreak: A cross-sectional study. In A. M. Musleh Al-Sartawi, A. Razzaque, & M. M. Kamal (Eds.), *European, Asian, Middle Eastern, North African Conference on Management & Information Systems* (pp. 65–77). Springer.

Hashlamoun, A., & Nafeth (2021). Cultural challenges eLearners from the GCC countries face when enrolled in Western educational institutions: A thematic literature review. *Education and Information Technologies, 26*(2), 1409–1422.

Hodges, C. B., Moore, S., Lockee, B. B., Trust, T., & Bond, M. (2020). The difference between emergency remote teaching and online learning. *Educause Review* https://er.educause.edu/articles/2020/3/the-difference-between-emergency-remote-teaching-and-online-learning

Hrastinski, S. (2008). Asynchronous and synchronous e-learning. *Educause Quarterly, 31*(4), 51–55.

Katz, J. (2013). The three-block model of universal design for learning (UDL): Engaging students in inclusive education. *Canadian Journal of Education, 36*(1), 153–194.

Krishnapatria, K. (2020). From 'lockdown' to letdown: Students' perception of E-learning amid the COVID-19 outbreak. *ELT in Focus, 3*(1), 1–8.

Mahfoodh, H. (2021, November). Reflections on online EFL assessment: Challenges and solutions. In *2021 Sustainable Leadership and Academic Excellence International Conference (SLAE)* (pp. 1–8). IEEE.

Potential Reforms in the GCC Higher Education Post COVID-19   25

Mahfoodh, H., & AlAtawi, H. (2021, November). Higher education in COVID-19: From emergency to sustainable remote education. In *2021 Sustainable Leadership and Academic Excellence International Conference (SLAE)* (pp. 1–7). IEEE.

Mahfoodh, H., & Hashim, S. (2021). Integrating employability skills in EFL speaking and writing curricula through digital platforms. *TESOL International Journal, 16*(6.1), 66–87.

Pace, C., Pettit, S. K., & Barker, K. S. (2020). Best practices in middle-level quaranteaching: Strategies, tips and resources amidst COVID-19. *Becoming: Journal of the Georgia Association for Middle Level Education, 31*(1), 2–13.

Palvia, S., Aeron, P., Gupta, P., Mahapatra, D., Parida, R., Rosner, R., & Sindhi, S. (2018). Online education: Worldwide status, challenges, trends, and implications. *Journal of Global Information Technology Management, 21*(4), 233–241.

Plattner, H. (2013). An introduction to design thinking. Institute of Design at Stanford (pp. 1–15). https://dschool.stanford.edu/s/Redesign-the-School-Lunch-Experience.pdf

Pokhrel, S., & Chhetri, R. (2021). A literature review on impact of COVID-19 pandemic on teaching and learning. *Higher Education for the Future, 8*(1), 133–141.

Rose, D. H., Harbour, W. S., & Johnston, C. S., Daley, S. G., & Abarbanell, L. (2006). Universal design for learning in postsecondary education: Reflections on principles and their application. *Journal of Postsecondary Education and Disability, 19*(2), 135–151.

Schultz, R. B., & DeMers, M. N. (2020). Transitioning from emergency remote learning to deep online learning experiences in geography education. *Journal of Geography, 119*(5), 142–146.

Scott, L. A. (2018). Barriers to implementing a universal design for learning framework. *Inclusion, 6*(4), 274–286.

UDL. (2014). *National Centre on Universal Design for Learning. About UDL: Learn the basics.*

United Nations. (1987). *Report of the World Commission on Environment and Development: Our common future.* United Nations-WCED-World Commission on Environment and Development. www.un-documents.net/our-common-future.pdf

World Bank. (2021). *World Bank Education and COVID-19, learning data compact – UNESCO, UNICEF, and the World Bank unite to end the learning data crisis.*

Zimmerman, J. (2020, March 10). Coronavirus and the great online-learning experiment. Chronicle of Higher Education.

2 Pandemic Upsurge

Insights from Higher Education Reforms in the Gulf

Muhammad Rehan Shaukat and Abdul Sami

Introduction

The global crisis caused by COVID-19 has had profound impacts on health, society, and the economy worldwide. The initial outbreak of the 2019 coronavirus pandemic which originated in China, led to a rapid spread of the virus across the globe. With the emergence of new coronaviruses causing severe respiratory diseases in various countries, the world finds itself grappling with a pandemic for which vaccine was then unavailable, including treatment, antivirals, screening, or prevention methods. These epidemics are fuelled by low immunity and a lack of preparedness. The virus, characterised by its complexity, spreads swiftly through contact, particularly amongst individuals with compromised immune systems. Its rapid growth has defied expectations, challenging the belief that a viral population of a disease can self-sustain. Nations worldwide have experienced fluctuations in cases, highlighting the lack of clinical management and treatment understanding amongst healthcare professionals and governments, which has contributed to the severity of this epidemic. Insufficient pandemic-ready infrastructure in many governments has left them unprepared for unexpected surges or new threats, resulting in a slow response to the pandemic. The international community recognises the need to provide greater information, skills, resources, and equipment to support their allies. While some may argue that this outbreak is an epidemic rather than a pandemic, it is crucial to differentiate between the two. An epidemic refers to a localised outbreak with a sudden increase in disease incidence, whereas a pandemic occurs when the infection spreads across regions and possibly countries (Khan & McIntosh, 2005). In recent cases, there has been resistance on the part of health providers as well as governments because they are sceptical about the methods adopted by researchers and health personnel (Bin Othayman et al., 2022). These research methods are considered to be novel, and some may fear the use of such methods for fear of losing their jobs. To a large extent, public health officials in these countries have not given sound advice and have remained slow in responding to the outbreaks. Despite all of this, there has been rapid spread of the virus by medical staff, international travellers, and other members of the population including close contacts.

DOI: 10.4324/9781003457299-4

The response by governments has been too slow to prevent further proliferation as well as possible disruption in academic life, rising deaths, and increased instances of microbiological infections especially due to poor water supply in many places

The outbreak poses significant challenges for all affected countries, altering the landscape of higher education and daily life (Ma et al., 2021). There is a dire need for higher education institutions (HEIs) to review their preparedness measures in order to ensure that they remain relevant, effective, and efficient in the wake of this global outbreak. During the COVID-19 period, higher education in Gulf countries witnessed a drop in students and many institutions were in the process of closing their doors, especially those that have no modern facilities or equipment to accommodate the current situation (Leo et al., 2021). The national governments as well as international agencies have proven themselves to be slow and reluctant to provide relief. As a consequence, the higher education sector is being ruined by the closing down of universities and colleges (Al-Fadhel et al., 2020). The outbreak has spread to different parts of the world which is an alarming sign. It is important for HEIs across gulf states to take precautions since they share similar characteristics with China, a country with 800 million citizens. While the number is not as high, it is still important for the institutions to take appropriate preventive measures. Many colleges and universities lack sufficient resources and equipment to deal with this pandemic situation (Abdulrahim & Mabrouk, 2020). The outbreak of this virus highlights the ignorance of previous researchers in regard to the severity of a virus and its rapid transmission amongst people. The previous research studies were conducted in places where there were less than 100 cases and a significantly lower population density compared to the current situation, which is due to global population growth.

This chapter describes the COVID-19 epidemic, its causes, and its day-to-day complications within the context of Gulf higher education. Many universities were forced to close as a result of the pandemic, necessitating the shift to online education to meet student demand during this period of global transformation. This chapter also examines how eLearning has evolved and expanded in Gulf states and how offline and online learning impact higher education in Gulf states, their efforts to continue higher education, and how HEIs offer multiple phases of transformation. It investigates COVID-19's impact on HEIs as well as how new online tools and technology may be utilised to continue education. At the height of COVID-19 pandemic, more data become necessary and accessible, demonstrating that technology is continually advancing and that HEIs can investigate new avenues to make learning accessible.

This chapter is guided by the following points of enquiry:

- How has the COVID-19 pandemic affected higher education practices in the Gulf region?
- What eLearning tools are often used in higher education?

28 *Muhammad Rehan Shaukat and Abdul Sami*

- What are the challenges that face universities in Gulf countries as a result of severe virus COVID-19?
- What eLearning opportunities are available during COVID-19 pandemic?
- What are the implications of eLearning during COVID-19?

This chapter examines problems with higher education reform in Gulf states. Interviews and document analysis were done as the analytical frame. Namey et al. (2016) suggest 5 to 11 interviews based on the proportion of subjects disclosed at a particular stage of analysis divided by the total number of themes identified in order to achieve 80% saturation. In-person interviews with relevant sources provided evidence, and all telephone and electronic mail interviews were conducted in English. College students, instructors, and laboratory personnel affected by the pandemic were questioned. Informants were selected through the use of a non-random sampling strategy. This strategy assured that only participants in eLearning were included. The individual's identity was not revealed in this chapter for privacy considerations. The interview data were examined to comprehend the reasoning behind specific problems. The chapter seeks information regarding the reforms made by Gulf HEIs during COVID-19.

COVID-19 Pandemic and Higher Education

The COVID-19 pandemic is one of the most catastrophic and widespread epidemics in recent history, capable of causing irreparable damage to the global education system. It has forced many countries to rethink how they teach and learn (Fauzi & Khusuma, 2020). One way that countries have responded is through offering online learning opportunities to their students, while other countries have closed their doors and offered a complete overhaul of their current teaching systems (Budur et al., 2021). In the U.S., the COVID-19 pandemic has created a number of challenges and obstacles for students and educators (Nguyen & Kieuthi, 2020). Universities have closed due to widespread staff and faculty illness, and many universities have been forced to cancel or postpone exams (Maican & Cocoradă, 2021). In some universities, particularly colleges, the pandemic has forced authorities to address student concerns about financial aid. Some institutions of higher education have actually gone so far as cancelling classes for those enrolled in a full-time degree program (Irfan et al., 2018).

The impact of COVID-19 on the education system goes well beyond these immediate issues; however, the educational system has been forced to reevaluate its methods of teaching and learning, as well as the role that technology should play in the classroom (Nguyen & Kieuthi, 2020). There are debates within governments, universities, and colleges, and even amongst parents on whether traditional face-to-face or homework learning is still possible in the modern world (Rich et al., 2017). This crisis has forced higher education system to change their daily schedules and the way they approach teaching new material. In some parts of the world, education authorities have decided that face-to-face lessons cannot be conducted for a certain number of hours each day because sick students cannot be attending class due to COVID-19 symptoms (Dempsey et al., 2022). In other cases, colleges have had to institute staggered schedules, encouraging students to attend class a few times per day. In some universities around the world, students who already have full-time jobs have taken over teaching duties in lieu of those ill (Ferdig et al., 2020). Others have had to cancel their classes during the day and replace their lessons with online formats instead. In some instances, students are provided with additional support from professionals in order to help them meet their academic obligations (Vargo et al., 2021). Some universities have even created a separate classroom for those unable to attend whether through illness or lack of time, so that they can still meet their daily requirements (Barton, 2020).

COVID-19 has affected many different subjects within the curriculum as well as across countries and continents. For example, in the U.S., higher education system had to postpone standardised testing for several weeks because of issues with staffing during the pandemic (Daniel, 2020). The virus has also forced many universities to cancel or postpone events such as inter-university sports competitions and art exhibits (Xie et al., 2020). Some education systems have even axed entire subject areas from their lesson plans because they could not adequately staff those classes. This is a particularly big issue at universities where professors are often responsible for overseeing more than one area of study or multiple classes at once (Cahapay, 2020).

Education is an essential human right, a fundamental human goal, and one of the most important institutions in society. The COVID-19 pandemic has severely impacted education systems in many countries (Mustapha et al., 2021). It has also forced educational leaders to reevaluate the way that they teach material, evaluate their students' progress, and even the role that technology should play in their curricula (Nasution & Nandiyanto, 2021). Such a major disaster has forced many governments to address the needs of both students and educators, as well as the future of education in their societies (Ahmed et al., 2021). As a result, education systems around the world have been forced to reevaluate their methods of teaching and learning. In some areas of the world where COVID-19 has greatly impacted student attendance at universities during certain hours of the day or days of the week, officials have begun supplementing face-to-face lessons with online learning opportunities (Crawford et al., 2020). Others offer staggered university schedules so that students can attend class multiple times per day for brief periods of time. Some instructors even use online assignments, study guides, and other digital resources in their classes. Officials have established special classrooms for ill children. While instructing these courses, professionals can meet the needs of students. There is an enormous amount of debate within many government college administrations as to whether traditional education methods or online learning methods are viable ways forward (Al-Fadhel et al., 2020). Some education systems have decided that face-to-face and traditional lesson delivery is not possible because of limited staff and student attendance. In some cases, this has forced

How COVID-19 Influences eLearning in the Gulf Countries Context

As we have seen the various virtual resources and the utility of eLearning, it is crucial to evaluate how online learning impacts higher education (Pan et al., 2020). Universities and colleges worldwide must enhance their services in the light of the COVID-19 pandemic. As new information and technology become available, learning will become easier and more efficient (Cox, 2021). Technology aids education. The majority of individuals can afford it. This makes it easier for instructors to construct online courses accessible at any time. Online courses benefit pupils and save time and money for instructors (Leo et al., 2021).

According to one interviewee, online education is innovative and not solely a novelty amongst students. At the advent of the digital age, many viewed traditional learning methods as antiquated and ineffective; consequently, schools and institutions began to implement online learning. Students can learn and implement more when eLearning is utilised. eLearning enhances the learning of students. There exist instructor-led, self-paced, and hybrid online courses. Professors or academic professionals such as learning management system instructors lead instructor-led courses. Self-paced courses are suitable for students with demanding schedules. Weekends and late evenings provide these. Blended courses consist of lectures, discussions, and small group assignments and activities. The blended course allows students to determine their own class periods. This is beneficial for students with demanding schedules.

Numerous studies have demonstrated that online learning is effective (Amarneh et al., 2021; Islam et al., 2021). Online education motivates students more than traditional methods. Online education enhances academic and individual performance. Students can study at their own pace with online courses (Gismalla et al., 2021). Without television, sports, or video games, students can concentrate better and complete their homework quicker (Nuseir et al., 2021). This instruction helps students effectively manage their time.

Another interviewee stated that institutions have recognised the benefits of online learning. Many institutions and colleges in the U.S. and abroad are employing online learning methods because they have observed its benefits for students. eLearning enables students to work faster by allowing them to learn at their own pace. Online courses allow students to learn at their own tempo. At home, studying is simpler.

Numerous studies demonstrate the advantages of online education (Ansari et al., 2022; Maican & Cocoradă, 2021). Al-Mamari et al. (2021) found that online learning systems increase academic achievement, professional interest, and overall development. Students may complete assignments at any time. Homework does not consume classroom time. Online courses allow students to determine their own tempo. When children are unable to attend school due to family obligations, parents need not fret (Amarneh et al., 2021). Universities and institutions provide online study resources. Students have 24/7 access to their assignments. No need to transport literature when leaving the house. They can obtain papers and other study materials without leaving their homes or visiting a library. This is helpful for online pupils who must sign in and out (O'Sullivan et al., 2021).

Another expert observed that online education enhances student learning. eLearning provides simplicity, adaptability, and cost-effectiveness. Online courses provide content not available on campus. Students gain real-world experience through online assignments (Ashour, 2021). Due to its many benefits, online education is now very prevalent.

Online education has aided combat COVID-19. Multiple modalities are utilised in online education. Technology has made online learning lectures, journals, audiobooks, and video lessons available (Urbina Nájera & Calleja Mora, 2017). The flexibility of online learning in terms of delivery time and cost has been demonstrated to meet the requirements of students (Fauzi & Khusuma, 2020). Since the advent of the Internet, distance education technology has advanced significantly. Internet connectivity permits us to study whenever, wherever. Multiple administrations are employing strategies to promote eLearning and educational technology because they can help close the digital divide (Barana et al., 2019).

"The term 'eLearning' is an umbrella term that encompasses all forms of learning facilitated by ICTs" (UNESCO, Luan & Tsai, 2021). eLearning is the use of a computer or digital device to acquire knowledge from multiple sources (Vartiainen et al., 2021). Distance, collaboration, and sharing of knowledge are eLearning methods. eLearning is dominated by distance learning. This term refers to Internet-based communication between physically distant individuals (Al-Hunaiyyan et al., 2021). Learning collaboratively requires collaboration. This type of eLearning allows participants to express their views on a topic via open conversations (Kučak et al., 2018). Sharing accurate information constitutes knowledge transfer (Surya, 2019).

According to one respondent, eLearning allows students to study at any time and place. It is a benefit for busy employees. Educators must utilise technology due to changes in the learning process. Many universities offer online education like University of Edinburgh now offers eLearning. Since eLearning is relatively new, its curriculum design and delivery should be enhanced. (Bell, 2020). The Internet has assisted in the development and distribution of eLearning programmes (Alshurideh et al., 2020). With all of these technological advancements, educators must begin utilising technology in the classroom. This article discussed one of the numerous advantages of employing technology in education.

eLearning Tools Used in Higher Education

There is ongoing scrutiny surrounding eLearning in higher education. In response, it is argued that an increasing number of universities are adopting eLearning technologies. Some institutions utilise video lessons, while others leverage social media platforms such as Facebook or Twitter to interact with students. Virtual technology plays a crucial role in facilitating these advancements.

We know that online social networks and eLearning tools assist students meet their learning requirements. Connecting them all? GN University uses social media to make learning more dynamic, engaging, and fun by Smart Linking all of these wonderful technologies on their website. GN University encourages other institutions to embrace this practise, which helps students reach their full potential and improves teaching. The Smart Link may be a "course hub" where students may access lessons, assignments, and assessments. Students may access all their "courses" or learning materials in one handy portal. Live discussions between professors and students are another great aspect of the course portal. Some colleges use these educational materials to enhance teaching and student–teacher interactions. Smart Linking lets teachers and students utilise the same resource to develop materials. For example, if a professor from one university teaches a course on "The History of Mathematics", then it is possible for him to compile his lesson plans using materials from any other university within his network (Leo et al., 2021). This will help professors save time by receiving all of their course materials in one convenient location.

Virtual environment has several advantages for HEIs. Professors may use social media and new teaching approaches to create more interesting content that helps students learn faster and better. These networks are only in the US, but other higher education systems are adopting a similar method. This shows how innovation and technology can make college more inexpensive and accessible. This will assist produce future leaders and innovators who can lead society into the next technology era. Universities must embrace innovative approaches to help students learn quicker, better, and more efficiently.

COVID-19 and eLearning Challenges

Informants address COVID-19 eLearning problems. One said the COVID-19 corona virus had devastated educational establishments worldwide. To meet demand, new eLearning modules must be developed. This requires addressing the following issues. First, virtual classrooms reduce expectations of face-to-face connection. This has transformed how we educate, making us concentrate more on content than procedure. Since these virtual classrooms have no characteristics, we cannot regulate their atmosphere and maintain student engagement. Due to the absence of physical touch between students and professors, many feel uncomfortable, but by giving their virtual persona their own gestures and personality, they may overcome this. Second, cultural values vary. English is the language of teaching and entertainment, but not culture. Instructors may captivate audiences with more than images and music. To promote cross-cultural understanding, teachers might applaud students who engage in class or urge them to sing a song or cheer in their native language. Third, most online eLearning solutions use a worldwide network instead of a specialised infrastructure where they manage everything. New features must comply with this standard, making implementation challenging. Fourth, social media usage in eLearning has increased dramatically. YouTube and other sites have a lot of conference, lecture, and presentation footage. It is pointless to re-record this when it's so accessible. The eLearning system used for this material cannot scan video or audio files for keywords. Another respondent says that with so much online materials accessible, administrators and teachers sometimes find it difficult to choose what to utilise for whatever topic or course. Their pupils need high-quality, relevant, and interesting information. This procedure is not always easy. Google Chrome and Firefox pose security risks; hence several universities don't let students use the Internet. This move may be acceptable given recent ISIL assaults on essential infrastructure, but also makes it impossible for professors to supply students with internet material that may be valuable in their everyday lives. An eLearning system's vulnerability to malware and spyware installation is often overlooked. Just open an email attachment. Instructors manage the eLearning system and its content, but administrators testing the system in the lab may have issues. With all of these challenges, it is critical that we do everything we can to keep our students engaged during the inevitable disruptions (Injadat et al., 2021).

COVID-19 and eLearning Opportunities

Educational institutions have come up with innovative ways to provide access to their courses during the COVID -19 coronavirus pandemic (Singh & Lal, 2013). The emergence of COVID-19 virus in Africa has posed a challenge for academics. Online learning opportunities are an ideal solution during the pandemic owing to its lower cost, enhanced learner engagement, and ease of use (Tan & Shao, 2015). The article discusses how online education can be utilised during the time when higher educations are closed due to this virus, facing strict health guidelines in order to prevent any negative effects which might happen in an open environment. The article also gives insight on what learners need to do in order to be eligible for this opportunity and some other helpful tips that make online learning easy and fruitful. Faculty members can play an important role in promoting eLearning as an alternative to face this challenge (Mahyoob, 2020).

One interviewee responded that eLearning has made it possible for academics to have insight into their course or subject even when they do not have access to a classroom or any other resources. The online mode of teaching and learning has replaced the traditional lecture system while simultaneously ensuring student engagement which facilitates learning (Maatuk et al., 2022). eLearning has also made it possible for academics to get information from Internet and interactive tools which might have been hard to obtain in a traditional learning process (Almaiah et al., 2020). With the aid of eLearning, teachers can easily share strategies that engage learners and provide them with useful content for reference and other measures, which help them reach their academic goals. This chapter also gives insights on how eLearning encourages an individual to be an active and independent learner. On top of the various benefits linked with eLearning, it also facilitates recruitment of new staff members in higher educations. This is important as these staff members bring experience along with them which is essential for the attainment of academic goals (Hermawan, 2021).

Another interviewee responded that eLearning has also made it possible for academics to have insight into their course or subject even when they do not have access to a classroom or any other resources. The online mode of teaching and learning has replaced the traditional lecture system while simultaneously ensuring student engagement which facilitates learning. eLearning has also made it possible for academics to get information from Internet and interactive tools which might have been hard to obtain in a traditional learning process.

COVID-19 and eLearning Implications

With the interference of the pandemic, many HEIs had to quickly change their method of teaching for the safety of all students and staff (Oke & Fernandes, 2020). Some of these changes included the use of interactive video lectures instead of traditional classrooms and professors. This is a very beneficial change for all involved, as the student now has greater access to teachers via video, which makes it easier for the teacher to respond quickly to individual questions (Acheampong, 2021). This is not only beneficial to the students, but it is also beneficial to professors who can save time looking for student requests or questions on-hand. Another advantage to this type of teaching is the ability for students to rewind/forward and pause videos as they please. It also would give students a chance to pause the video and make their own notes while re-watching portions of the lecture that they might have missed before (Alhumaid et al., 2020). As with any new change, there are always some risks and advantages. In this case, one big disadvantage would be the loss of student–teacher interaction which some might see as a waste of time or a momentary distraction from their studies. On the other hand, there is a good possibility that students would be more engaged in their classes if they knew how to conduct their own research and ask their professors for extra help when needed (Alhumaid et al., 2020). In the end, this teacher–student interaction can be beneficial and this is simply a change that occurred after the pandemic. Overall, this example of interactive video lectures shows great potential for both professors and students as well as increasing accessibility to higher education for all.

Another great example of future education is the use of virtual reality (VR) technology. VR uses systems to create computer-simulated environments that one could experience in reality. For example, VR technology can be used to create a tutorial setting where students could put on their headsets and step inside an interactive house designed to teach them how to properly build a home (Jaoua et al., 2022). This would allow students to see, hear, and feel the

Pandemic Upsurge   35

environment as if they were truly there. This not only provides the real-life experience needed to prepare them for the working world, but also gives all students access to the same lesson and expands their overall knowledge of the subject matter (Keržič et al., 2021). The use of VR technology in education has already started to take off in some areas of Europe; however, there is still much room for improvement. One of these improvements involves the ability for students to physically interact with their surroundings. For example, being able to blow up a virtual wall or use a virtual hammer and nails to build the home would help students further understand the concepts they are learning (Talafha, 2022). Another area of improvement is the need for more realistic environments that allow students to learn from their mistakes. These types of systems would be huge in helping patients prepare for upcoming surgeries and allow them to get a better understanding of what will happen (Elnagar et al., 2021).

Conclusion and Recommendations

This chapter discusses how COVID-19 influences teaching techniques, student results, and national debate on higher education. It also suggests solutions. Students agreed that online learning works for skills-development material. Online learning was largely seen as ineffective for science and technology subjects by students. This may be due to insufficient training and support for online learning. Students also needed face-to-face lab facilities at HEIs due to a lack of virtual labs.

The COVID context of higher education reform in the Gulf is complicated because of fast socio-economic and political developments impacting institutions and society. Technology should be used more for social transformation. Over time, governance difficulties in our area have become more complicated, and conventional higher education models no longer work.

After showing the many advantages and drawbacks of virtual learning in higher education, there are still potentials for development. This chapter showed us the relevance of technology in higher education. COVID-19 had a major influence on all people at the end of 2021 and the first part of 2021, forcing the globe to adjust to an online platform. These online media foundations were not only for human engagement and connection, but also for employment and survival. Higher education has to support students and the industry. Due to the continuous usage of virtual education, institutions have cancelled or banned face-to-face sessions in favour of online classrooms for all courses and required students to enrol and practise with more online resources. This established a new market for apps and programmes to fulfil the needs of HEIs, students, and teachers. Teachers, students, and parents needed to adapt to the latest educational technology and instruments. Thus, self-education became easier. Virtual classrooms may save many schools money on real estate and other support systems and resources. To sustain learning continuity during a pandemic, this should be seen as a transient event, since the educational institution's ultimate goal is to create a literate community regardless of distribution method. However, considerable obstacles must be overcome. Due to the rapid move to online education, colleges and universities were unable to experiment to see whether this way of teaching was effective or even acceptable. Lack of research has prevented institutional boards and online platform providers from making quick education improvements. Google Classroom, Blackboard Learn, Ultra Collaborative, Zoom, and others are problematic for offline courses.

Faculty and students will struggle to communicate and finish tasks. Faculty will supervise and assess open-book examinations to ensure systematic invigilation. Wi-Fi makes cheating simpler since students may use internet resources and chat with peers without their teachers' knowledge. Institutions and students struggle with cybercrime and privacy. With more individuals online, criminals have a broader market to exploit. With a greater online audience, hackers have more access to information formerly solely accessible to institutions or students, which might cause bigger issues that need rapid treatment.

Implications

As suggested by the previous study, there are a multitude of implications for future research regarding the effects of the COVID-19 pandemic on higher education in the Gulf. These repercussions could aid institutions in recognising the impact of the pandemic on their operations and in devising strategies to face the impending challenges. The COVID-19 pandemic has had a significant impact on HEIs in the Gulf region, and its effects are expected to last for decades. The following are some potential research implications regarding the effects of COVID-19 on higher education in the Gulf. Due to the pandemic, HEIs in the Gulf region were compelled to implement online learning swiftly. Policy makers may examine the effects of online education on students, instructors, and institutions. For instance, studies could investigate the impact of online education on educational quality, student engagement, and student retention rates. The pandemic has highlighted the need for robust technology infrastructure in colleges and universities. How institutions in the Gulf region have adapted their technological infrastructure to facilitate online learning and remote work could be investigated. In addition, the analysis could investigate the difficulties and opportunities associated with implementing new technologies. As a result of the pandemic, enrolment in HEIs has been significantly disrupted. The short- and long-term effects of the pandemic on enrolment in Gulf HEIs could be investigated. In addition, the research could examine the factors that influence student enrolment decisions, such as safety concerns, financial considerations, and online learning accessibility. Due to the pandemic, a number of colleges and universities in the Gulf region are experiencing financial difficulties. It is possible to investigate the post-pandemic financial viability of Gulf HEIs, including the impact on tuition, research grants, and donations. The pandemic has impeded the internationalisation efforts of a number of Gulf-based HEIs. In response to the pandemic, HEIs in the Gulf

Pandemic Upsurge 37

may have modified their internationalisation strategies as well as re-examined the long-term effects of the pandemic on international student recruitment, faculty mobility, and research partnerships.

References

Abdulrahim, H., & Mabrouk, F. (2020). COVID-19 and the digital transformation of Saudi Higher Education. *Asian Journal of Distance Education*, 15(1), 291–306.

Acheampong, T. Y. (2021). Impact of Covid-19 on e-commerce in the European Union. *ENTRENOVA-ENTerprise REsearch InNOVAtion*, 7(1), 89–98.

Ahmed, S., Taqi, H. M., Farabi, Y. I., Sarker, M., Ali, S. M., & Sankaranarayanan, B. (2021). Evaluation of flexible strategies to manage the COVID-19 pandemic in the education sector. *Global Journal of Flexible Systems Management*, 22(2), 81–105.

Al-Fadhel, H., Al-Jalahma, A., & Al-Muhanadi, M. (2020). The reporting of technological readiness of higher education institutions in GCC countries: A situational analysis of COVID-19 crisis. In *2020 Sixth International Conference on E-Learning (Econf)* (pp. 296–301). IEEE.

Alhumaid, K., Ali, S., Waheed, A., Zahid, E., & Habes, M. (2020). COVID-19 & E-learning: Perceptions & attitudes of teachers towards E-learning acceptance in the developing countries. *Multicultural Education*, 6(2), 100–115.

Al-Hunaiyyan, A., Alhajri, R., & Bimba, A. (2021). Towards an efficient integrated distance and blended learning model: How to minimise the impact of COVID-19 on education. *International Journal of Interactive Mobile Technologies*, 15(10), 173–193.

Almaiah, M. A., Al-Khasawneh, A., & Althunibat, A. (2020). Exploring the critical challenges and factors influencing the E-learning system usage during COVID-19 pandemic. *Education and Information Technologies*, 25(6), 5261–5280.

Al-Mamari, K., Al-Zoubi, S., Bakkar, B., & Al-Shorman, A. (2021). The impact of e-learning during COVID-19 on teaching daily living skills for children with disabilities. *Journal of E-Learning and Knowledge Society*, 17(3), 135–145.

Alshurideh, M., Al Kurdi, B., Salloum, S. A., Arpaci, I., & Al-Emran, M. (2020). Predicting the actual use of m-learning systems: A comparative approach using PLS-SEM and machine learning algorithms. *Interactive Learning Environments*, 31(3), 1214–1228.

Amarneh, B. M., Alshurideh, M. T., Al Kurdi, B. H., & Obeidat, Z. (2021). The impact of COVID-19 on E-learning: Advantages and challenges. In A. E. Hassanien, et al. *Proceedings of the International Conference on Artificial Intelligence and Computer Vision (AICV2021). Advances in Intelligent Systems and Computing*, vol 1377. (pp. 75–89). Springer. https://doi.org/10.1007/978-3-030-76346-6_8

Ansari, M., Alshammari, F., Alqahtani, H., Alshammari, R., Althubyani, M., Al Hagbani, T., & Alshammari, B. (2022). Healthcare students' perceptions towards using e-learning, and self-reported drivers and barriers during COVID-19 pandemic. *Journal of Young Pharmacists*, 14(1), 89.

Ashour, S. (2021). How COVID-19 is reshaping the role and modes of higher education whilst moving towards a knowledge society: The case of the UAE. *Open Learning: The Journal of Open, Distance and e-Learning*, 1–16.

Barana, A., Brancaccio, A., Conte, A., Fissore, C., Floris, F., Marchisio, M., & Pardini, C. (2019). The role of an advanced computing environment in teaching and learning mathematics through problem posing and solving. In *Proceedings of the 17th International Scientific Conference on eLearning and Software for Education* (vol. 2, pp. 11–18), Bucharest, Romania, April 22–23, 2021.

Barton, D. C. (2020). Impacts of the COVID-19 pandemic on field instruction and remote teaching alternatives: Results from a survey of instructors. *Ecology and Evolution, 10*(22), 12499–12507.

Bell, J. (2020). *Machine learning: Hands-on for developers and technical professionals.* John Wiley & Sons.

Bin Othayman, M., Mulyata, J., Meshari, A., & Debrah, Y. (2022). The challenges confronting the training needs assessment in Saudi Arabian higher education. *International Journal of Engineering Business Management, 14*, 1–13.

Budur, T., Demir, A., & Cura, F. (2021). University readiness to online education during Covid-19 pandemic. *International Journal of Social Sciences & Educational Studies, 8*(1), 180–200.

Cahapay, M. B. (2020). Rethinking education in the new normal post-COVID-19 era: A curriculum studies perspective. *Aquademia, 4*(2), ep20018. https://doi.org/10.29333/aquademia/8315

Cox, A. M. (2021). Exploring the impact of Artificial Intelligence and robots on higher education through literature-based design fictions. *International Journal of Educational Technology in Higher Education, 18*(1), 1–19.

Crawford, J., Butler-Henderson, K., Rudolph, J., Malkawi, B., Glowatz, M., Burton, R., Magni, P., & Lam, S. (2020). COVID-19: 20 countries' higher education intra-period digital pedagogy responses. *Journal of Applied Learning & Teaching, 3*(1), 1–20.

Daniel, S. J. (2020). Education and the COVID-19 pandemic. *Prospects, 49*(1), 91–96.

Dempsey, A., Lanzieri, N., Luce, V., de Leon, C., Malhotra, J., & Heckman, A. (2022). Faculty respond to COVID-19: Reflections-on-action in field education. *Clinical Social Work Journal, 50*(1), 11–21.

Elnagar, A., Afyouni, I., Shahin, I., Nassif, A. B., & Salloum, S. A. (2021). The empirical study of e-learning post-acceptance after the spread of COVID-19: A multi-analytical approach based hybrid SEM-ANN. *ArXiv Preprint ArXiv:2112.01293.*

Fauzi, I., & Khusuma, I. H. S. (2020). Teachers' elementary school in online learning of COVID-19 pandemic conditions. *Jurnal Iqra': Kajian Ilmu Pendidikan, 5*(1), 58–70.

Ferdig, R. E., Baumgartner, E., Hartshorne, R., Kaplan-Rakowski, R., & Mouza, C. (2020). *Teaching, technology, and teacher education during the COVID-19 pandemic: Stories from the field.* Association for the Advancement of Computing in Education.

Gismalla, M. D.-A., Mohamed, M. S., Ibrahim, O. S. O., Elhassan, M. M. A., & Mohamed, M. N. (2021). Medical students' perception towards E-learning during COVID 19 pandemic in a high burden developing country. *BMC Medical Education, 21*(1), 1–7.

Hermawan, D. (2021). The rise of e-learning in covid-19 pandemic in private university: Challenges and opportunities. *IJORER: International Journal of Recent Educational Research, 2*(1), 86–95.

Injadat, M., Moubayed, A., Nassif, A. B., & Shami, A. (2021). Machine learning towards intelligent systems: Applications, challenges, and opportunities. *Artificial Intelligence Review, 54*(23), 3299–3348.

Irfan, A., Rasli, A., Sulaiman, Z., Sami, A., & Qureshi, M. I. (2018). Use of social media sites by Malaysian universities and its impact on university ranking. *International Journal of Engineering and Technology(UAE), 7*(4.28 Special Issue 28), 67–71.

Islam, M. A., Nur, S., & Talukder, M. S. (2021). E-learning in the time of COVID-19: Lived experiences of three university teachers from two countries. *E-Learning and Digital Media, 18*(6), 557–580.

Jaoua, F., Almurad, H. M., Elshaer, I. A., & Mohamed, E. S. (2022). E-learning success model in the context of COVID-19 pandemic in higher educational institutions. *International Journal of Environmental Research and Public Health, 19*(5), 2865.

Kahn, J. S., & McIntosh, K. (2005). History and recent advances in coronavirus discovery. *The Pediatric infectious disease journal, 24*(11), S223–S227.

Keržič, D., Alex, J. K., Pamela Balbontín Alvarado, R., Bezerra, D. S., Cheraghi, M., Dobrowolska, B., Fagbamigbe, A. F., Faris, M. E., França, T., & González-Fernández, B. (2021). Academic student satisfaction and perceived performance in the e-learning environment during the COVID-19 pandemic: Evidence across ten countries. *PLoS One, 16*(10), e0258807.

Kučak, D., Juričić, V., & Đambić, G. (2018). Machine learning in education-a survey of current research trends. In *Proceedings of the 29th International DAAAM Symposium 2018* (pp. 0406–0410). DAAAM International. https://doi.org/10.2507/29th.daaam.proceedings.059

Leo, S., Alsharari, N. M., Abbas, J., & Alshurideh, M. T. (2021). From offline to online learning: A qualitative study of challenges and opportunities as a response to the COVID-19 pandemic in the UAE higher education context. In M. T. Alshurideh, A. E. Hassanien, & R. Masa'deh (Eds.), *The effect of coronavirus disease (COVID-19) on business intelligence* (pp. 203–217). Springer.

Luan, H., & Tsai, C.-C. (2021). A review of using machine learning approaches for precision education. *Educational Technology & Society, 24*(1), 250–266.

Ma, G., Black, K., Blenkinsopp, J., Charlton, H., Hookham, C., Pok, W. F., Sia, B. C., & Alkarabsheh, O. H. M. (2021). Higher education under threat: China, Malaysia, and the UK respond to the COVID-19 pandemic. *Compare: A Journal of Comparative and International Education, 52*(5), 841–857.

Maatuk, A. M., Elberkawi, E. K., Aljawarneh, S., Rashaideh, H., & Alharbi, H. (2022). The COVID-19 pandemic and E-learning: Challenges and opportunities from the perspective of students and instructors. *Journal of Computing in Higher Education, 34*(1), 21–38.

Mahyoob, M. (2020). Challenges of e-learning during the COVID-19 pandemic experienced by EFL learners. *Arab World English Journal (AWEJ), 11*(4), 351–362.

Maican, M.-A., & Cocoradă, E. (2021). Online foreign language learning in higher education and its correlates during the COVID-19 pandemic. *Sustainability, 13*(2), 781.

Mustapha, I., Van, N. T., Shahverdi, M., Qureshi, M. I., & Khan, N. (2021). Effectiveness of digital technology in education during COVID-19 pandemic. A bibliometric analysis. *International Journal of Interactive Mobile Technologies, 15*(8), 136–154.

Namey, E., Guest, G., McKenna, K., & Chen, M. (2016). Evaluating bang for the buck: A cost-effectiveness comparison between individual interviews and focus groups based on thematic saturation levels. *American Journal of Evaluation, 37*(3), 425–440.

Nasution, A. R., & Nandiyanto, A. B. D. (2021). Utilization of the google meet and quiziz applications in the assistance and strengthening process of online learning during the COVID-19 pandemic. *Indonesian Journal of Educational Research and Technology, 1*(1), 31–34.

Nguyen, D. T., & Kieuthi, T. C. (2020). New trends in technology application in education and capacities of universities lecturers during the covid-19 pandemic. *International Journal of Mechanical and Production Engineering Research and Development (IJMPERD), 10*, 1709–1714.

Nuseir, M. T., El-Refae, G. A., & Aljumah, A. (2021). The e-learning of students and university's brand image (post COVID-19): How successfully Al-Ain University have embraced the paradigm shift in digital learning. In M. T. Alshurideh, A. E. Hassanien, & R. Masa'deh (Eds.), *The effect of coronavirus disease (COVID-19) on business intelligence* (pp. 171–187). Springer.

Oke, A., & Fernandes, F. A. P. (2020). Innovations in teaching and learning: Exploring the perceptions of the education sector on the 4th industrial revolution (4IR). *Journal of Open Innovation: Technology, Market, and Complexity, 6*(2), 31.

O'Sullivan, S. M., Khraibi, A. A., Chen, W., & Corridon, P. R. (2021). Lessons learned transitioning from traditional premedical and medical education to E-learning platforms during the COVID-19 pandemic within the United Arab Emirates. *Journal of Medical Education and Curricular Development, 8*, 23821205211025860.

Pan, S. L., Cui, M., & Qian, J. (2020). Information resource orchestration during the COVID-19 pandemic: A study of community lockdowns in China. *International Journal of Information Management, 54*, 102143.

Rich, P. J., Jones, B., Belikov, O., Yoshikawa, E., & Perkins, M. (2017). Computing and engineering in elementary school: The effect of year-long training on elementary teacher self-efficacy and beliefs about teaching computing and engineering. *International Journal of Computer Science Education in Schools, 1*(1), 1–20.

Singh, S., & Lal, S. P. (2013). Educational courseware evaluation using machine learning techniques. *2013 IEEE Conference on E-Learning, e-Management and e-Services* (pp. 73–78). IEEE.

Surya, L. (2019). Machine learning-future of quality assurance. *International Journal of Emerging Technologies and Innovative Research, 6*(5), 1078–1082.

Talafha, A. H. (2022). E-learning challenges and opportunities for students with special needs during COVID-19 pandemic. *Technium Social Sciences Journal, 28*, 89–105.

Tan, M., & Shao, P. (2015). Prediction of student dropout in e-learning program through the use of machine learning method. *International Journal of Emerging Technologies in Learning, 10*(1), 11–17.

Urbina Nájera, A. B., & Calleja Mora, J. (2017). Brief review of educational applications using data mining and machine learning. *Revista Electrónica de Investigación Educativa, 19*(4), 84–96.

Vargo, D., Zhu, L., Benwell, B., & Yan, Z. (2021). Digital technology use during COVID-19 pandemic: A rapid review. *Human Behavior and Emerging Technologies, 3*(1), 13–24.

Vartiainen, H., Toivonen, T., Jormanainen, I., Kahila, J., Tedre, M., & Valtonen, T. (2021). Machine learning for middle schoolers: Learning through data-driven design. *International Journal of Child-Computer Interaction, 29*, 100281.

Xie, X., Siau, K., & Nah, F. F.-H. (2020). COVID-19 pandemic–online education in the new normal and the next normal. *Journal of Information Technology Case and Application Research, 22*(3), 175–187.

3 Towards a Self-Sustainable Higher Education Quality Assurance System

The NFCFFE Model for Gulf and South Asian Nations

Radha Krishan Sharma

Introduction

COVID-19 pandemic has affected education systems throughout the world. Sudden lockdown to stop the spread of virus during the first wave of the pandemic stunned academicians, administrators, regulators, students, and other stakeholders. Majority of higher education institutions (HEIs) throughout the world, in general, and the Gulf and South Asian countries, in particular, had no clue how to survive in the situation. Academicians and students who were used to 'face-to-face' teaching-learning methods found themselves in highly challenging situations. This was mainly because they were left with no 'access to infrastructure' and 'training to handle such a situation'. Educational administrators were confused as they had no clue what and how to build infrastructure and train stakeholders to quickly respond to the challenging situation. Non-availability of facilities, 'expensive, weak or no internet connectivity', particularly in remote locations of the Gulf and South Asian countries, suddenly became a matter of concern to governments and policy makers. Following lessons learned from the first wave, a big majority of the stakeholders prepared themselves for the second wave of the pandemic. By that time, most of the stakeholders were mentally prepared to face the challenge; however, investing in expensive ICT equipment remained a challenge to a vast majority, throughout the developing countries, particularly at the time when a large population lost their employment and had been struggling for livelihood. El Said (2021) highlighted the significance of online teaching-learning in future. All this together, made the academic world realise the significance of working on online and distance learning in a post-pandemic world.

During COVID-19 pandemic, many new Edtech start-ups have introduced online and app-based student support systems and programmes. Certificate courses offered by online platforms like 'Coursera', 'LinkedIn', and 'MOOC',

DOI: 10.4324/9781003457299-5

42 *Radha Krishan Sharma*

among others, have gained popularity during this pandemic. A few well-equipped universities and colleges have also introduced online postgraduate (PG) and undergraduate (UG) programmes. Even some regulators like UGC (India) are actively supporting and promoting Open and Distance Learning and Online education. However, in contrast to growing stakeholders' confidence in online certificate courses, online PG or UG programmes are still struggling to gain recognition by stakeholders. Pre-pandemic quality of HEIs' physical campus-based programmes was already in question, and the pandemic has further increased concern for stakeholders. During this period, on the one hand, HEIs throughout the globe have lost revenue of trillions of dollars, on the other, they have to spend a big part of it to build and/or improve online and blended teaching-learning infrastructure at par with societal expectations in order to maintain quality. For a considerable number of HEIs, this has become a question of survival; hence, this huge cost needs to be handled very carefully and efficiently.

Pre-pandemic models of quality management adopted by HEIs left them helpless during the strike of COVID-19 pandemic. HEIs, regulators, and all other stakeholders of the Gulf and South Asian countries are concerned about refining and reshaping systems to meet dynamic needs of employment market and society at large. Along with others, one of the key concerns is to develop fresh standards, norms, and other modalities to support, monitor, and regulate quality of offline as well as online higher education (HE). HEIs and stakeholders took a long time to develop, implement, review, and improve the HE system; now working afresh in new scenario is certainly a big challenge. HEIs and stakeholders are still struggling to cope with the situation. Hence, this chapter proposes a sustainable quality improvement and assurance (QIA) model, i.e. 'NFCFFE Model', for HEIs around the globe, specifically for the Gulf and South Asian countries. 'NFCFFE Model' is primarily a conceptual model to open debate for the future of HE in post-pandemic world. This model has built upon the '5 Layers GQA Model' proposed by Sharma et al. (2019). 'NFCFFE Model' is a six-layered model. The first layer highlights the areas where quality assurance (QA) is 'Needed'; the next layer talks about stages where QA must have customised 'Focus'; the third one recommends a strategy to develop QA 'Culture'; the fourth layer talks about QA 'Framework' while the fifth one offers practical suggestions and efficient QA 'Feedback' mechanism; and the sixth layer defines 'Essentials' for sustainable QA. The chapter attempts to highlight key shadow areas and explain how each of six layers will help to develop systems to meet pandemic-related challenges. The model has been developed with out-of-the-box thinking and problem-solving ideas shared by different stakeholders of different countries.

Pre-Pandemic

Education reforms and increase in number of HEIs created an opportunity to learners in the Gulf and South Asian countries, but this has brought some challenges too. *Materu (2007) highlighted 'countries are becoming conscious of the need for effective quality assurance and quality improvement'; he further mentioned that fast increase in enrolments, insufficient numbers of qualified academicians, low efficiency (internal and external), and poor governance are some factors contributing to the decline of higher education quality.* Odhiambo (2011) highlighted that diminishing income, brain drain, increasing government interference, and negative aspects of globalisation are contributing to diminishing HE quality; further in 2014, he stressed upon the need of a strong internal and external QA framework. Sharma et al. (2019) highlighted the pressure of QA on HEIs in India and Oman. They stressed the need for a sustainable QA system focused on continuous improvement, for HE QIA. According to study, '... *Not only Quality Assurance but continuous improvement of QA system is also a must, to match the output quality with ever-changing market needs. A sustainable QA system should be adaptive, dynamic and also focus on continuous informed improvement based on rational feedback of different stake holders of HEIs...'.* They proposed a '5-Layered Generalised Quality Assurance' (GQA) Model for sustainable internal QIA for HEIs. The paper also concludes that review feedback collected from a group of stakeholders with diversified personality needs to be *'carefully assessed and scientifically filtered'* before using for improvement. Similarly, Sharma (2020) mentioned '... *the demand for higher education is rapidly increasing along with the challenges of quality and sustenance'.* According to him, quality and fitness of purpose is not paid required attention, which resulted to *skill gaps, research gaps, relevance gaps,* etc., and '... *got converted into issues like access, equity, quality and employability...'.* UNESCO in its Global Convention on the Recognition of Qualifications Concerning Higher Education at 40th session highlighted the need of building cooperation among member countries for HE QIA. *'Higher education institutions (HEIs) are increasingly being held accountable for maintaining quality in their activities by governments, industry, students, and the community as a whole'* Al-Amri et al. (2020).

Post-Pandemic

Sudden closure of HEIs due to COVID-19 pandemic made the situation worse and disclosed the reality of vast majority of HEIs. Roy and Brown (2022) highlighted that despite the use of Learning Management System by a few premier public and private sector HEIs, majority of HEIs suffered because of unpreparedness. Based on experience during the pandemic, authors classified HEIs in three categories *'prepared', 'quick responders',* and *'unprepared'* and concluded that majority of them were unprepared. Study also places doubt on institutional leadership and stresses upon the need of more studies and a sustainable solution. Similarly, Agrawal (2021) revealed that during the pandemic *'45% of students never joined an online class during the entire session. Further analysis demonstrated that 13% of students*

44 *Radha Krishan Sharma*

do not have their own mobile phone, nearly 18% could not join due to poor internet connectivity, 21% of students faced unfavourable study environment at home and 3% of students have other reasons'. The condition was worse in rural areas where education is not one among priorities. Authors urge, *'to promote education in COVID 19 era strong strategies are urgently needed'.* Gandhi and Rani (2020) also questioned the preparedness of HEIs to handle this crisis. They highlighted the struggle of stakeholders, particularly teachers and students, to upgrade themselves for online teaching-learning without any support, guidance, and training. The paper discusses key problems that arise because of the pandemic, e.g. *Mental Health, Quality of Teaching-Learning, Health Issues, Social Divide, Missing of Real Touch,* etc. The paper further suggests some positive effects of the pandemic on education sector, e.g. *Skill Enhancement, Transition in methods of teaching and learning, Positive Mindset, The Emergence of a new model of learning, Local to Global,* etc. Authors also provide some suggestions to government and other stakeholders to overcome the scenario. Sarkar et al. (2021) highlighted post-pandemic crisis of education system in Bangladesh like the rest of the world. Their findings also match with others, i.e. difficulty faced by students with sudden shift to online classes. They observed more participation and positive approach of urban students, those too more female students compared to male, and students with access to ICT facilities with Wi-Fi connection had more positive perception towards online teaching-learning. The study also proposes *essential guidelines for better policy development in future.*

Rodriguez et al. (2022) in World Bank document revealed that according to World Bank report 2020 'School closures and the economic downturn severely affected education systems. While schools were closed, learning gains that students previously achieved were partially lost'. They further observed that *'However, several LMICs reacted quickly to mitigate these shocks to their respective education systems ... most of the countries were focused on coping with the emergency by designing and implementing remote learning programs aimed at reaching all students and teachers, but less on monitoring progress and designing programs for remedial learning'.*

The World Bank twin report 2022 highlights that technology and its access are crucial for the success of Edtech for effective remote learning. The teacher's role has become more critical, and hence they must be trained and supported for using technology and upgrading pedagogy for teaching in person or remotely. Use of the most appropriate technology will help teachers as well as students to interact meaningfully in local context even if they are interacting remotely (Muñoz-Najar et al., 2021).

Overall, pre-pandemic as well as post-pandemic literature expressed concern about QIA mechanism and resulted deterioration in quality of HE. The literature highlights the need of development and adoption of a self-sustainable QIA system/model by HEIs.

Available Quality Improvement and Assurance Models

PDCA Cycle

Deming's PDCA cycle is a high-level model generally used as a TQM tool for continuous improvement by starting change with a small size to test results on improvement in overall organisational outcomes. According to Lodgaard and Aasland (2011), sufficiency of Time, Recourses, and Commitment are crucial for better outcomes using PDCA. Maruyama and Inoue (2016) defined 'P (Plan): Contents and Levels of Learning and Educational Achievement Goals' and suggested four levels of learning, i.e. '1-Know', '2-Conceive', '3-Act', and '4-Master', 'D (Do): Educational Method, Program Design for Goal Achievement', 'C (Check): Evaluation Method to Assess Goal Achievement', and 'A (Act): Improvement of Overall Education Program Based on Assessment Results'. They proposed a leadership education programme design flowchart through PDCA and concluded that by applying and repeating PDCA cycle from 2008 to 2013, learning level 3 (Act) and 4 (Master) had been achieved.

Plan-Implement-Evaluate-Act Model

Luxton (2005) mentioned that 'In practice quality improvement is concerned with an ongoing cycle of agreeing on a set of standards and/or goals, gathering relevant information, evaluating feedback and ensuring the implementation of change'. The author characterised quality institution as 'culture of evaluation and change', 'High level of satisfaction of stakeholders', 'agreement and implementation of quality improvement with high commitment of all', continuous measurable improvement', 'open communication', and 'institutional commitment and confidence' and suggested seven principles for quality management structures and improvement processes. In replacement to PDCA Model, the author proposed Plan-Implement-Evaluate-Act model and also proposed a working chart of organisational structure. The conclusion stresses upon involvement of all stakeholders throughout the organisation and commitment of management for establishing organisational culture for quality improvement.

European Foundation for Quality Management Excellence Model

This generalised model introduced by the European Foundation for Quality Management (EFQM) is not confined to any one or few sectors, rather the model is equally useable by all types of institution, sectors, industries, etc. The model is a self-assessment tool for continuous evaluation and improvement. 'RADAR logic' of the model makes it sustainable and useful to all at all the time. (Uygur & Sümerli, 2013). EFQM claims that the model is helpful

46   *Radha Krishan Sharma*

to *'define a strong purpose, inspire leaders at every level and create a culture committed to driving performance, while remaining agile, adaptive and able to evolve for THE FUTURE'.*

Five-Layered Generalised Quality Assurance Model

The conceptual model was proposed by Sharma, Jain, and Kumar at GRM 2019 in Cambridge, UK. In the first layer, i.e. QA Need, the model highlights areas of HEI teaching-learning process where QIA is needed. In its first layer, the model stresses upon QA need at four stages of HEI's operations: 'Prepare', 'Conceive', 'Groom', and 'Deliver' (PCGD). The second layer argues that there are three different stages in the life cycle of HEIs, i.e. 'Formation', 'Operation', and 'Monitoring' and all these three need different focus from QA point of view. The third layer of the model suggests a pathway to establish quality culture in HEIs with the help of continuous orientations, training, and reminders. Layer four of the model defines QA framework consisting of cycle of 'Improve', 'Implement', and 'Review' for sustainable continuous improvement. The fifth layer of the model argues about the significance of continuous collection, assessment, filtering, and then use of stakeholders' feedback. The paper argues that most of the time feedback is influenced by an individual's personality traits. Hence, feedback collected from different stakeholders must be scientifically filtered before using for improvement.

Future Higher Education Models

Orr et al. (2020) suggested four models of HE in 2030, i.e. Tamagotchi, Jenga, Lego Set, and Transformer models. This is not a quality improvement or assurance model, but this is a guide, as the model talks about the future of HEIs. According to them, 'Tamagotchi model' is the same as the current classical model starting with school passing through UG, PG, and leading to employment. 'Jenga model' is quite like Tamagotchi model because of the shorter period of learning and its focus to self-learning makes it popular among non-traditional students. Rather than one compact unit, the 'Lego Set model' is a self-reliant and non-standardised learning path. It is a combination of modules of different sizes. On the other hand, 'Transformer model' is for those who discontinued their education for some time because of one reason or another and now willing to rejoin HE for their own career growth.

Objectives of the Chapter

This chapter is an attempt to propose a model showing sustainable internal quality adoption, implementation, improvement, and assurance, particularly for HEIs in the Gulf and South Asia. It is evident from the literature that the quality of HE is not a new concern for the world. Post-pandemic crisis has

Self-Sustainable Higher Education Quality Assurance System 47

placed a question mark on sustainability of prevailing QIA models particularly adopted by HEIs in the Gulf and South Asian countries. Many researchers, academicians, administrators, employers, regulators, and other stakeholders from developed as well as developing countries have expressed their apprehension and stressed upon the need of a more refined and sustainable internal QIA model forHE.

The discussions were based on primary and secondary qualitative data. In the first stage of primary data collection, formal as well as informal, semi-structured interviews, discussions, and observations were conducted. Once a basic draft was developed, 'Focused Group Discussions (FGD)' with different stakeholders separately was organised for developing an in-depth understanding of opinion, issues, and ideas of that group of stakeholders. After compiling and incorporating information and ideas of different stakeholders, in the draft, finally the improved draft was shared with experts, already working in QIA of HEIs of different countries in different capacities and a FGD was conducted to reach to final outcome. For all FGDs, attempts were placed to open participants by giving them more opportunity to raise issues and share ideas, using open-ended questions and limited intervention by moderator. For better FGDs' outcome, the numbers of participants were limited between six and eight. In some situations of FGDs, Delphi method (Adler & Ziglio, 1996) was used for minimising differences or to reach consensus of opinions, ideas, and suggestions. Secondary data have been collected from research publication, government, and independent accreditation agencies' websites, media, and other online and offline sources. After every stage of data collection, data has been compiled in the form of tables and/or write-ups for easy understanding, better analysis, and interpretation.

Voices from HEI Staff

Most of the faculty members and administrative staff of HEIs in the Gulf and South Asian countries are not happy with the planning process. A common opinion is that plans are made at the top level with top-down approach. Many times, plans are developed in isolation without collecting and/or considering inputs from different stakeholders, too high targets are set, and planning for development of infrastructure and other facilities for achieving targets is not considered. Plans are more focused towards short-term competition rather than a sustainable and study growth. In addition to this, majority of HEIs of the Gulf and South Asian countries in general and public sector in particular are slow in planning and decision making. Most of the time, plans are reactive and not proactive.

A big number of stakeholders are not aware and/or do not have a clear understanding of broader common organisational goals, policies, procedures, plans, and other important information. This is mainly because of poor communication strategy, over confidence on self-learning habits of employees, and

48   *Radha Krishan Sharma*

the negligence of employees. As a result, synchronisation of different activities becomes a challenge.

Preparation for implementation of plans is a basic requirement. However, many a time, because of poor understanding, preparation is not in line with plans and resulted in disasters. If at all, planning and understanding of employees is good, still availability of resources becomes crucial. Many a time, implementation is started with partial preparation and non-availability of some of the resources in the middle of the process turns all efforts useless. Procuring qualified, experienced, and efficient faculty members is still a big challenge to HEIs. Research is not among the priorities; hence, support is very weak in the majority of HEIs in Gulf and South Asian countries. In most of the cases, research is supported for fulfilling regulatory requirements, and therefore quantity became more important than quality; as a result, Gulf and South Asian countries like India have a huge number of publications with no or very little impact and a big number of patents are not commercialised. All the participants were of the consensus that because of the above, operational team feels suffocated and bulldosed and blamed for poor performance and/or failures.

The low level of motivation, due to the above shortcoming, resulted in deterioration of dedication, determination, and discipline. Subsequently, poor/weak delivery of the academic programmes has resulted in deficiency of achievement of programme outcomes. Most of the programmes are more focused to knowledge rather than development of skills. Students are also more focused towards securing employment at the earliest. Even though Indian government has initiated outcome-based teaching-learning, but majority of the HEIs in private as well as public sector have no or little understanding of this initiative and faculty members are confused about methods of implementation. Training to faculty members is crucial for successful implementation of the initiative. All participants agreed that maintaining a high level of motivation is a challenge for most of the HEIs.

A big number of HEIs in Gulf and South Asian countries failed to support graduates for securing employment. On one hand, graduates complain about non-availability of employment, on the other, industry complains about non-availability of skilled workforce. Employers blame HEIs for not considering market needs while developing and/or updating programmes and HEIs blames industry for not contributing to academic development. Alumni interaction is poor, and HEIs are not taking interest in development of database for interaction with alumni. Alumni also do not take interest because of their personal commitments. Some alumni expressed their unwillingness as they are not happy with HEIs' approach towards inviting/accepting feedback. They mentioned 'Institute want us to publicize but don't want to change themselves to meet market requirement'. A big number of HEIs still have resistance to change, particularly public sector HEIs. Affiliated HEIs have no or very little freedom to incorporate new things. They must pass through a long process for any improvement. This makes implementation ineffective.

A huge number of HEIs do not have an effective internal monitoring system. In many of the HEIs, internal quality system is considered an unimportant thing and wastage of resources. These HEIs have internal quality monitoring systems, just for formality. This is mainly because of poor vision and short-term goals. Post-pandemic digitalisation has made external monitoring a bit easy; however, there is a long way to achieve desired results in Gulf and South Asian countries like India, Oman, and Bangladesh. To the best of our knowledge, there is no model available specifically for the HE sector except GQA Model. Almost all available models are developed either for the manufacturing sector or for the service sector, focused on customers. HE is an entirely unique sector without customers. Most of the institutions are following PDCA Model with modification and customisation for their needs. That needs a lot of effort and failed to maintain consistency throughout the sector.

NFCFFE Model

NFCFFE is a six-layered model which is actually an extension of Five-layered GQA Model proposed by Sharma et al. (2019). The model is a combination of six models, one for each layer. The first layer, 'PCPGDR Model', highlights six functional areas of a HEI, where QIA is needed. These are Plan (P), Conceive (C), Prepare (P), Groom (G), Deliver (D), and Review (R). The second layer, 'FOM Model', splits activities in three stages, i.e. Formation (F), Operation (O), and Monitoring (M). The model argues that all these three stages are Focus point from QIA point of view and advocates adopting different approaches of QIA at all three focus points. The third layer, 'OTR Model', stresses upon significance of continuous Orientation (O), Training (T), and Reminders (R) to inculcate quality culture throughout organisation. The fourth layer, 'RII Model', proposes continuous quality improvement framework consisting of cyclic Review (R), Improvement (I), and Implementation (I). The fifth layer, 'Feedback', proposes 'CAFU Model'. The model details the significance of feedback in quality improvement using systematic Collection (C), careful Assessment (A), efficiently Filtered (F) (prioritised), and effectively Used (U). The sixth layer stresses upon existence '4D' for success of sustainable QIA system which is 'Essential' at all levels of organisation. These 4D are Dedication, Determination, Discipline, and Direction. All six models/layers are complementary to each other, and hence ignoring any one model or a part will result in non-achievement of desired quality of graduates and research.

Layer 1 – QIA Need: PCPGDR Model

The model is cyclic. Planning, Conceiving, and Preparing are most crucial parts of the model. As rightly said, *'Most projects fail in beginning, not at the end'*. Planning is one of the most crucial phases for success of a HEI. A well-thought-of plan built upon carefully collected and filtered information from all stakeholders, with prefixed priorities, is the first step of success. HEIs are dealing with thoughtful young brains from diversified backgrounds with different personalities. The objective is to transform them into skilled, socially responsible, ethical global citizens for a nation building and serving the world community. Hence, this is not possible to develop and test plans like any other products or service. The PDCA Model allows failures and then improvement. This is permissible in other sectors, but in HEIs because of their unique characteristics, checking after implementation is not acceptable. This is mainly because in other sector a mistake can be undone or its negative effects can be neutralised. Also the cost of failure is mainly limited to financial and for a limited period. On the other hand, failure in the HE sector is not limited to financials only; a failure can't be undone, and its effects spread all around and pass through generations. This would not be wrong to say that 'for scientists their lab is whole world but for HEIs whole world is a lab'. Not only planning, equally important is conceiving these plans in their totality. Many a time, plans are good, but implementation team have not understood the plan and/or the core idea behind it. This results in 'sailing a boat in different direction by different sailors'. If these plans are not well communicated to the implementation team, the outcomes will be a disaster for sure. A strong communication strategy with verification process to check that message communicated has been conceived with its true objective is one among the most important foundation of success of plans. Once plans are communicated effectively, preparation must be done efficiently well in advance. Without providing resources at the right time, in the right quantity, and of right quality, desired outcomes cannot be achieved. Hence, adequate preparation before implementation is another basic requirement for successful delivery. Once preparation is done and tested, the real implementation, i.e. grooming of learners took place – this is the real test of previous three stages. The role of the operational team becomes crucial here. They are not only accountable for the implementation of plans but also responsible to keep reviewing plans in dynamic real-world environment and pass feedback for quick improvements. The responsibility is not limited to enhancing skills and knowledge but inculcating ethics and value becomes more important. This is the stage where real work of shaping the future is undertaken; most of the faculty members become role models of a set of students or another. At HEIs, teaching-learning process is not limited to delivery and experiments alone, but these mature learners learn by observation too. Hence, along with knowledge and skills of faculty members, their personality, community engagement, and values also become a source of life-long learning to students. Thus, the role of faculty members and administrators becomes crucial for creating and delivering the future of society. Creating an employment-ready workforce is undoubtedly a challenging task for HEIs, along with helping learners as well as employers matching right skills with the right opportunity which has also become an important priority of HEIs. Most of the learners in HEIs are expecting the right employment at the end of their studies; similarly, employers and society look towards HEIs in expectation of getting rightly skilled people at the right time. Delivering this is not an event;

it is a continuous activity, to be paid attention to. The obligation of HEIs does not end at delivery but continuous review of performance of delivered workforce and changing expectation of employers provides input for continuous improvement of plans.

Figure 3.1 is a pictorial presentation of PCPGDR Model. Though all six stages need serious QIA efforts, Plan, Conceive, and Preparation stages are highly crucial, hence requiring a rigorous approach. This helps to reduce required efforts at Groom, Review, and subsequently success as reflected from the quality of Delivery. PCP is not the responsibility of top management alone; this is the activity which every stakeholder needs to perform at all levels. Figure 3.1 also demonstrates key activities to be performed in a HEI. Vision, Mission, Values, Quality Philosophy, Benchmarks, Graduate Attributes, Programme Outcomes, Course Outcomes, Financials, Infrastructure Policies, Procedures, Infrastructure, Faculty and Staff, Programme Structure, Course Structure, Assessments, Mapping with outcomes, Research and Innovation, etc. must be planned, conceived, and prepared. At different stages of students' progression, grooming must be done with appropriate Pedagogy, Andragogy, Heutagogy, or blending of some or all of these. Value driven, socially responsible, ethical, and skilled workforce and research and innovation for global social welfare must be delivered. For further improvement, continuous self, regulatory, and stakeholders' review and feedback must be used.

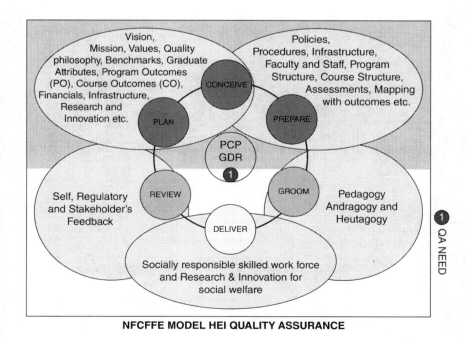

Figure 3.1 Layer 1 – QIA Need: PCPGDR Model.

Layer 2 – QIA Focus: FOM Model

Applying single QIA approach at all six levels of PCPGDR might not work efficiently. Therefore, these six levels have been divided in three stages, i.e. Formation stage (F), Operation stage (O), and Monitoring stage (M). Planning and Conceiving is a Formation stage activity. This require prediction or formation of future and hence futuristic Preactive and/or Proactive approach is more appropriate at this stage. Preparation, Grooming, and Delivering are grouped under operation stage. At this stage, some unplanned minor issues may need to be addressed, and hence at this stage QIA approach must be Reactive to solve these issues with speed to avoid any effect on desired outcomes. Monitoring stage covers all six levels of PCPGDR; however, Review is the main activity of this stage. Both internal and external monitoring are desired for achieving broader common organisational goals. Internal monitoring might be performed by Self-monitoring by individuals and units, Peer Review, Administrative monitoring, and by Internal Quality Audit/Assurance. External monitoring is the task of Regulatory Bodies, External public and private Audit/Accreditation, Ranking and Rating agencies, etc. Figure 3.2 provides a pictorial presentation of FOM Model of QIA Focus.

All HEIs, irrespective of their size, domain, and location, must ensure that appropriate QIA approach must be followed at all three FOM stages. This will help to develop an integrated organisation with quality culture.

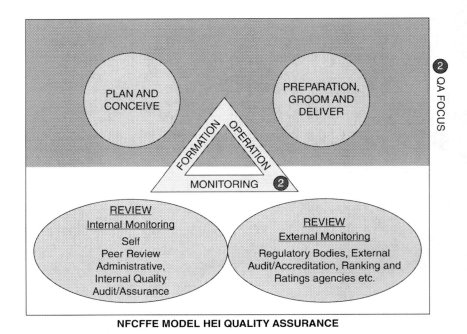

Figure 3.2 Layer 2 – QIA Focus: FOM Model.

Layer 3 – QIA Culture: OTR Model

Humans are naturally forgetful and prioritise tasks. Individuals remember and practise things only of their priority. This is the obligation of HEIs to add institutional tasks and goals among individual stakeholders' priority. OTR Model suggests a strategy to develop quality culture throughout the organisation. This can be achieved by continuous Orientations (O) for making new stakeholders familiar with HEI and its broader common organisational goals, Modalities, Environment, Infrastructure and Facilities, Expectations, Code of conduct, Culture, etc., to help them adopt new system quickly and walk with organisations' vision, mission, and objectives; also to make existing stakeholders familiar with new things introduced in the HEI. Training (T) is important for enhancing stakeholders' competencies for making them competent to achieve tasks at par with organisational standards and expectations. This not only helps to guide stakeholders but two-way communication during these sessions add value to existing systems by collecting their views and using their expertise for improvement. Repeated Reminders (R) is required to bring broader common organisational goals on the top of stakeholders' mind and to keep them motivated for putting their collective efforts for achieving these goals together. Figure 3.3 displays the OTR Model in a pictorial form.

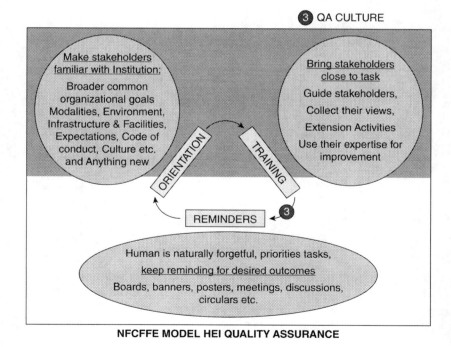

Figure 3.3 QIA Culture: OTR Model.

54 Radha Krishan Sharma

The success of OTR Model is in its continuity. HEIs must maintain continuous communication with stakeholders in one way or the other. This will bring belongingness among them and will gradually make them all quality conscious. Once quality culture is established, then all other tasks will become very easy to achieve.

Layer 4 – QIA Framework: RII Model

Layer 4 guides methodology for establishing a QIA Framework using RII Model: Periodic Review (R), Improvement (I), and Implementation (I) of improved broader common organisational goals, Modalities, Environment, Infrastructure and Facilities, Expectations, Code of conduct, Programme and Course Structure and Outcomes, Delivery Methods, Assessments, Feedback formats and mechanism, Mapping of outcomes with attributes, Research and Innovation, Extension Activities, community engagements, etc. This framework must be cyclic throughout the life of HEIs with futuristic approach. This is also important in order to align institutional practices with national goals. Figure 3.4 shows the RII Model.

RII Model's success depends on carefully collected and efficiently filtered feedback from all stakeholders.

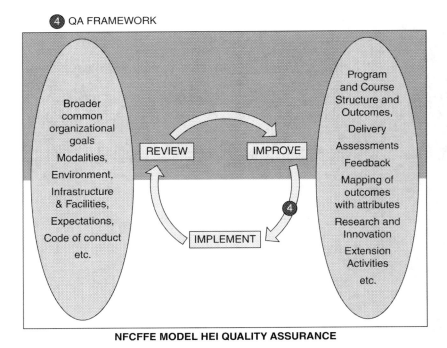

Figure 3.4 QIA Framework: RII Model.

Layer 5 – QIA Feedback: CAFU Model

CAFU Model was originally introduced by Sharma et al. (2019). The study used OCEAN Big 5 Personality Traits Model and tested using SEM Model. They concluded that feedback by stakeholders of HEIs is influenced by their personality traits and, hence, needs to be assessed and filtered efficiently before planning for improvement. CAFU Model argues that an efficient feedback about all aspects of HEIs' operations and performance, e.g. broader common organisational goals, Modalities, Environment, Infrastructure and Facilities, Programme, Course, Assessments, Research and Innovation, community engagement, etc., must be Collected (C) very carefully from different groups of stakeholders, e.g. Students, Alumni and Parents, Faculty and Staff, Industry, Scholars, Community representatives, Regulators, Audit/Accreditation and Rating Agencies, etc. Since stakeholders in a group have different personalities, a respondent group's personality must be Assessed (A) and based on the result feedback outcomes must be Filtered (F) and prioritised for Use (U) to improve. Figure 3.5 shows the CAFU Model.

The model suggests that any flaw in QIA Feedback will destroy all efforts; hence, CAFU process suggests that genuine feedback from fair stakeholders must be incorporated in planning and decision making.

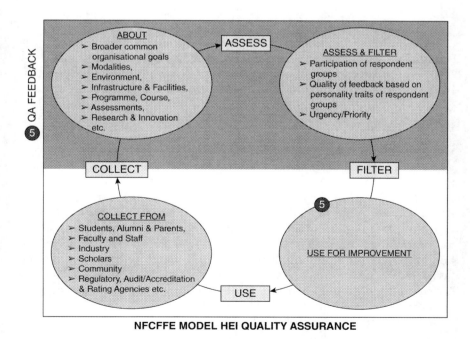

Figure 3.5 QIA Feedback: CAFU Model.

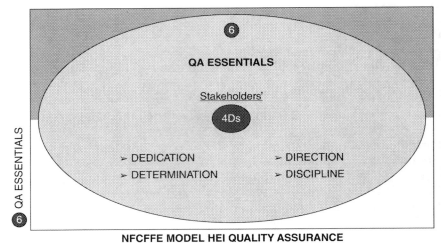

Figure 3.6 QIA Essentials: 4D Model.

Layer 6 – QIA Essentials: 4D Model

Layer 6 proposes 4D Model as QIA Essential. The model argues that 4Ds, i.e. Dedication, Determination, Discipline, and Direction, are the foundation of QIA for all HEIs in the Gulf and South Asia, in particular, and globally, as a whole. In the absence of any one of these, HEIs cannot imagine for any improvement. These are essential conditions to be maintained by all stakeholders (internal and external) and public and private HEIs in all organisational levels. Figure 3.6 demonstrates 4D carpet at which the whole NFCFFE Model is built. If any one of these is missing, the whole quality system will collapse.

NFCFFE Model

Figure 3.7 demonstrates the NFCFFE Model in a comprehensive manner. The figure also demonstrates that layer 1 ('PCPGDR Model') is the primary task where QIA needs to be implemented. Layer 2 ('FOM Model') groups PCPGDR in three stages and explains that one single QIA approach at all stages will not bring desired results; each stage needs a different approach of QIA. Layer 3 guides method to implement quality culture throughout the organisation using 'OTR Model'. Layer 4 suggests a QIA Framework to be established using 'RII Model'. Layer 5 suggests how to establish an efficient feedback system using 'CAFU Model', and Layer 6 provides Essential 4D characteristics required to be maintained throughout the organisation. All six layers are interlinked and interdependent; hence, implementing the entire model is essential for sustainable QIA.

Linkage and dependency of the six layers of NFCFFE Model makes it sustainable. This is mainly because all layers interact in continuation. Deficiency

Self-Sustainable Higher Education Quality Assurance System 57

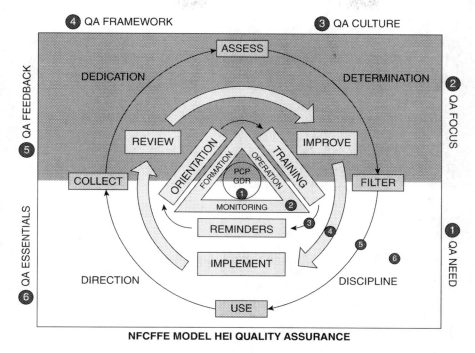

Figure 3.7 NFCFFE Model.

at any place will be automatically highlighted or discovered, and hence can be improved immediately. Though maintaining the presence of 4Ds at all levels all the time is not easy, the presence of 4Ds at other places will discover and will encourage improvements. The 4Ds at the top level will automatically spread downwards and the model will be proven sustainable.

Limitation of the Model

Since the NFCFFE Model is an outcome of experiences and opinions of different stakeholders and experts working on quality of HE at different HEIs in the Gulf and South Asian countries, the model can be relied upon. However, the small number of participants in FGDs from Gulf and South Asian countries only may be a limiting factor and, hence, leaves a scope for further study and testing of model with larger participants from other countries. Examining each layer with different research design will certainly help HEIs and community at large, and will add value to the existing debates and knowledge. We also invite researchers, academicians, administrators, and regulators to critically evaluate the model for statistical testing and real-life implementation.

Conclusion

The world has been shaken because of the COVID-19 pandemic, so are the HEIs in the Gulf and South Asian countries. The pandemic has certainly pushed the economy decades back, and HEIs are not an exception to this. However, along with challenges, the pandemic has forced HEIs to think out of the box and explore and test new methods to deal with such conditions. The proposed NFCFFE Model for HEIs' QIA is a step forward in this direction, especially if the model is fully implemented. The model is an attempt to provide a sustainable QIA model for the HEIs of Gulf and South Asian countries struggling to establish QIA systems in their organisation. Since the model is an outcome of experience, observations, experts' and stakeholders' opinions, further testing and implementation is desired.

References

Adler, M., & Ziglio, E. (1996). *Gazing into the Oracle: The Delphi Method and its application to social policy and public health.* Jessica Kingsley Publishers.

Agrawal, J. (2021). Effect of lockdown on education of rural undergraduate students during covid-19 pandemic in Umarban (Dhar), M.P., India. *Innovare Journal of Education, 9*(3), 14–18. https://doi.org/10.22159/ijoe.2021v9i3.41647

Al-Amri, A. S., Mathew, P., Zubairi, Y. Z., & Jani, R. (2020). Optimal standards to measure the quality of higher education institutions in Oman: Stakeholders' perception. *Sage Open, 10*(3), 2158244020947440. https://journals.sagepub.com/doi/10.1177/2158244020947440

El Said, G. R. (2021). How did the COVID-19 pandemic affect higher education learning experience? An empirical investigation of learners' academic performance at a university in a developing country. *Advances in Human-Computer Interaction, 2021,* 6649524. https://www.hindawi.com/journals/ahci/2021/6649524/

Gandhi, A., & Rani, K. (2020). Online education during COVID-19 and future concerns: India perspective. *Educational Quest, 11*(2), 53–58. https://ndpublisher.in/admin/issues/EQv11n2b.pdf

Lodgaard, E., & Aasland, K. E. (2011). An examination of the application of plan-do-check-act cycle in product development. In DS 68-10: Proceedings of the 18th International Conference on Engineering Design (ICED 11), Impacting Society through Engineering Design, Vol. 10: Design Methods and Tools pt. 2. https://www.designsociety.org/publication/30737/AN+EXAMINATION+OF+THE+APPLICATION+OF+PLAN-DO-CHECK-ACT+CYCLE+IN+PRODUCT+DEVELOPMENT

Luxton, A. (2005). *Quality management in higher education.* General Conference Department of Education, Higher Education Management Series No 2. https://www.adventist.education/wp-content/uploads/2017/10/Quality-Management-in-Higher-Education.pdf

Maruyama, T., & Inoue, M. (2016). Continuous quality improvement of leadership education program through PDCA cycle. *China-USA Business Review, 15*(1), 42–49. https://doi.org/10.17265/1537-1514/2016.01.004

Materu, P. N. (2007). *Higher education quality assurance in Sub-Saharan Africa: Status, challenges, opportunities and promising practices* (No. 124). World Bank Publications. https://openknowledge.worldbank.org/handle/10986/6757

Muñoz-Najar, A., Gilberto, A., Hasan, A., Cobo, C., Azevedo, J. P., & Akmal, M. (2021). *Remote learning during covid-19: Lessons from today, principles for tomorrow.* The World Bank.

Odhiambo, G. O. (2011). Higher education quality in Kenya: A critical reflection of key challenges. *Quality in Higher Education, 17*(3), 299–315. https://doi.org/10.1080/13538322.2011.614472

Odhiambo, G. O. (2014). Quality assurance for public higher education: Context, strategies and challenges in Kenya. *Higher Education Research & Development, 33*(5), 978–991. https://doi.org/10.1080/07294360.2014.890578

Orr, D., Luebcke, M., Schmidt, J., Koschutnig-Ebner, M., Wannemacher, K., Ebner, M., & Dohmen, D. (2020). Four Models of Higher Education in 2030. In *Higher education landscape 2030* (pp. 25–42). Springer.

Rodriguez, M. B., Cobo, C., Muñoz-Najar, A., & Ciarrusta, I. S. (2022). *Remote learning during the global school lockdown: Multi-country lessons.* World Bank Group. http://documents.worldbank.org/curated/en/668741627975171644/Remote-Learning-During-the-Global-School-Lockdown-Multi-Country-Lessons

Roy, S., & Brown, S. (2022). Higher education in India in the time of pandemic, sans a learning management system. *AERA Open, 8,* 1–15. https://doi.org/10.1177/23328584211069527

Sarkar, S. S., Das, P., Rahman, M. M., & Zobaer, M. S. (2021). Perceptions of public university students towards online classes during COVID-19 pandemic in Bangladesh. *Frontiers in Education, 6,* 703723. https://doi.org/10.3389/feduc.2021.703723

Sharma, S. C. (2020). *Inducing quality and relevance in Indian higher education institutions some thoughts* (P. Mittal & S. R. Devi Pani, Eds.). Association of Indian Universities. https://aiu.ac.in/documents/AIU_Publications/Reimagining%20Indian%20Universities/16.%20Inducing%20Quality%20And%20Relevance%20In%20Indian%20Higher%20Education%20Institutions%20Some%20Thoughts%20By%20S%20C%20Sharma,%20Director,%20National%20Assessment%20And%20Accreditation%20Council%20Bangalore.pdf

Sharma, R. K., Jain, V., & Kumar, S. (2019, July 15–18). Significance of personality dimensions to feedback and its impact on quality assurance in higher education: Comparative study of Oman and India (Workshop 8). In *10th Gulf Research Meeting.* Center of Islamic Studies, University of Cambridge. https://gulfresearchmeeting.net/archives-main-page/2019

Uygur, A., & Sümerli, S. (2013). EFQM excellence model. *International Review of Management and Business Research, 2*(4), 980. https://asset-pdf.scinapse.io/prod/2106858110/2106858110.pdf

4 Pandemic Challenges of Higher Education

Reconsidering Core Values

Mariam Orkodashvili

Introduction

The quality of online instruction has become questionable, especially regarding examinations, tests and various types of assessments that are conducted online. This in, its turn, has put the validity of credentials, degrees and diplomas under scrutiny in certain contexts. Especially, if we consider that quality of education is closely associated with global rankings, it acquires high-stakes feature and makes online instruction debatable.

Tied on to the above issue, conferring degrees and credentials as a result of questionable assessments has put the validity of these credentials under question as well. The chapter analyses the core concepts of education, such as quality evaluation, access to study materials and online classes, and validity of conferred credentials as a result of online assessments. It offers three dynamic models that discuss the introduction of innovations in higher education institutions (HEIs) and their operation in terms of online or hybrid mode of education.

Critical Analysis of Gulf Higher Education

This section presents a comparative critical analysis of education institutions in different GCC countries. It mainly bases its postulates on the secondary sources obtained through the official websites of GCC countries, education institutions and universities. To provide illustrative examples of online instruction, the chapter analyses the cases of universities with well-branded names such as Doha's Education City, Dubai's Knowledge Village, Sharjah's University City and other universities offering world class courses. Qatar's Education City has tried to brand itself as the largest concentration of universities in the world – it brings prestigious institutions such as Northwestern University, Carnegie Mellon, Texas A&M, Cornell and Georgetown to Qatar's shores. Similarly, NYU has just built a huge international campus in Abu Dhabi. In fact, Qatar University – the only public university in Qatar – enrols 91 percent of Qatari students, while the elite universities at the Education City enrol only 9 percent (Stasz et al., 2007). The study programmes are also different at local universities and international universities. Therefore, the issues of standards,

DOI: 10.4324/9781003457299-6

Pandemic Challenges of Higher Education   61

quality and decision-making power are constantly debated in the GCC countries. The online questions were also sent out to students and staff of the universities that asked them to share their experiences of online education during the lockdown period and evaluate both positive sides and challenges that the new mode of instruction posed to their universities.

Education Field: Online Classes and Access to Education

As technology has been influencing all the spheres of human activity, it has not left out the education field either. Thanks to technological advances, there has been enormous development and transformation within the entire education system and new modes of instruction have emerged. For instance, during the lockdown period, modern language teachers have been using the newest available technological devices such as computers, laptops, mobile phones, smartphones, tablets, OHPs, e-books, blackboard software, digital flashcards, particularly frequently. This fact has caused changes in teaching trends, and since the transformations within instruction have been changing, the requirements for the teachers to vary their teaching strategies and methodologies accordingly have been increasing as well.

To acquire the newest teaching methods and strategies, the teachers need to upgrade courses, attend training programmes, conferences, workshops and seminars/webinars, which are also mostly online, again due to isolation and pandemics. In connection with this, *new terms describing online education features* have been spreading, *zoom-meetings, web-classes, online presentations, file share, microphone and camera check, digital boards, smart boards, computers, mobile devices* being just a few examples among many others. Therefore, online classrooms and webinars have impacted not only teaching styles in education, but have engendered *new quality characteristics of education* as well. This process is reflected in the production of new terms, concepts and practices associated with virtual interaction.

Pre-recorded classes and lectures are yet another feature of pandemic-era education. These classes are informative talks that are geared to teach the students with the basic or background comprehensive knowledge about the subject and share with them new and innovative ideas that happen in their specialised fields. These recorded web-classes form a web-library for educational institutions that are free both for teachers and learners, and are useful for teaching and learning tasks. A number of large libraries and universities have opened up their online resources for free access to the public during the pandemic period. This fact has accumulated huge amount of teaching and learning resources almost in any field of science or scholarship. With this online-library-recoded storage facility, the institutions can give training to everybody. These also are useful in teaching new concepts to their learners and, therefore, the learners get the chance to concentrate on the recorded web-classes whenever they need them.

62   Mariam Orkodashvili

The traditional teaching and learning methods and approaches have been replaced by the newest techniques and drastic changes have been made to the concept of teaching as well, which in many cases means more reliance on independent information search through online sources. This type of scenario is reflected in language, especially in English, which has become most adaptable and flexible under the current conditions. For instance, an organisation TEACHINGENGLISH offers free webinars for educators. These webinars provide educators with ideas and motivation which are also available live and on-demand. All of these webinars are free of charge, and participants are eager to join, contribute and grow in their learning. *Web-classes, e-classes, web-lectures, web-libraries, e-libraries, web-sources, web-discussions, web-platforms and online drop-boxes* are just a few *catchphrases* that have been spreading at a particularly high speed in the sphere of education over the past couple of years during the lockdown period.

Online Classes and Quality of Education

There exists extensive research on the resilience and adaptation of universities (Leslie & Fretwell, 1996; Tierney, 1998). The studies have focused on issues such as resource constraints (Tierney, 1998, Sporn, 1999); new internal relationships between faculty and administration, outcomes and external needs (Sporn, 1999); environmental trends, financial situation, effective management and scarce resource allocation, strategic planning, entrepreneurship, pressure for deep change and continuous learning from experimentation (Leslie & Fretwell, 1996,); resource dependence (Pfeffer & Salancik 1978); contingency approach: external conditions causing high differentiation and integration at universities (Dill & Sporn, 1995; Lawrence & Lorsch, 1986). The professional bureaucracy existing in academia can be a possible impediment to the introduction of any innovations.

The ability of universities to adapt to the changing external environment and of the professional bureaucracy existing in them can be analysed together. Universities have been traditionally considered as organisations that are slow to respond to changes in the external environment. As Sporn (1999) notes, 'Universities are among the oldest organizations in the world and have proven resilient over several centuries of socioeconomic and political change' (Sporn, 1999, p. 6). Compared to other types of organisations, universities are usually resistant to any type of change or innovation. It can be assumed that resilience to change is, in the majority of cases, caused by various bureaucratic structures that exist in universities. It is common knowledge that any organisation possesses bureaucratic features. As Mintzberg et al. (2003) state, this is because organisations are created to replace uncertainty with stability that is usually achieved through adhering to rules and regulations. This fact in its turn breeds bureaucracy. 'We ought not to be surprised that organizations resist innovation. They are supposed to resist it. The reason an organization is created is in large part to replace the uncertain expectations and haphazard activities of

Pandemic Challenges of Higher Education 63

voluntary endeavours with the stability and routine of organized relationships' (Mintzberg et al., 2003, p. 357).

The specific nature of academic institutions and complex bureaucratic organisation make them resistant to changes in the external environment. Sporn (1999) names five major trends that seem to be important parts of the external environment influencing academia. These are restructuring of the economy, changing role of the state, shifting demographics, new technologies, and increasing globalisation (Sporn, 1999, p. 8). These externalities often necessitate the introduction of innovations and reorganisation of universities to a certain degree. However, the process of innovating or reorganising academia is usually accompanied by controversy and resistance often intensified by the bureaucracy. However, it is technological innovations that most actively triggered fast-paced transformations in education institutions during the pandemic.

Mintzberg (1980) offers five basic organisational structures of bureaucracy: simple structure, machine bureaucracy, professional bureaucracy, divisionalised form and adhocracy. He claims that an effective organisation will often use a combination of these conurations, 'some sort of logically consistent clustering of its elements – as it searches for harmony in its internal processes and consonance with its environment. But some organizations will inevitably be driven to hybrid structures as they react to contradictory pressures or while they affect a transition from one configuration to another, and hence too it is believed that the typology of five can serve as a diagnostic tool in organizational design' (Mintzberg, 1980, p. 322). Universities are considered as functioning on professional bureaucracies. Mintzberg (1980) gives the following description of professional bureaucracy: 'The professional bureaucracy relies on the standardisation of skills in its operating core for coordination; jobs are highly specialised but minimally formalised, training is extensive and grouping is on a concurrent functional and market basis, with large sized operating units, and decentralization is extensive in both the vertical and horizontal dimensions; this structure is typically found in complex but stable environments, with technical systems that are simple and non-regulating' (Mintzberg, 1980, p. 322). Hence, universities are characterised by highly specialised and minimally formalised jobs carried out by 'functional groups based on knowledge or skills' (Mintzberg, 1979). In addition, the environment in academia is stable. And the pace of change is slow because academic staff is considered particularly resistant to innovations.

However, during 2020–2022, universities faced the challenges of overcoming bureaucracies and rigid resistance during the pandemic, since switching to online flexible instruction had to be conducted quickly and efficiently to adapt to the changing world. Therefore, it could be conjectured that the rigid bureaucracies, so characteristic of universities, were shattered by the shockwaves of online instructions and online modes of teaching materials and methods.

Regarding horizontal and vertical decentralisation, universities (especially in the U.S.) are highly decentralised organisations. Weick (1976) even refers to the university as a loosely coupled system (that could be perceived as an

64   *Mariam Orkodashvili*

extreme form of decentralisation), where the introduction of innovation in one unit (department) might not affect other units (Weick, 1976). Weick states that functional loose-coupling refers to the low level of cooperation and coordination required by teaching and research activities within HEIs (Weick, 1976). Therefore, it can be assumed that a professionalised bureaucracy (that strengthens the resilience of academia) and loose-coupling (that distorts interdepartmental coordination for implementing new policies) are two factors that might cause confusion and paradoxes for universities when trying to adapt to a changing external environment. The paradox is that while a professionalised bureaucracy (Mintzberg, 1980) might lead to extreme authoritative power and constrained organisation, loose-coupling might engender another extreme of unregulated system and chaos (Musselin, 1996; Weick, 1976). Hence, it is at this point that the strategy of *organisational isomorphism* (DiMaggio & Powell, 1983) might be useful. As DiMaggio and Powell (1983) suggest, an optimal way to deal with the problem is through one type of *organisational isomorphism,* called *mimetic isomorphism,* which involves adapting business strategies to academic institutions (DiMaggio & Powell, 1983). Through *mimetic isomorphism,* academia decreases the level of bureaucracy and makes itself adaptable to the external environment. In the case of technological adaptations, universities had to go through *mimetic isomorphism* of introducing online modes of instructions.

Another strategy to transform the highly bureaucratised university has been introduced by Burton Clark (1998). According to him, there is an imbalance between environmental demand and institutional response. Therefore, he proposes *an interactive instrumentalism,* which implies the creation of a climate of innovation within the university. Lockdown period naturally created the environmental demand for institutional changes. Sporn (1999, pp. 280–281) analyses the development of universities from the perspective of influencing the external environment and presents *a comprehensive theory of adaptation.* As she (1999) states, 'successful organisational adaptation for colleges and universities will require new and innovative strategies to respond to the changing environment for higher education' (Sporn, 1999, p. 6). Referring to different scholarly sources, Sporn (1999) names the perspectives from which the environment of HEIs has been analysed. 'These include threats and opportunities; the degree of complexity (Cameron & Tschirhart, 1992); sources of institutional demands (Berdahl & McConnell, 1994; Gumport & Sporn, 1985); and resource providers (Salancik & Pfeffer, 1974; Slaughter & Leslie, 1997). These perspectives can be integrated at a higher level of cross-national societal dynamics influencing higher education systems' (Sporn, 1999, p. 8). Therefore, 2020–2022 drastic changes in different fields had shockwave spillover effects on education as well.

Online Classes and Validity of Credentials

Validity of credentials, such as exam results, diplomas and degrees conferred by universities, has become even more topical during the pandemic in view of

Pandemic Challenges of Higher Education   65

increasing numbers of online classes. A widely held belief regarding the future development of academia is that the real genius of higher education system is the provision of high-quality education on a mass level. This means achieving independent quality inquiry for all. However, growing student numbers and resource constraints often turn this genius goal into mission impossible.

Institutional isomorphism comes into play at this point. Mimetic isomorphism engenders when academia tries to apply market-oriented strategies, while coercive pressures come from internal or external forces, and natural tendency of academia to manipulate with the concept of *quality* put higher education governance at stake and often engender corruption. Especially, as higher education funding and governance depend on certain performance criteria, the probability of manipulating with the term *quality* rises. When there are no fixed criteria, norms and rules, the risk of engaging in dishonest and corrupt practices for personal or institutional gain rises substantially. Such uncertainty in HEIs is a powerful force that encourages both imitation, i.e. mimetic isomorphism, and coercion, i.e. coercive isomorphism. Defining quality criteria for online education, especially for online tests and examinations, has become even blurrier and nebulous a task than existed ever before.

The objective of the chapter is to also identify and analyse higher education governance challenges when academia tries to implement quality enhancement strategies. Nebulous nature of *quality* allows for manipulations with its definitions or measurement criteria and gives rise to corrupt practices. Most importantly, the paper states that online classes should not cause the loss of credential values.

Overview of *High-Stakes* Concept

The chapter suggests and supports the idea that putting high stakes on any public good corrupts that public good. Higher education is no exception. In fact, it might be perceived as one of the most easily vulnerable public spheres that often become prone to various violations, distortions, misconduct and corruption. The fact that people have natural tendency of corrupting the sphere on which high social stakes are put naturally requires many-sided analysis of the processes involved in human agency. The paper introduces the idea of *counterbalancing* any given sphere that falls prone to manipulations due to its high social, economic or public stakes. Counterbalancing accreditation with university rankings at this point presents most challenging tasks, especially if we consider that online instruction has required reconsideration of criteria for university rankings.

As Campbell's Law states: 'The over-reliance on high-stakes testing and competition has serious negative repercussions that are present at every level of the public school system' (Campbell, 1979). A number of scholars also claim that 'the pressures of high-stakes testing…erode the validity of test scores and distort the integrity of education system. …It appears that the greater the social consequences associated with a quantitative indicator – such as test scores – the

66 *Mariam Orkodashvili*

more likely it is that the use of the indicator itself will become corrupted, or the more likely it is that the use of indicator will corrupt the social processes it was intended to monitor' (Sahlberg, 2009, p. 143). The paper assumes that in different countries the nature of corrupt practices corresponds to the priorities that corrupt individuals attach to such factors as prestige, job stability, income and promotion. If online education challenges are to be plugged in at this point, the concept of *high stakes* becomes even more controversial and debatable.

Overview of Broadband Benefits for the Development of Countries

The project undertaken by the Global Information and Communication Technologies Department and the Development Economics Data Group of the World Bank Group came to significant conclusions regarding the influence of information and communication technology (ICT) on economic development of countries around the globe (Barro & Sala-i-Martin, 2003; Waverman et al., 2005). Countries that adopt policies enabling convergence among telecommunications, media and computing services will enhance the impact of ICT on economic development. Technological innovation and market demand are driving the ICT sector towards convergence. Convergence is shorthand for several changes occurring in the ICT sector. Broadly speaking, convergence refers to the erosion boundaries among previously separate services, networks, and business models in the sector (Barro & Sala-i-Martin, 2003; Waverman et al., 2005).

The empirical findings suggest that broadband's benefits are major and robust for both developed and developing countries, although the significance is higher for the former, which have a longer track record of broadband diffusion. As the number of broadband subscribers increases and the applications supported by broadband reach a critical mass, the benefits could show the same statistical significance in developing economies, as with all other communications technologies

Broadband deserves a central role in national development strategies. Once longer periods of data are available on broadband penetration, a subperiod analysis could be conducted, thus establishing multiple data points for each economy in an endogenous growth regression. This approach would make it possible to study individual dynamics, give information on the ordering of events and control for individual unobserved heterogeneity, addressing the endogeneity issue better. Second, it may be useful to look at how broadband affects key variables that are good for growth, such as trade, foreign investment, education and innovation. Third, the microeconomic foundations of broadband's impact should be further explored with specific reference to developing countries. The current largely anecdotal analysis needs to advance to systematic impact evaluation. The effect of broadband on the creation and expansion of social and political networks could also be explored further in

Pandemic Challenges of Higher Education 67

both developed and developing countries (Barro & Sala-i-Martin, 2003; Waverman et al., 2005).

The Barro cross-sectional endogenous growth model was used to look at long-term average growth rates. Waverman et al. (2005) used a similar model to test the impact of mobile telephony on economic growth in developing countries. This endogenous technical change approach, which uses period averages and initial values, is therefore less prone to data errors. Given the poor data availability in a large number of developing countries, this model may prove more successful in obtaining sensible estimates.

The growth benefit that broadband provides for developing countries was of similar magnitude as that for developed economies – about a 1.38 percentage point increase for each 10 percent increase in penetration. But the coefficient on average broadband penetration for middle- and low-income countries (BBNDL) was statistically significant at 10 percent but not at 5 percent, perhaps reflecting that broadband is a recent phenomenon in developing countries and penetration has not yet reached a critical mass to generate aggregate effects as robust as in developed countries. In 2006, 3.4 percent of the population in low-income countries and 3.8 percent in middle-income countries had broadband, compared with 18.6 percent in developed economies (Barro & Sala-i-Martin, 2003; Waverman et al., 2005).

Despite its shorter history, broadband seems to have a higher growth impact relative to communications technologies such as fixed and mobile telephony and the Internet. Thus, current differences in broadband penetration among countries may generate significant long-run growth benefits for early adapters. Moreover, the significant and stronger growth effects of other technologies in developing countries suggest that the growth benefit of broadband in developing countries could be on a similar path (Barro & Sala-i-Martin, 2003).

Three Types of Dynamic Model of Quality Assessment for Online Instruction

As noted, institutional isomorphism is one of the ways of structural reorganisation that is aimed at quality enhancement. Uncertainty in organisations, and in HEIs, is a powerful force that encourages both imitation, i.e. mimetic isomorphism, and coercion, i.e. coercive isomorphism. 'Modeling is a response to uncertainty' (DiMaggio & Powell, 1983, p. 117). It is a powerful tool for academia, especially in transition countries, to reform organisation, assessment criteria and quality enhancement mechanisms.

The chapter offers a *dynamic model* of quality evaluation and enhancement strategy that will enable educators to tackle coercive and manipulative forces, and make higher education governance efficient. Therefore, the present chaper offers continuous evaluation process through customer, public and private sector feedback on the performance of HEIs. It suggests that through the *dynamic model of quality assessment*, the HEIs will improve governance and quality by continuous feedback analysis. This might appear effective for

68 Mariam Orkodashvili

the transition countries where the socioeconomic conditions change rapidly and need constant update on the changing environment and on the directions and policies necessary for the adjustment to the worldwide developments of the pandemic period and online modes of education.

Besides, evaluating how effectively HEIs adhere to their mission statements will become easier and more vivid through *dynamic model*, since it will allow the policymakers to differentiate between the efficiency of HEIs' fulfilling the mission statement and the niches in study programmes that they might offer but still might not be able to adhere to the mission statement. In order to administer the dynamic model, the present research offers horizontal and vertical models of policy diffusion (Leader-Laggard Model, Regional Diffusion Model and Vertical Influence Model, source: Berry & Berry, 1999).

The first model that the article offers is *Vertical Influence Model*. The model would be initiated by the governmental bodies and urge all HEIs to set up online instruction as a required component of being accredited. This would enhance chances of the students to engage in online classes and listen to online lectures from different parts of the world. The model would significantly decrease the gap between elite groups and low SES communities.

The implementation of *Vertical Influence Model* would encounter least obstacles, since it would be officially sanctioned. As a consequence, the probability of innovation would be high, as most resources would be directed from governmental bodies. As for the level of motivation, it would be moderate owing to the governmental involvement. However, *Vertical Influence Model* might increase probabilities of coercion from the governmental organisations due to the new types of hierarchical structures and power relations that will emerge in the organisations officially entitled 'to oversee' the implementation of the policies. Any official requirement or policy coming from the higher levels of governmental structures could induce the formation of certain power relations, impositions and power struggles that might grow into coercion.

To address the issue of coercion, horizontal models, such as *Organisational Diffusion Model* and *Leader-Laggard Model,* would balance and 'monitor' the susceptibility of the *Vertical Influence Model* to coercive practices. *Organisational Diffusion Model* should be implemented and monitored by the HEIs themselves. This should be envisaged as a next stage, further development of *Vertical Influence Model.* Having introduced the innovation, the governmental bodies should put the monitoring power of the practice into the hands of HEIs. The incentive of attracting student bodies and establishing reputation on the job market would foster inter-institutional competition of contacting and contracting as many employers as possible. However, the motivation of implementing the innovative ways of online practices would increase motivation of individual universities for achieving success.

Another option would be the *Leader-Laggard Model*, where less successful organisations follow the examples of more successful organisations or pioneer organisations. The novel policies would be first implemented and tested by the most resourceful HEIs and further diffused to other institutions. In addition

Pandemic Challenges of Higher Education 69

to the features of *Organisational Diffusion Model*, the *Leader-Laggard Model* would include the component of 'successful/less successful' institution that would affect the public image of HEIs. This would highly increase competition between institutions. However, the drawbacks would be that it might leave certain universities with fewer resources at a considerable competitive disadvantage, while advantaging others significantly. Laggards would, therefore, have less motivation, while leader institutions would be highly motivated. However, both horizontal models would increase competition and transparency in higher education.

Besides, the increased competition in assisting the graduates to succeed on the job market would consequently incentivise all HEIs to enhance quality of instruction and study programmes. Table 4.1 summarises the main features, advantages and drawbacks of each model.

Table 4.1 Summary of the suggested policy introduction-implementation models

Model	Description	Assessment
Vertical Influence Model	Government initiates and influences the introduction and implementation of new policies that spread throughout the country gradually.	Decreases collusion and nepotism, however, might increase coercion from the government due to the new types of hierarchical structures and power relations that will emerge in the organisations officially entitled 'to oversee' the implementation of the policies. Least obstacles, high probability of innovation, most resources, moderate level of motivation owing to the governmental involvement.
Organisational Diffusion Model	Institutions introducing new policies that spread from one organisation to another. Unlike Leader-Laggard Model, successful/less successful institution variable is not considered.	Assumed to foster more competition. Most obstacles, hence, low probability of innovation, least resources, high degree of motivation if implemented efficiently.
Leader-Laggard Model	Less successful institutions following the policy examples of more successful institutions or pioneer institutions.	Fosters competition and influences the public image of an institution. Less obstacles for laggards than in Organisational Diffusion Model due to the earlier precedents, most obstacles for leaders as they pave the first path; moderate probability of innovation, moderate amount of resources, moderate degree of motivation for laggards, high degree of motivation for leaders.

Source: Author.

70   *Mariam Orkodashvili*

The three proposed models should be implemented with continuous evaluation. Cross-institutional comparative analysis of the degree of success of implementing the offered policies will enable policymakers and educators to adjust those policies to the ongoing socioeconomic changes and developments. Continuous assessment and evaluation of the offered models will also enable HEIs to efficiently enhance their study programmes and requirement standards and to adapt to online modes of teaching, learning, material design and distribution.

The important questions that should be put at this point are: which universities have managed most successful adaptation to online modes of instruction: private or public? One could assume that private institutions would be able to adapt to online instruction faster; however, the research so far has found out that private institutions might lack resources for technological upgrade, whereas public institutions received subsidies from the governments to introduce online technologies during the pandemic. Thus, it could be assumed that vertical diffusion model acted most prominently in this case.

Another issue would be, which departments and specialties would be quicker in adapting to online studies. The research so far has yielded the results that IT and business departments appeared most flexible and quick to respond to the pandemic challenges. Therefore, they could be considered as *leaders* in Leader-Laggard Model of introducing innovations.

Reconsidering Criteria for University Rankings: New Variables Plugged In?

On the one hand, it could be argued that introducing online classes across the world has created opportunities for students to join the courses at their desirable universities from different countries and from different parts of the world. The easy access to electronic resources and study materials, to video recordings of classes or to live online streaming of lectures has facilitated the spread of education all over the world. This in itself has given rise to the possibilities of students to obtain certificates, diplomas, credits, degrees and qualifications based on online assessments and evaluations. However, the online access to education requires certain IT equipment and the availability of the Internet, which is not always provided in economically disadvantaged parts of the world. This fact puts number of students at a disadvantage relative to others.

Taking a step further, the above discussed and offered models of quality enhancement and assessment of online instruction at HEIs make it necessary to reconsider the criteria for university rankings. The online mode of instruction has clearly revealed the pitfalls in the existent criteria and has engendered controversies and debates in this respect. On the one hand, quick and timely switch to online classes and lectures has been perceived as one of the positive indicators of university's ability to adapt to novel types of instruction and to keep up with the stressing demands of global lockdown. It has been even felt that the pace at which education institutions managed to switch from face-to-face to online style of instruction has served as an indicator of success, and hence high quality and better access, of any specific institution. This adaptability has been perceived as a kind of quality indicator across education institutions.

In this respect, timely and flexible switch to online and/or hybrid mode of teaching/learning can be plugged in the university ranking assessment formulas as new variables. That would make the assessment even more diverse and would allow the flexible rearrangement of the variables when identifying the position of a university in global rankings. On the other hand, the lack of rigid and transparent regulations of monitoring the progression of education through online tests and examinations has engendered debates on how reliable and valid credentials acquired through such online assessment methods are.

Developing the argument further, conferring credentials, diplomas and degrees based on online modes assessments has raised further issues of quality control, university ranking criteria and the related issues. Therefore, the degree of success of a certain university in conducting online assessments and credential checks would be yet further variables that could be plugged into university ranking formulas. This process would make the assessment process and quality check more complex and diverse, but at the same time, it would take the education quality standards to further level of development and could give rise to the issues and details that have not been considered so far (e.g. making students more employable for the rising tele-working market and adaptable to hybrid modes of multitasking). Therefore, the positive technological developments that triggered different modes of instructions in academia have also necessitated the reconsideration of quality check and university ranking components that need to be added as further new variables to the global framework of assessments.

Concluding Remarks

The challenging questions that remain for academia in the future regarding online study mode adaptations are: How and who would monitor the quality enhancement plans in HEIs? What policies would cause the decrease of the instances of quality manipulation and coercion in HEIs? How should the dilemma of accountability vs. autonomy dichotomy be resolved in mimetic and coercive isomorphic clashes? What variables and how should they be incorporated into global university ranking process?

Regarding the impact of COVID-19 on the higher education in the Gulf countries, it could be stated that there has been a double-sided influence of the pandemic on the universities. On the one hand, the prestigious universities in GCC countries, Doha's Education City, Dubai's Knowledge Village, Sharjah's University City and other universities offering world class courses, have managed to adapt to online instruction mode quickly and efficiently. The majority of them possessed the necessary technologies to switch to online classes in a

72 Mariam Orkodashvili

short span of time. On the other hand, the local national universities were slower to respond to the changes either due to the lack of high-level technologies, or due to highly bureaucratised administrative sector, that hindered timely and efficient implementation of online class deliveries and schedules. Therefore, this discrepancy between various universities has created a gap that could be reflected on the quality of education.

The second important implication could be the fact that while prestigious universities considered timely switch to online education as one of the assets, or positive indicators, in reconsidering university ranking criteria, the laggard universities could be claiming the online mode of instruction as an obstacle to high-quality education. Therefore, this divergence in the perception of online mode of instruction could affect the uniformity in the indicators of university rankings. Thus, the two implications need to be considered carefully while redrafting the criteria for university rankings in the Gulf States.

References

Barro, R. J., Sala-i-Martin, X. (2003). *Economic growth* (2nd ed.). Massachusetts: MIT Press.

Berry, W. F., & Berry, F. S. (1999). Innovation and diffusion models in policy research. In P. A. Sabatier (Ed.), *Theories of the policy process* (pp. 169–200). Westview Press.

Berdahl, R., & McConnell, T.R. (1994). *Autonomy and accountability: Some fundamental issues.* In P. Altbach, R. Berdahl, & P. Gumport (Eds.), *Higher education* in American society (pp. 55–72). Amherst, NY: Prometheus Books.

Cameron, K.S. & Tschirhart, M. (1992). Postindustrial Environments and Organizational Effectiveness in Colleges and Universities. *The Journal of Higher Education,* 63(1), 87–108.

Campbell, D. T. (1979). "Assessing the impact of planned social change". *Evaluation and Program Planning,* 2(1), 67–90.

Clark, B. R. (1998). *Creating entrepreneurial universities: Organizational pathways of transformation.* Pergamon Press.

Dill, D. & Sporn, B. (1995). *Emerging Patterns of Social Demand and University Reform: Through a Glass Darkly.* http://lst-iiep.iiep-unesco.org/cgi-bin/wwwi32. exe/[in=epidoc1.in]/?t2000=007149/(100).

DiMaggio, P., & Powell, W. (1983). The iron cage revisited: Institutional isomorphism and collective rationality in organizational fields. *American Sociological Review,* 48(1), 147–160.

Gumport, P. J., & Sporn, B. (1985). Institutional adaptation: Demands for management reform and university administration. In J. Smart & W. G. Tierney (Eds.), *Higher education handbook of theory and research* (Vol. XIV, pp. 103–145). Agathon Press.

Lawrence, P. R., & Lorsch, J. W. (1986). *Organization and Environment: Managing Differentiation and Integration.* Harvard Business Review Press.

Leslie, D.W.; Fretwell, E.K. Jr. (1996). Wise Moves in Hard Times: Creating & Managing Resilient Colleges & Universities. *The Jossey-Bass Higher and Adult Education Series. First Edition.* Jossey-Bass.

Mintzberg, H. (1979). *The structuring of organizations.* Prentice-Hall.

Mintzberg, H. (1980). Structure in 5'S: A synthesis of the research on organization design. *Management Science*, 26(3), 229–344.

Mintzberg, H., Lampel, J., Quinn, J. B., & Ghoshal, S. (2003). *The strategy of process. Concepts, contexts, cases* (4th ed.). Pearson Education, Prentice Hall.

Musselin, C. (1996). Organized anarchies: A reconsideration of research strategies. In M. Warglien & M. Masuch (Eds.), *The logic of organizational disorder* (pp. 55–72). De Gruyter.

Pfeffer, J. and Salancik, G. (1978) *The External Control of Organizations: A Resource Dependence Perspective*. Harper & Row, New York.

Sahlberg, P. (2009). Creativity and Innovation through Lifelong Learning. *Journal of Lifelong Learning in Europe*, 14, 53–60.

Salancik, G. and Pfeffer, J. (1974). The Bases and Use of Power in Organizational Decision Making: The Case of a University. *Administrative Science Quarterly*, 19(4), 453–473.

Slaughter, Sh. and Leslie, L. L. (1997). Expanding and Elaborating the Concept of Academic Capitalism. *SAGE Journals*, 8(2), 154–161.

Sporn, B. (1999). *Adaptive university structures. An analysis of adaptation to socio-economic environments of US and European Universities*. Higher Education Policy Series 54. Jessica Kingsley Publishers.

Stasz C., et al. (2007). RAND Corporation. Post-secondary Education in Qatar: Employer Demand, Student Choice, and Options for Policy, Doha, Qatar.

Tierney, W. (1988). Organizational Culture in Higher Education. *The Journal of Higher Education*, 59, 2–21. 10.2307/1981868.

Waverman, L., et al. (2005). The Impact of Telecoms on Economic Growth in Developing Markets. *The Vodafone Policy Paper Series*, 1(2), 10–23.

Weick, K. E. (1976). Educational organizations as loosely coupled systems. In M. W. Peterson (Ed.) (1991). *Organization and governance in higher education* (4th ed., pp. 103–117). ASHE Reader Series. Pearson Custom Publishing.

5 Higher Education in the COVID-19 Environment

ICT-Based Perspective for GCC Countries

Umara Noreen, Attayah Shafique, and Bello Musa Yakubu

Introduction

There is a long history of pandemics in the world since 1200 BC. A total of 249 pandemics have been recorded throughout the world including the COVID-19 of today. Some of the popular pandemics include Black death, Ebola, Smallpox, Spanish Flue, the plague of Justinian, MERS, SARS, COVID-19, etc. During COVID-19, the educational sector is one of the most affected areas. Most countries of the world did not have the proper educational infrastructure to combat these situations. The immediate transfer of education from face-to-face mode to online was difficult for most countries because of lack of resources and training.

With the rest of the world, Gulf countries (Saudi Arabia, Kuwait, Qatar, Bahrain, United Arab Emirates, and Oman) also face challenges in the education sector. After the outbreak of the pandemic, more than 100 countries, including the Gulf countries, ordered the closure of schools and universities and think about another way of teaching. Thus, it was decided that higher educational institutions (HEIs) were shifted to the online system to continue the education of students across the world (Asad & Kashif, 2021; Crawford et al., 2020).

For the last 15 years, the Gulf Cooperation Council played a vital role in the betterment of education in the Gulf Countries. Day by day the world becomes modernised, and the demands of society including the students are drastically changed. Therefore, the GCC has decided to invest enough resources for educational purposes. This will help achieve the goals and prepare their economies and societies for an increasingly globalised and competitive world. In achieving the long-term sustainable educational goals, the GCC countries made and adopted an ambitious and comprehensive education reform agenda. Development of the educational sector in GCC countries gives opportunities to teachers, academicians, and researchers to enhance, explore, and improve their knowledge and skills. This leads to the expansion and diversification of HEIs, as well as the provision of accreditation and quality assurance programmes, in addition to collaborations with local and worldwide universities.

DOI: 10.4324/9781003457299-7

According to the Encyclopaedia of Computer Science: *"Information Communication Technology (ICT) is an imprecise term frequently applied to broad areas of activities and technologies associated with the use of computers and communications".* In the early 1980s, ICT started to be introduced in several organisations by catering to all fields (Zhang & Aikman, 2007). Meanwhile, in the same era, the educational sector also tried to upgrade its standards by introducing computer labs in the schools and college levels (Bransford et al., 2000; Grimus, 2000; Yelland, 2001). They focused on computer literacy and arranged computer training programmes for the faculty members and other related staff.

Like the developed countries, the developing and Gulf countries also worked for the development and implementation of ICT at all levels. They made huge investments in this development. In the educational sector, ICT offered a wide range of methods to enhance the classroom teaching and learning of students (Qiao, 2009). *These include the increased potential for taking into account individual differences; providing feedback to the learner; increasing achievement in language learning; supporting the acquisition of learning skills and computer literacy; acquiring positive digital habits; speeding up the learning process; developing problem-solving skills; diversifying learning experiences; consolidating concepts; reinforcing historical learning; and reducing the burden on the teacher.*

Several studies have been done to highlight the importance of ICT in the educational field (Kozma, 2005). The founder and initiator of ICT also launched the advanced technologies from the platform of ICT, which lead to more advancements in information communication technology in the future (Somekh, 2007). As already discussed, ICT plays an important part in the social and economic development of any society. But there are certain challenges linked with the usage and integration of ICT in the education sector (schools, colleges, universities, etc.), so it is the need time that important steps will be taken for integration, to lead to the improvement in the quality of education through learning and teaching. Therefore, it is concluded that, with the introduction of new technology, there are challenges attached to it.

Due to COVID-19, educational institutions (schools, colleges, and universities) had been closed in March 2020. Across the globe, the pandemic affects educational institutions adversely, and face-to-face interaction between students and teachers has been changed to online teaching methods. Hence, the most powerful tool used for this purpose is ICT.

The developing and developed countries were not prepared to combat the situations that arise from the pandemic in all aspects. Although the developed countries introduced ICT in all fields of life but in educational sector, the interaction of students and teachers online was less before COVID-19. The situation in underdeveloped countries was worse than in developed countries. The educational institutions were closed, and the teacher and students were not enough trained or skilled that they immediately understand, implement, and use it in the classroom or for educational purposes.

The GCC region will have great work on the educational sector by introducing educational reforms in the last decade. The main purpose is to produce highly educated workforce from the Gulf countries so that they can compete at any forum globally. To fulfil that aim, they started facilitating the faculty members, academicians, researchers, scholars, and students on a priority basis and allocation of a major part of the resources. ICT is one of the emerging technologies and is integrated into the educational sector also. The GCC countries also implement ICT tools in educational institutions.

The implementation and usage of the ICT tools are also accompanied by certain challenges during COVID-19. Lack of understanding, training, skills, resources faced by the teachers and students, etc. are pointed out as the main and crucial challenges now in the present day. Therefore, this chapter is designed to identify the teachers' views related to ICT in their teaching and the impact of ICT on students' learning during the COVID-19 located in Bahrain, Kuwait, Oman, Qatar, Saudi Arabia, and the United Arab Emirates during the COVID-19. It also investigates the challenges in the implementation and usage of ICT tools by teachers and students during COVID-19 by examining the following questions:

1 What are the perception and views of teachers on the impact of ICT on their teaching during COVID-19 while teaching in the GCC region?
2 What will be the impact of ICT on the learning of students in the GCC region?
3 What are the main challenges faced by the teachers and students in the usage of ICT during COVID-19?

Objectives of the Chapter

The purpose of this chapter is to determine the impact of ICT in the HEIs concerning the teachers and students in the GCC countries during a pandemic. It explored the challenges of using the ICT tools by the teachers and students during COVID-19. Two different questionnaires were developed separately for faculty and students by using the study of Ghavifekr et al. (2016) with few modifications. Questionnaires were developed by using the Google Form and circulated randomly in the higher education institutions (HEIs) of the GCC. Questionnaires were sent by email personally to the faculty members of the Gulf HEIs.

The period for the collection of data was from March 2022 to May 2022. The questionnaires developed for faculty and students consisted of three parts. In both questionnaires, the first part was related to the demographics of the faculty members and students. The second and third sections were designed for the faculty related to teachers' perception of using ICT and challenges faced in using the ICT during COVID-19. Similarly, the second and third sections of the students' questionnaire consisted of questions related to the impact of ICT on the learning of students and the challenges faced by the

Higher Education in the COVID-19 Environment 77

students in the usage of ICT during COVID-19. Five-point Likert scale was used ranging from strongly agree (05) to strongly disagree (01). Three hundred questionnaires each were distributed to the teachers and students at different HEIs in GCC.

Three hundred and ninety-nine usable questionnaires were received from the teachers and students from the GCC region, which are completed in all respects. Cronbach's alpha was greater than 0.7, therefore reliable. Descriptive data analysis was used to see a clear picture of data through mean and standard deviation. ANOVA analysis was used to determine the difference in perception of teachers related to ICT among the difference. An in-depth analysis was carried out by using the correlation and regression analysis using the EVIEWS-10 software.

Impact of ICT on Teaching and Learning

Digital learning has been used in higher education in Saudi Arabia in the post-COVID-19 era (Shahzad et al., 2021). Al-Fadhel et al. (2020) conducted a study on higher education technology readiness to face the sudden pandemic hit. The study showed that some countries in the GCC had a smoother transaction from the offline education to an online education experience as they were technology equipped. However, other countries had a rough start and took time for the technology implementation. The study concludes with a recommendation to enforce and raise technology awareness and usage for the GCC countries to avoid similar situations.

Another study has shown the university's role in community service during the pandemic was clear as universities contributed with research support and initiatives. Universities were able to protect the welfare of their students and faculty members while maintaining the university's teaching standards (Bensaid & Brahimi, 2020). A study has recommended that training services for the university staff and effective work distribution among faculty members will enhance effectiveness.

Other than the technical difficulties the higher education encountered during the pandemic, psychological implications such as stress, anxiety, and fear of the unknown, among other things, have significant effects on the higher education institutions in the GCC region. Furthermore, the following study introduces the fourth Industrial Revolution (4IR) in higher education in the GCC and its impact and effectiveness on the learning phase during the pandemic COVID-19 phase. The study explains the 4IR benefits in transforming virtual education for the country's advancement as Saudi Arabia has implemented that in their higher education approach as part of the 2030Vision. In conclusion, results showed that the 4IR has a significant role in the student's learning outcomes, staff productivity, work environment, and the enhancement of the faculty member's capabilities.

Shedding light on the varied assessment approach in the GCC, some countries, such as Saudi Arabia, had postponed the assessment to the second semester.

Others gave the student the chance to choose whether to include the first semester counted in their total GPA or not. In conclusion, the study ended on a positive note. The accounting educators' changes have coped with the changes enforced upon them and have improved the lecturer's effectiveness and good usage of the lecture time compared to traditional education (Sarea et al., 2021).

Aldulaimi et al. (2021) find the opportunities and challenges of E-Learning as explained by higher education faculties members in the GCC. The study starts by listing the positive outcome of E-learning during COVID-19, as universities were able to accommodate many students in one place and time compared with traditional education; it had its time and space limitations. However, providing large Networks and large equipment to the student was one of the challenges faced. The study concluded with the need to omit and change some of the universities' laws to match the fast pace of technology developments. The following study explores the challenges imposed on students and staff of higher education institutions in the GCC. At one of the universities in Oman, the students and the staff members could not access the university educational system during the lockdown. The high demand for laptops and other equipment needed for virtual learning faced a shortage of supplies. Besides, some universities faced shorts in finance to provide the right equipment in time for their members. Moreover, the study shed light on student entrepreneurship careers, as a significant number of student start-ups suffered during the pandemic lockdown, which resulted in major losses (Orkodashvili, 2021).

Participants have highlighted some of the improvements universities should consider for improving future advancements (Altwaijry et al. 2021). Another study discusses the need for educational innovation in higher education. The study about the iPad intuitive in the GCC implemented exploring the four-frame by Bolman and Deal (1991). Such research allows higher education to be prepared in times of crises such as COVID-19. The iPad intuitive applied by the university was able to provide psychological support for its students and faculty members alongside technological training. In conclusion, the study emphasised that universities need to explore more such initiatives to be more equipped for the future with the right knowledge and readiness to face any challenges.

According to Khan et al. (2021), in this competitive era, every university is looking towards qualitative and cost-effective methods of examination. Online assessment is gaining more popularity during the ongoing COVID-19 outbreak. E-exams must be authentic, dependable, secure, and compliant in promoting learning and ensuring alignment with intended learning outcomes. Most of the teachers lack the expertise required to manage the online examination judiciously. Blended learning can provide students with flexibility and accessibility that cannot be found elsewhere. This helps students define goals, make decisions, and evaluate their progress, which would improve the learning outcome. The concept of blended learning is new in the country with only a small number of Saudi universities offering it (Bamoallem & Altarteer, 2022).

The COVID-19 crisis caused several countries to close off their educational institutions. Most countries have issued new regulations on the learning method at every stage of education. The Kingdom of Bahrain did not impose a lockdown because of the presence of large numbers of expatriate employees. However, other strict measures were taken to control the spread of the COVID-19 pandemic. The education institutions in Bahrain were planning to transfer to blended learning at the beginning of the academic year 2020–2021.

Malik and Ahmad (2020) concluded that HEIs in Saudi Arabia must reconsider the integration of soft skill in all study majors during the COVID-19 crisis. Instructors who utilise the use of ICT in a virtual learning environment have accomplished the tasks assigned to them. Most universities around the world are equipped with LMS, but instructors are not well prepared to deliver their courses virtually. Some studies found that E-learning takes more time per student than traditional learning. Others found that traditional learning takes more time than E-Learning (Sarea et al., 2021). During the pandemic, many universities had to change their method of teaching for the safety of all students and staff. Universities introduced Zoom, Blackboard collaborate, WebEx, Google meets, and other such online platforms to conduct classes and have students participate in online classes as well as lectures. These tools created a virtual classroom with interaction and provided the professors with a chance to conduct their lectures in an equivalent way to how they would normally (Leo et al., 2021).

E-Learning assists in gaining knowledge in depth escalating self-motivation and accomplishes the adult learning values. On the other hand, financial issues for fixing, operating, and maintenance of the E-Learning platform has been improved. It is necessary to develop the infrastructure and hire IT experts. The absence of face-to-face interaction is one of the biggest challenges. Lack of tutor support, particularly in the case of complex subjects, is also a drawback (Hoq, 2020). Challenges include poor internet connection that hinders students from accessing virtual platforms to attend their classes.

Despite the major benefits of M-learning, the widespread and effective application of technologies in teaching and learning processes has remained low among Saudi students during the COVID-19 pandemic. Furthermore, university management support, university culture, and awareness, all have a major influence on students' acceptance of M-learning (Almaiah et al., 2022).

Challenges Faced by Faculty in Using ICT during COVID-19

The questionnaire developed for the faculty comprises ten questions on the teachers' perception related to the ICT and six questions were asked about the challenges they faced while using ICT during COVID-19. Other than these questions, five questions were asked to the faculty to know about their personal and professional characteristics.

80 Umara Noreen, Attayah Shafique, and Bello Musa Yakubu

Table 5.1 Descriptive statistics of faculty's demographics

Country	n	%	Gender	n	%	Age group	n	%
Bahrain	43	24.7	Male	93	53.4	26-35	40	23
Kuwait	16	9.2	Female	81	46.6	36-45	53	30.6
Oman	13	7.5				46-55	48	27.5
Qatar	13	7.5				More than 55	32	18.4
Saudi Arabia	57	32.7						
UAE	32	18.4						
Total	174	100		174	100		174	100

There were 174 faculty members from GCC countries who participated in this survey. Table 5.1 gives the country, gender, and age of the respondents. Table 5.2 shows information such as teaching experience and level of computer literacy.

Most of the faculty members participated from Saudi Arabia (32.7%), then from Bahrain (24.7%). From Qatar and Oman, only 7.5% of faculty members show their representation. In terms of gender, 53.4% were male teachers while 46.6% were female teachers. Likewise, most of the teachers were between 36 and 45 years of age. More than half of faculty members have ten years and above of teaching experience. The level of computer literacy was also "better" (38% proficient) among the teachers serving in the Gulf countries.

Cronbach's alpha is a very important measure to determine the internal consistency of the variables that as a group the variables are consistent. If the value of the Cronbach's alpha is more than 0.70, then it is considered to be acceptable and overall data is reliable. The value of Cronbach's alpha for the perception of the teacher on the impact of ICT on their teaching during COVID-19 was 0.72. Likewise, Cronbach's alpha of the challenges faced by the teacher by using the ICT shows a value of 0.78, both the values are higher than 0.70. Therefore, it was declared that the overall data was reliable and consistent. The perception/views of teachers on the impact of ICT on their teaching were determined in terms of achieving pedagogical and curricular aspects, student involvement and technical skills, and accessing the ICT tools.

The results of the equality to check the mean difference among different GCC countries and the perception of teachers of achieving pedagogical and

Table 5.2 Descriptive statistics of faculty teaching experience and computer literacy

Teaching experience variable	n	%	Level of computer literacy	n	%
1–5 years	36	21	Basic	58	33
6–10 years	43	24	Intermediate	50	29
11–15 years	36	21	Proficient	66	38
16–20 years	59	34			
Total	174	100		174	100

Higher Education in the COVID-19 Environment 81

Table 5.3 ANOVA analysis of achieving pedagogical and curricular aspects

Countries	n	Mean	Std. Dev.	Std. Err of Mean
Bahrain	43	3.495581	0.784700	0.119666
Kuwait	16	3.791875	0.696996	0.174249
Oman	13	3.564615	0.567826	0.157487
Qatar	13	3.539231	0.789403	0.218941
Saudi Arabia	57	3.678772	0.736772	0.097588
UAE	32	3.563125	0.588341	0.104005
All	174	3.603678	0.709725	0.053804

Method	df	Value	Probability
ANOVA F-test	(5, 168)	0.595295	0.7036
Welch F-test*	(5, 49.1877)	0.545388	0.7410

curricular aspects by using ICT during COVID-19 are shown in Table 5.3. According to the results, there was no difference in the mean level of perception of achieving pedagogical and curricular aspects among the GCC countries. Among all the countries, the teachers in Kuwait's higher institutes show the highest mean which was 3.79 in the perception that ICT helps during COVID-19 in achieving their pedagogical and curricular aspects and impacted positively their teaching. The mean value of other countries was also close to or higher than 3.5, and therefore it was concluded that teachers benefitted by using the ICT tools during COVID-19. The reason would be that the faculty members from the GCC countries were proficient in computer usage and had enough experience in teaching. Therefore, they can manage their teaching activities during that period in a better way. Hence, the null hypothesis that there is no difference in means in terms of achieving pedagogical and curricular aspects is accepted.

Table 5.4 represents the ANOVA analysis of teacher views on students' involvement and technical skills that also impacted their teaching during COVID-19.

Table 5.4 ANOVA analysis of student's involvement and technical skills

Countries	n	Mean	Std. Dev.	Std. Err of Mean
Bahrain	43	3.525581	0.449387	0.068531
Kuwait	16	3.487500	0.478714	0.119678
Oman	13	3.400000	0.424264	0.117670
Qatar	13	3.476923	0.666025	0.184722
Saudi Arabia	57	3.533333	0.614507	0.081393
UAE	32	3.581250	0.435103	0.076916
All	174	3.521839	0.519988	0.039420

Method	df	Value	Probability
ANOVA F-test	(5, 168)	0.259979	0.9343
Welch F-test*	(5, 48.8133)	0.347632	0.8813

82   *Umara Noreen, Attayah Shafique, and Bello Musa Yakubu*

Table 5.5 ANOVA analysis of accessing ICT

Countries	n	Mean	Std. Dev.	Std. Err. of Mean
Bahrain	43	3.453488	0.800401	0.122060
Kuwait	16	3.718750	0.729583	0.182396
Oman	13	3.384615	0.767948	0.212990
Qatar	13	3.384615	0.893352	0.247771
Saudi Arabia	57	3.000000	0.958980	0.127020
UAE	32	3.562500	0.904737	0.159936
All	174	3.339080	0.897956	0.068074

Method	df	Value	Probability
ANOVA F-test	(5, 168)	2.897428	0.0155
Welch F-test*	(5, 49.4341)	2.667938	0.0327

The results show that there was no difference among the GCC countries concerning this. In other words, all teachers have the same perception that students' involvement and technical skills enhance their teaching skills irrespective of the country. The reason might be that the students would be well trained and facilitated throughout the period so that they performed well. Hence, the null hypothesis that there is no difference in means in terms of teachers' perception regarding the student's involvement and technical skills by using the ICT tool during COVID-19 is accepted.

Table 5.5 shows the ANOVA analysis of assessing the ICT impact on their teaching during COVID-19. The result shows the significant difference among the Gulf countries in accessing the ICT tools by the students which ultimately affect the teaching of the teacher. The reason would be some Gulf countries have better facilities for ICT tools. Secondly, they trained their students well in time in the period of COVID-19. The p-value was also less than o.o5, which also depicts the significant differences. Therefore, the null hypothesis that there is no difference in the mean values in accessing the ICT impact on teachers' view was rejected.

Table 5.6 shows the descriptive statistics of challenges faced by the faculty members of the higher institutes in the GCC region. Using the ICT tool, a time-consuming activity has a mean of 3.49 with deviations from the mean

Table 5.6 Descriptive statistics of challenges faced by faculty by using ICT

Challenges faced by teachers	n	Mean	Std. Deviation
Using ICT tool is a time-consuming activity	174	3.494253	0.802792
Lack of knowledge and skills in using computer	174	3.574713	1.087312
Lack of resources	174	3.373563	1.055452
Lack of technical support	174	3.528736	1.084191
Lack of training	174	3.402299	1.152627

Higher Education in the COVID-19 Environment   83

Table 5.7 Ranking of challenges by using ICT tools

Challenges	Percentage	Rank
Using ICT tool is a time-consuming activity	41.38	1st
Lack of technical support	32.76	2nd
Lack of resources	32.18	3rd
Lack of knowledge and skills in using computer	28.74	4th
Lack of training	25.86	5th

being 0.80. Likewise, the means for the lack of knowledge, lack of resources, lack of technical support, and lack of training are 3.57, 3.37, 3.52, and 3.40 with the deviation from the mean being 1.08, 1.05, 1.08, and 1.15, respectively. It represented that teacher's response related to the challenges lies between sometimes and often. They agreed that they were facing different challenges in using the ICT tools during COVID-19.

Table 5.7 shows the ranking of challenges faced by the teachers or faculty members serving in the GCC countries. According to the results, 41.38% of teachers declared that using ICT tools is a time-consuming activity and they were challenged to manage the time of their lectures while using the ICT tools. 32.76% of teachers rank second the lack of technical support as a challenge. Likewise, lack of resources, lack of knowledge, and lack of training ranked third, fourth, and fifth with 32.18%, 28.74%, and 25.86%, respectively. The teachers were well educated, experienced, and well trained before the period of COVID-19, so they did not face any challenges in this respect, but before COVID-19, they did not interact or use enough ICT tools; therefore, during that period, they put more efforts in using and managing these tools.

Challenges Faced by Students in Using ICT during COVID-19

The questionnaire made for the students comprises 16 questions. Eleven questions are related to the impact of ICT on the learning of students and five questions are related to the challenges faced by the students by using ICT tools during COVID-19. The questions follow the Likert scale ranging from 1 *(strongly disagree)* to 5 *(strongly agree)*. Demographic information like gender, country, educational level, and computer literacy was also obtained.

Table 5.8 shows the personal and educational demographics of the students. Almost equal number of students participated from each country in the GCC region; 29% of students had A-level or equivalent; 86% had a Bachelor's Degree, and 33% of them were enrolled in Postgraduate degrees. More than half of the students are computer literate.

The internal consistency or reliability of all the items in the questionnaire was checked by using Cronbach's alpha. The variables related to the impact of ICT on the learning of students during COVID-19 had the value of Cronbach's alpha 0.79. Likewise, the value of Cronbach's alpha of the items related

Table 5.8 Descriptive statistics of student demographics

Country Variable	n	%	Gender Variable	n	%	Educational level	n	%	Computer literacy	n	%
Bahrain	37	16.4	Male	123	54.6	A-levels or equivalent	65	29	Yes	182	81
Kuwait	39	17.4	Female	102	45.4	Graduate (BS level)	86	38	No	43	19
Oman	37	16.4				Postgraduate (MS, Ph.D.)	74	33			
Qatar	40	17.7									
Saudi Arabia	36	16									
UAE	36	16									
Total	225	100		225	100		225	100		225	100

to the challenges faced by the students was 0.81. Thus, it was concluded that the data used in the analysis was reliable and consistent.

The impact of ICT was defined by using four independent variables, namely, Effectiveness of ICT, Availability of ICT, Usage of ICT, and Knowledge about the ICT. The dependent variable is the learning of students during COVID-19. Table 5.9 shows the descriptive statistics of dependent and independent variables.

Table 5.10 represents the correlation analysis between the dependent and independent variables. Correlation analysis depicts the interdependency of variables. One unit change in the effectiveness of ICT brings 0.513 units of

Table 5.9 Descriptive statistics of dependent and independent variables

Variables	n	Mean	Std. Deviation
Learning of students	225	3.611937	0.814833
Effectiveness of ICT	225	4.124444	1.005599
Availability of ICT	225	3.915556	0.771697
Usage of ICT	225	4.008889	0.850373
Knowledge of ICT	225	3.888889	0.774084

Table 5.10 Correlation analysis

Variables	Learning of students	Effectiveness of ICT	Availability of ICT	Usage of ICT	Knowledge of ICT
Learning of students	1	0.513	-0.024	0.051	-0.025
Effectiveness of ICT	0.513	1	-0.020	0.077	0.006
Availability of ICT	-0.024	-0.020	1	0.001	0.044
Usage of ICT	0.051			1	0.048
Knowledge of ICT	-0.025	0.006	0.044	0.048	1

Higher Education in the COVID-19 Environment 85

Table 5.11 Regression analysis

Variables	Coefficient	Std. Error	t-Statistic	Prob.
Learning of students	2.019277	0.433442	4.658696	0.0000
Effectiveness of ICT	0.414955	0.047001	8.828625	0.0000
Availability of ICT	-0.013155	0.061124	-0.215211	0.8298
Usage of ICT	0.012642	0.055634	0.227241	0.8204
Knowledge of ICT	-0.030336	0.060996	-0.497342	0.6194

change in the learning of the students during COVID-19. Likewise, the usage of ICT tools also brings positive to the learning of the students (0.051). Furthermore, the availability and knowledge of ICT show the inverse relationship with the learning of the student during COVID-19.

The relationship between ICT and the learning of students during COVID-19 is shown in Table 5.11. The results depict that there is no statistically significant relationships between availability, usage, and knowledge of ICT with the learning of students during COVID-19 as the p-value for these variables was higher than 0.05 and the t-value was also less than 2. It may be explained that the students from Gulf HEIs already have enough ICT knowledge, and ICT tools are also accessible so there was no new impact or effect on the learning of the students during COVID-19. The effectiveness of ICT shows a positive and significant impact on the learning of students with a p-value less than 0.05.

Descriptive statistics of challenges faced by students by using ICT during COVID-19 is shown in Table 5.12. Time management was one of the challenges faced by the students during COVID-19. It has a mean value of 3.35 with deviations from the mean being 1.04. Likewise, the means for the implementation of ICT tools in the classroom, lack of resources, and lack of training and skills of the students are 3.32, 2.54, and 4.00 with the deviation from the mean being 1.22, 1.12, and 1.27, respectively. The findings depict that students' challenges lay between neutral and agree except for the lack of resources. Moreover, the students disagree that they lack resources of using ICT during COVID-19.

The ranking of challenges faced by the students in using the ICT tools is shown in Table 5.13. As shown, 51% of students identified lack of training in

Table 5.12 Descriptive statistics of challenges faced by students in using ICT

Challenges faced by students	n	Mean	Std. Deviation
Time management	225	3.35	1.04
Implementation of ICT tools	225	3.32	1.22
Lack of resources	225	2.54	1.12
Lack of training and skills	225	4.00	1.27

86 Umara Noreen, Attayah Shafique, and Bello Musa Yakubu

Table 5.13 Ranking of challenges faced by students by using ICT tools

Challenges	Percentage	Rank
Lack of training	51.56	1st
Time management	40.00	2nd
Lack of resources	33.89	3rd
Implementation of ICT tools	28.00	4th

using the ICT tools during the COVID-19. Some students agreed on time management (40%) and lack of resources (33.89%) and the least challenge they faced was the implementation of ICT tools in the classroom.

Conclusion

Over the last decade, the educational reforms play an important role in enhancing the quality of education in GCC counties (Bahrain, Kuwait, Oman, Qatar, Saudi Arabia, and the United Arab Emirates) by improving the curricula, teaching standards through training and development, increasing professional freedom, and use of ICT in HEIs. The major change in educational institutions was the shifting of physical teaching or learning to online teaching or learning. At that stage, in developed countries, ICT makes it possible to continue educational activities online by providing better services in this respect. However, many countries did not have proper resources for implementing advanced informational technologies.

This chapter presented the teachers' views related to ICT in their teaching and the impact of ICT on students' learning during COVID-19 in Bahrain, Kuwait, Oman, Qatar, Saudi Arabia, and the United Arab Emirates. It was shown that there was a significant difference in accessing the ICT tools by the students among the GCC countries. It was also known that there is a positive significant impact of the effectiveness of ICT on the learning of students in Gulf HEIs. This means that if the students used ICT tools effectively in their educational activities, their learning and performance would increase. The major challenges identified by the teachers and students during COVID-19 in using the ICT tools include the usage of a time-consuming activity, lack of technical support, training, and resources. The pandemic was so sudden that no country would be prepared to deal with it. Before the pandemic, face-to-face teacher mode was used but due to COVID-19, it is immediately shifted to online learning without adequate training and resources, which posed as major challenges by both students and teachers during that period.

Policy makers, heads of HEIs, and other key stakeholders are encouraged to continue or implement a combination of online and face-to-face teaching even after the pandemic. This will enhance the learning of the students because of the continuous interaction with the ICT tools and other advanced technologies. In addition, the students will be well prepared to work or cope with similar situations in the future. Proper allocation of resources, provision of technical support, and proper training of the students and teachers are also important in the implementation and use of ICT in Gulf HEIs. Curriculum development is also recommended, focusing on the ICT integration in the HEIs in the Gulf. This will help in the teaching and learning activities of both teachers and students. Furthermore, the educational reforms of the GCC countries are renewed after the pandemic by introducing teaching pedagogy as a new scientific field in education.

References

Aldulaimi, S. H., Abdeldayem, M., Abo Keir, M. Y., & Al-Sanjary, O. (2021). E-learning in higher education and COVID-19 outbreak: Challenges and opportunities. *Psychology and Education Journal, 58*(2), 38–43.

Al-Fadhel, H., Al-Jalahma, A., & Al-Muhanadi, M. (2020, December). The reporting of technological readiness of higher education institutions in GCC Countries: A situational analysis of COVID-19 Crisis. In *2020 Sixth International Conference on e-Learning (econf)* (pp. 296–301). IEEE.

Almaiah, M. A., Ayouni, S., Hajjej, F., Lutfi, A., Almomani, O., & Awad, A. B. (2022). Smart mobile learning success model for higher educational institutions in the context of the COVID-19 pandemic. *Electronics, 11*(8), 1278.

Altwaijry, N., Ibrahim, A., Binsuwaidan, R., Alnajjar, L. I., Alsfouk, B. A., & Almutairi, R. (2021). Distance education during COVID-19 pandemic: a college of pharmacy experience. *Risk Management and Healthcare Policy*, 2099–2110.

Asad, M., & Kashif, M. (2021). Unveiling success factors for small and medium enterprises during COVID-19 pandemic. *Arab Journal of Basic and Applied Sciences, 28*(1), 187–194.

Bamoallem, B., & Altarteer, S. (2022). Remote emergency learning during COVID-19 and its impact on university students perception of blended learning in KSA. *Education and Information Technologies, 27*(1), 157–179.

Bensaid, B., & Brahimi, T. (2020, April). Coping with COVID-19: Higher education in the GCC countries. In *The international research & innovation forum* (pp. 137–153). Springer.

Bolman, L. G., & Deal, T. E. (1991). Leadership and management effectiveness: A multi-frame, multi-sector analysis. *Human Resource Management, 30*(4), 509–534.

Bransford, J. D., Brown, A. L., & Cocking, R. R. (2000). *How people learn* (Vol. 11). National Academy Press.

Crawford, J., Butler-Henderson, K., Rudolph, J., Malkawi, B., Glowatz, M., Burton, R., Magni, P. A., & Lam, S. (2020). COVID-19: 20 countries' higher education intra-period digital pedagogy responses. *Journal of Applied Learning & Teaching, 3*(1), 1–20.

Ghavifekr, S., Kunjappan, T., Ramasamy, L., & Anthony, A. (2016). Teaching and learning with ICT tools: Issues and challenges from teachers' perceptions. *Malaysian Online Journal of Educational Technology, 4*(2), 38–57.

Grimus, M. (2000, August). ICT and multimedia in the primary school. In *16th conference on educational uses of information and communication technologies* (pp. 21–25).

Hoq, M. Z. (2020). E-learning during the period of pandemic (COVID-19) in the kingdom of Saudi Arabia: An empirical study. *American Journal of Educational Research, 8*(7), 457–464.

Khan, M. A., Vivek, V., Khojah, M., Nabi, M. K., Paul, M., & Minhaj, S. M. (2021). Learners' perspective towards e-exams during COVID-19 outbreak: Evidence from higher educational institutions of India and Saudi Arabia. *International Journal of Environmental Research and Public Health, 18*(12), 6534.

Kozma, R. B. (2005). "National policies that connect ICT-based education reform to economic and social development." *Human Technology 1*(2), 117–156.

Leo, S., Alsharari, N. M., Abbas, J., & Alshurideh, M. T. (2021). From offline to online learning: A qualitative study of challenges and opportunities as a response to the COVID-19 pandemic in the UAE higher education context. In M. Alshurideh, A. E. Hassanien, & R. Masa'deh (Eds.), *The Effect of Coronavirus Disease (COVID-19) on Business Intelligence* (pp. 203–217). Springer.

Malik, A., & Ahmad, W. (2020). Antecedents of soft-skills in higher education institutions of Saudi Arabia study under COVID-19 pandemic. *Creative Education, 11*(7), 1152–1161.

Orkodashvili, M. (2021). Quality enhancement through internationalisation at GCC universities. In R. G. Segumpan & J. McAlaney (Eds.), *Higher education in the Gulf* (pp. 47–63). Routledge.

Qiao, A. (2009, July). Using ICT for enhancing English teaching: A quasi-experimental study. In *2009 International Conference on Information Technology and Computer Science* (Vol. 2, pp. 301–304). IEEE.

Sarea, A., Alhadrami, A., & Taufiq-Hail, G. A. M. (2021). COVID-19 and digitizing accounting education: Empirical evidence from GCC. *PSU Research Review, 5*(1), 68–83.

Shahzad, A., Hassan, R., Aremu, A. Y., Hussain, A., & Lodhi, R. N. (2021). Effects of COVID-19 in e-learning on higher education institution students: The group comparison between male and female. *Quality & Quantity, 55*(3), 805–826.

Somekh, B. (2007). *Pedagogy and learning with ICT: Researching the art of innovation*. Routledge.

Yelland, N. (2001). *Teaching and learning with information and communication technologies (ICT) for numeracy in the early childhood and primary years of schooling*. Department of Education, Training and Youth Affairs.

Zhang, P., & Aikman, S. (2007, July). Attitudes in ICT acceptance and use. In *International conference on human-computer interaction* (pp. 1021–1030). Springer.

6 Application of Risk Management on COVID-19 by Universities in the Gulf Cooperation Council (GCC)

Wan Norhayate Wan Daud, Fakhrul Anwar Zainol, Reynaldo Gacho Segumpan, and Joanna Soraya Abu Zahari

Introduction

A pandemic is a disease spread worldwide. It can infect and be efficiently transmitted among human or animal populations, affecting large populations (Porta, 2014). Pandemics are identified by their geographic scale rather than the severity of illness. Most people do not have immunity when, for instance, a new influenza virus emerges and spreads worldwide (WHO, 2010). The latest pandemic in the world is traced to the end of December 2019. The Chinese city of Wuhan has reported novel pneumonia caused by coronavirus disease 2019 (COVID-19), spreading domestically and internationally. The virus was defined as severe acute respiratory syndrome coronavirus 2 (SARS-CoV-2) or COVID-19. Information from the National Health Commission of China noted that the cases affected by COVID-19 in mainland China had increased tremendously, including in other international countries, especially the USA. Over the last two years, almost 248 million people have been diagnosed with the COVID-19 pandemic, leading to more than 5 million deaths. As of June 2023, the World Health Organization (2023) reported 6,941,095 deaths due to COVID-19.

In the Gulf, the first COVID-19 case in the United Arab Emirates (UAE) was announced on 29 January 2020. It reported a confirmed case of a 73-year-old Chinese woman, after which the number of cases increased exponentially. Three months after being declared a global health emergency, the GCC countries were hit hard by this pandemic, where 58,055 new cases were reported. Saudi Arabia had the largest number of cases (22,753), followed by UAE (12,481), Qatar (13,409), and Kuwait (4,024). Bahrain and Oman had fewer reported cases, with 3,040 and 2,348, respectively. At the height of the COVID-19 pandemic, domestic travel were discouraged, and countless global and regional plans and programmes have been cancelled or postponed. Many international travels were forbidden, and countries were forced to enforce several preventive measures following recommendations from international and

DOI: 10.4324/9781003457299-8

90   W. N. W. Daud, F. A. Zainol, R. G. Segumpan, et al.

local health organisations. These measures included social distancing, working remotely, and wearing face masks, which have become the new norm due to health risks. Remote access and working from home increased social media use, where people shared their opinions using social media platforms.

The GCC countries took unprecedented steps to contain the virus. For instance, Saudi Arabia suspended *Umrah* daily and Friday prayers in about 80,000 mosques and public transportation and shut down all workplaces except essential services. The Saudi Ministry of Education also announced the temporary closure of all schools and universities nationwide. The UAE also imposed strict restrictions on movement and travel. Citizens had to stay home unless necessary, and a 14-day mandatory quarantine was imposed on individuals entering the borders. Kuwait also enforced the closure of all public and private schools and higher education institutions (HEIs), while in Qatar, dining in restaurants and cafes was banned. Similarly, the Sultanate of Oman closed its borders, and all of its transportation services. Bahrain has issued electronic bracelets to self-isolated citizens, which could notify the station when they are 15 metres away from their phone.

This chapter critically analyses the coping strategies of HEIs in the Gulf against COVID-19 from a risk management perspective. The first part explores the impact of COVID-19 on HEIs, while the next segment discusses the mitigation plans to address each COVID-19-related risk impact on higher education in the Gulf.

Impact of COVID-19 in Gulf Education

Pandemic risk is the expected value of widespread infectious diseases in human health that affects economies and communities. A characteristic of this risk is that it combines a probability of occurrence, potentially catastrophic, and global impact. For example, the most severe of the flu pandemics in the last 100 years, the 1918 epidemic, killed 50–100 million people in a worldwide population of less than 2 billion.

Focusing on health impacts alone makes people and governments underestimate the real risk and neglect policies, prevention, and preparedness actions to increase resilience and enable business and household continuity. Substantial negative impacts will occur more broadly in economic sectors than in the health sector and society. Government, businesses, and consumers reacted to the 2003 SARS outbreak (which was arrested after 8,000 cases and 800 fatalities). It gave rise to economic costs of $54 billion, confirming that contagion impacts outside the health sector predominate, possibly by an extensive margin.

Other costs related to the pandemic would be lost productivity due to high staff absenteeism, amounting to about 28% of total expenses. During this period, 40% of staff cannot work due to sickness and related health issues. Sometimes, the employees cannot go to work because they need to care for ill family members. At the same time, many employees were affected due to school and daycare closures. Many academic conferences also had to be cancelled, some institutions asked staff to work from home (WFH), and schools asked students not to return to school until further advice. This kind of distribution of impacts means that the health sector cannot be expected to undertake, on its own, an adequate level of pandemic risk management for influenza and similar highly transmissible diseases. Some of the impacts of the pandemic are the high cost of delays and, too often, detection, diagnosis, and control of disease outbreaks.

The COVID-19 pandemic has dramatically affected many industries, including the educational sector. There is a strong possibility of deteriorating mental health because of the resulting sense of uncertainty and anxiety among students and faculty members. Almost top universities turned towards innovative ways of teaching and learning, such as applying Massive Online Open Courses (MOOC) and makerspace. It caught the attention of educators in not only higher education but also the interest of high schools. Many researchers and organisations have documented the impact of COVID-19 pandemic on the education landscape in the Gulf and how they dealt with the impact of the pandemic, among which are summarised as follows:

- Kingdom of Bahrain has issued electronic bracelets to track its active cases of COVID-19. Universities switched to online teaching and learning systems after the closure of the educational institutions on 25 February 2020. Several artificial intelligence applications and technologies were used during the COVID-19 crisis, such as the mobile apps *BeAware Bahrain* and *SkipLino* (Al-Rawi et al., 2021).
- In the UAE, schools (both private and government) temporarily closed their facilities to staff and students starting in March 2020. The Ministry of Education (MOE) actively provided online information and expanded and implemented distance learning approaches. The MOE also issued guidelines on students' online behaviour, information about free satellite broadband services for remote areas, free mobile internet packages, and existing e-learning, m-learning, and distance learning programmes and tutorials (Erfurth & Ridge, 2020).
- The Sultanate of Oman has also implemented similar measures, such as switching to online teaching and learning in all levels of education (primary to higher education), closure of restaurants and other service establishments and rise of mobile applications (e.g. *Talabat* and *Akeed*) for shopping and home delivery, limiting and, to a certain extent, prohibiting overseas travels (there were times when local and international flights were cancelled), and implementing curfew hours to ensure that residents are at home at certain times of the day.
- The scenario in the Kingdom of Saudi Arabia is similar to other GCC countries, with the former focusing on HEIs' rapid transition to remote learning.

It provided infrastructure and developed capacity to deliver high-quality online learning across the following dimensions (O'Keefe et al., 2020):

a Leadership (Governance, Strategies, Policies, Processes, Resource Allocation, Periodic Review and Updating, and Innovation);

b Curriculum Design and Planning (Instructional Design Methods & Universal Design for Learning, Alignment with Standards, Course Syllabi, Course Materials and Content, and Innovation);

c Online Teaching and Learning (Communication, Engagement, Expectation Setting, Outcomes, Course Interaction, Feedback, Teaching and Learning Resources, and Innovation);

d Assessment (Assessment Strategies, Assessment Processes, Assessment Methods, Assessment Types, and Innovation);

e Technology (Centralized Online Education Infrastructure, Coverage, Innovation, Internet Access, Information Technology Service Management Compliance, Modality, Operability, Reliability, and Security);

f Student Support (Student Orientation, Equity, Accessibility, Compliance Standards, and Innovation);

g Training and Support (Technical Assistance, Professional Development, Orientation, Mentoring, and Innovation); and

h Evaluation and Continuous Improvement (Evaluation of Course Outcomes and Program Quality, Student Satisfaction, Faculty Satisfaction, Staff Satisfaction, and Innovation).

- In Qatar, a number of initiatives were spearheaded by Qatar University (QU) to increase awareness of the coronavirus and preventive methods. QU leads some practical initiatives such as conducting online workshops and seminars; analysing global surveys and data related to COVID-19 procedures and disseminated the results of this analysis with the community; publishing several articles that informed the public on healthcare and community health; producing educational videos for the public; offering expertise by QU faculty members in local and international TV interviews; and strict implementation of social distancing, among many others.
- Kuwait implemented the following measures: (a) full curfew, (b) restrictions in travels, (c) suspension of inbound commercial flights, (d) closure of educational institutions (i.e. schools and universities), (e) banning public gatherings and celebrations, and (f) suspension of non-essential matters in governmental institutions, among others (United Nations Sustainable Development Group, 2023).

According to UNESCO (2020), some of the harmful effects of HEI closures are interrupted learning and students were deprived of opportunities for growth and development. Lack of access to technology or good internet connectivity for continued education during HEI closures also harms the institutions. Social isolation is another harmful effect because educational institutions

Application of Risk Management on COVID-19   93

are hubs for social activity and human interactions. Closures of HEIs can deprive youth of some social communications and socialisation that are essential to learning, development, and creativity. Thus, HEIs in Gulf countries must have an optional plan called a mitigation plan to recover the potential risks. By taking these steps, they will be better positioned to reduce the impact of a pandemic in their operations.

Mitigation Plans Risk for GCC Higher Education Institutions

COVID-19 affected not only students and teachers but also triggered economic and social issues and opportunities such as new avenues for digital learning. As a result of COVID-19, universities across the GCC region have closed their campuses, with most moving to online learning to ensure the uninterrupted delivery of knowledge using reliable and appropriate tools to facilitate distance teaching (Ahmed, 2020).

HEIs in GCC countries offer flexible grading systems and give students the right to accept or decline their cumulative Grade Point Average when unsatisfied with the evaluation system (Ahmed, 2020). Universities started offering 24 hours of e-library services to support students' and faculty members' research. This e-library contains several electronic databases of journals, e-books, and academic articles (Solomon, 2020). Several technology initiatives have been developed and expanded rapidly to promote distance learning and the Internet for learning from home, support countries in their effort for continuous education through remote learning, and work actively with Ministries of Education. In the context of the GCC, internet users are already high, which facilitates the move to distance learning. According to the Internet World Stats, as of 31 December 2019, the internet penetration rates in each GCC country exceed 90% (Wansink, 2019).

In preparation for virtual courses, several universities in KSA organised workshops and announced unique mechanisms for the final exams. When the first case of COVID-19 was reported in the UAE, all universities transitioned to online teaching, which put all universities in a quandary of dealing with the digital delivery of education. Zayed University adopted Adobe Connect, the University of Sharjah and United Arab Emirates University used Blackboard systems, and Heriot-Watt University Dubai used the Vision learning tool. Among all universities in the UAE, Hamdan Bin Mohammed Smart University is the first university to demonstrate extensive experience in online teaching. Henceforth, it facilitated the rest of the universities to successfully implement online classes (Crawford et al., 2020). Khalifa University trained its faculty members and staff on online delivery tools' instruction.

The University created an online learning ecosystem based on four interconnecting layers. At first, they ensured that all employees and students were on the same online learning page. Secondly, they initiated a Learning Management System to connect faculty with students to share course material, conduct online discussions, tests, quizzes, and assignments, and administer feedback. At the third level, the university initiated virtual classroom platforms such as Big Blue Button, MS Teams, and Blackboard Connect. Lastly, it compiled a repertoire of content development and management tools to ensure faculty develop their lessons without hindrance (Salama, 2020). The Saudi Research and Innovation Network and The Integrated Telecom Company collaborated to develop a portal dedicated to sharing resources with teachers, parents, and students to ensure the provision of high-quality virtual classrooms and learning platforms. This free-of-cost portal consists of apps, websites, and other resources that support teachers, parents, and students in distance learning (Draycott, 2020). For example, King Abdullah University of Science and Technology (KAUST) initiated online teaching and implemented work-from-home to ensure the safety of employees and students. The entirely virtual educational model ensures instructions' uninterrupted delivery (KAUST, 2020a).

The government of Bahrain also issued directives to close all public and private universities. At the time, all training and community centres have been closed. Universities moved to online teaching and online learning systems, successfully imparting education smoothly. Using Microsoft Teams and Blackboard, Bahrain University started digital classrooms and e-learning to access instructional content and allow students and faculty to communicate through chat rooms and live broadcasts.

Similarly, in Kuwait, authorities announced a two-week suspension of all schools and public and private universities to contain the spread of COVID-19. The American University of Kuwait rolled out an e-learning platform for students to review course material and connect with faculty with plans not to hold assessments (American University of Kuwait, 2020). The University of Kuwait used Blackboard Collaborate to continue the teaching and learning process during the pandemic. The government developed a strategic initiative called Risk Mitigation and Recovery Plan under COVID-19 (RMRP), a collaborative effort spearheaded by the United Nations Country Team (UNCT) to help Kuwaiti Stakeholders in dealing with the socio-economic impact of the COVID-19 pandemic (United Nations Sustainable Development Group, 2023).

In Oman, the Ministry of Higher Education instructed all institutions of higher learning to use online teaching methods to complete the current academic year. Sultan Qaboos University, for instance, initiated an e-learning programme in which lectures are delivered in written, audio, or visual format with queries conducted through virtual chatrooms. Alternative assessment options, such as final reports, case studies, projects, and independent research studies, are also adopted.

However, extensive support is being provided to both faculty members and students to ensure the smooth implementation of the programme, and follow-ups are conducted to assess the progress of the educational process.

The classes were delivered online, with assessments conducted using the best alternative strategies to assess the learning accurately. Most universities also moved their classes online.

Khalifa University in the UAE provides remote mental health services and online development courses on leadership, managing stress, and positive thinking (Solomon, 2020).

Regarding the universities' community service during the pandemic, 19,533 volunteers from across 27 universities in the Kingdom of Saudi Arabia participated in efforts to combat COVID-19. They worked to provide awareness and education under educational and community programmes for epidemic control (Umm Al-Qura University is leading). Saudi universities have also made individual contributions to fight the pandemic. More recently, KAUST made the Supercomputer Core Laboratory (KSL) (KSL, n.d.), including the supercomputer "Shaheen-II" resources available to support projects, research, and innovation to fight the COVID-19 pandemic. It also launched the "Community COVID-19 Innovation Challenge", which includes education during COVID-19, social connectivity, community management, and other open challenges related to developing new and creative approaches to control the coronavirus's short- and long-term effects. Many universities organised workshops on distance learning, online communication tools, and online exam preparation.

Based on the above actions by many universities in the Gulf countries, emphasis on how to deal with the pandemic influenza should be essential to a HEI's disaster recovery and risk management plan. Even though the pandemic directly affects employees' health, it would be risky to consider the response the sole responsibility of the institution's Benefits or Human Resource Department. Pandemic influenza is an example of why enterprise risk management has emerged as a powerful management tool. Due to the fact that all employees could be affected by pandemic influenza, all departments play an essential role in managing risks and health programmes. A risk management framework engages the HEIs to reduce negative impacts from events; thus, reducing the pandemics' impact is imperative.

As an initial step, an assessment is a great initiative when HEIs in the Gulf do not know what their business continuity programme should comprise. Readiness templates and pandemic-specific templates may allow an institution to analyse the operations with the intention to identify mitigation, recovery, and management of risk and health issues and concerns. HEIs should complete a risk assessment of their core business processes to identify and prioritise new risks or issues in their existing controls for new scenarios for pandemics. When prompted with threats, first-level managers are in the best position to plan and assess how the scenarios will impact their areas of responsibility as a second step. Practising risk management is one of the assessments that can serve different scenarios, so a HEI will always be ready for many unexpected risks. A company should immediately set up decision-making teams for significant temporary issues, such as an "Emergency Response Team" or "Major Emergency Management Committee". The purpose is to build the whole objectives and new plan and ensure the Gulf HEIs can make the fastest possible decisions in various situations. The committee members can evaluate their professional strengths and, if necessary, bring professionals to match their business and regional characteristics.

Many big companies have established "emergency contingency plans" or "business sustainability plans" for significant emergencies. If a higher education institution has no such plan, it should comprehensively assess all risks, including employee, outsourcing, government, public, and supply chain issues. According to risk assessment, the higher education institution should respond to problems around office space, production plans, procurement, supply and logistics, personnel safety, and financial capital, as well as arrange other significant matters related to emergency plans and division of labour.

Not all risks within a higher education institution should be treated the same way. In step three, a business impact analysis allows higher education institutions to identify which parts of the business are critical to their operations. The results will determine which sections of the higher education institution to focus on during a business continuity plan event to maintain the activities. After an outbreak, HEIs should cooperate with downstream customers to understand client and market condition changes and confirm the impact of resumption, order delivery, demand, and market changes.

Policies need to be revised, updated, and communicated. For example, reviewing and revising a WFH policy is imperative where the institutions should identify and evaluate those contracts whose performance could be affected, promptly notify the related party to mitigate possible losses, and assess whether it is necessary to sign a new contract and retain evidence to use in potential civil lawsuits. The risk assessment and prioritisation of impact are essential for revising policies and procedures to ensure clear communication of their execution. For example, the Gulf HEIs developed a WFH plan for concise and ad hoc needs. The WFH policy plan to be tied to a Key Performance Indicator for a pandemic WFH can turn into a duration of six-week to six-month requirement. The performance needs to be monitored to ensure goals are achieved with leading indicators rather than lagging ones.

Moreover, change management is needed to analyse the effectiveness of mitigation and policy activities. Many HEIs were recommended to immediately establish a flexible vacation and work mechanism, using technical means to develop non-face-to-face or off-site work parameters during particular periods of pandemics. The HEIs also need to create a staff health monitoring system and keep employees' personal health information confidential. Strictly cleaning and disinfecting workplaces to ensure a safe working environment based on hygiene management requirements for periods of major infectious diseases should also be a priority of the company. It also recommended that

Application of Risk Management on COVID-19   97

the company strengthen epidemic safety education, establish fact-based employee self-protection guidelines, and increase awareness of safety and risk prevention. The HEIs should also establish a proper employee database and register internal and outsourced personnel, suppliers, partners, and other staff with whom they have contact. They should also formulate information security response plans to ensure security and stability.

The Future of Higher Education Institutions

Gulf higher education holds a promising future as its landscape is contoured by proactive actions from educational leaders and the educational community, including government bodies and private institutions. Any recurring pandemic in the future may overwhelm the teaching-learning systems put in place to mitigate their health, societal, and economic effects. Risk transfer mechanisms (such as specialised insurance facilities) offer an additional tool to manage this risk. Risk-based insurance products for pandemics require specific characteristics, such as the following:

1 Insurance policies should be designed to release discretionary funds early during an outbreak.
2 Because pandemics do not stay contained within national borders, a strong case can be made for mobilising bilateral and multilateral financing of insurance premiums as a cost-effective way to improve global preparedness and support mitigation efforts.
3 Risk transfer systems require the availability of rigorously and transparently compiled data to trigger a payout.

Insurance facilities can create positive incentives to invest in planning and capacity building. Insurance mechanisms may have other positive externalities: the potential release of funds may provide a strong incentive for the timely reporting of surveillance data. However, insurance facilities also may introduce perverse incentives and potential moral hazards.

Relative to investments in essential health provision, building capacity in infectious disease surveillance systems and other dimensions of pandemic preparedness has uncertain and potentially distant benefits. It can complicate the political and economic logic for investing in pandemic preparedness (Buckley & Pittluck, 2016). Innovations in pandemic financing have been developed in response to the significant burden a country can place on financial resources.

Risk transfer mechanisms such as insurance offer financial resources to help insured parties rapidly scale up disease response activities. As such, the utility of risk transfer mechanisms depends mainly on the absorptive capacity of the insured party. A country must use insurance payouts effectively to access additional human resources (clinicians, community health workers), personal protective equipment and other medical equipment consumables, and vaccines and therapeutics from domestic or international support. Nevertheless, HEIs in the Gulf could face unexpected risk events at any moment – it may be a question of when and its magnitude. Therefore, the HEIs should establish or upgrade their risk management systems to identify the risk register and build a risk mitigation plan. Strengthening the risk management system is just as important as dealing with adverse events when it arises. Due to COVID-19, HEIs were affected by the closure of schools and universities, social distancing, and the shift from face-to-face teaching and learning to e-learning. Those changes caused inconvenience to both students and educators but also gave a glimpse at how education could change rapidly and forced educational policymakers and managers to look at new models of intellectual creativity and innovation.

While most students worldwide could find a solution in face-to-face learning, some were active internet users as of April 2020, which may further increase the gap in education quality worldwide for students living in less developed areas. In response to the COVID-19 crisis, HEIs across the GCC countries rushed towards implementing their online learning effectively, thanks to their early GCC digital transformation plans to move to intelligent education and competent government. The key initiatives that helped HEIs maintain the learning cycle while protecting students' learning trajectories were mainly linked to swift administration and policy steps, access to resources, financial support, and the help provided in GCC's respective higher education ministries. However, the dearth of studies on similar pandemic issues in the past and the uncertainty related to when there would be potential treatments and vaccines have only contributed to the difficulty of forecasting possible future solutions. In the context of the GCC, a more collaborative yet strategic agenda on higher education and research is needed.

This direction would be for the GCC universities to further boost their collaboration on teaching, research, joint financing, and community service, in addition to increased industry and private sector engagement, to ensure effective reverse linkage between universities and the business world. There is also a need to encourage and support students, entrepreneurship training, and development. The institutions must build Quality Assurance systems to their full strength to create new networks among regional HEIs. Also important is for GCC HEIs to give more attention to the GCC context of job market analyses and trends to guide students and society.

Conclusion

One of the key challenges for the Gulf HEIs is to put mitigation plans to address each COVID-related risk. Through close coordination with their governments, the Gulf HEIs must promote the safety and welfare of the students, faculty, staff, and other stakeholders while paying attention to their roles in implementing risk management to reduce, avoid, or eliminate the risks.

Any planned research should explore the future of HEIs in the post-coronavirus era by emphasising crisis and risk management. Moreover, Gulf HEIs need to anticipate the future impact of COVID-19 to avoid critical disruptions in the teaching-learning processes. Proactive measures, from policy framework to practice-oriented curricula and programmes, must be explored, implemented, monitored, and assessed collaboratively.

References

Ahmed, Q. A., Memish, Z. A., & Allegranzi, B. (2020). COVID-19 and the Hajj: Pandemic risks, current prevention, and recommendations. *Travel Medicine and Infectious Disease, 37*, 101807.

Al-Rawi, Y. O. M., Al-Dayyeni, W. S., & Reda, I. (2021). COVID-19 impact on education and work in the Kingdom of Bahrain: Survey study. *Information Sciences Letters, 10*(3), 427–433.

American University of Kuwait. (2020). Voice Quarantine Issue (Publication No. v16-Quarantine-Issue-OCT2020).

Buckley, P., & Pittluck, R. (2016). Health Risk Framework: Pandemic Financing Workshop Summary. Board on Global Health; Institute of Medicine; National Academies of Sciences, Engineering, and Medicine. National Academies Press.

Craven, M., Singhal, S., & Wilson, M. (2020). *Risk practice: COVID-19: Briefing note.* McKinsey & Company.

Crawford, J., Butler-Henderson, K., Rudolph, J., & Glowatz, M. (2020). COVID-19: 20 countries' higher education intra-period digital pedagogy responses. *Journal of Applied Learning & Teaching, 3*(1), 1–20.

Doug, A., Smith, B., Johnson, C., & Lee, D. (2020). On pandemics: The impact of COVID-19 on the practice of neurosurgery. *Journal of Neurosurgery, 133*(1), 1–2.

Draycott, T. (2020). Covid-19 pandemic, outbreak educational sector and students online learning in Saudi Arabia. *Journal of Entrepreneurship Education, 23*(3), 23.

Erfurth, M., & Ridge, N. (2020). The impact of COVID-19 on education in the UAE. Sheikh Saud Bin Saqr Foundation for Policy Research. URL: https://www.academia.edu/43952488/The_Impact_of_COVID_19_on_Education_in_the_UAE

KAUST, 2020a. Coping COVID-19: Higher Education in the GCC Countries. Paper presented during Research and Innovation Forum, Athens, Greece, 15–17 April 2020.

Lai, J., Ma, S., Wang, Y., Cai, Z., Hu, J., Wei, N., Wu, J., Du, H., Chen, T., Li, R., Tan, H., Kang, L., Yao, L., Huang, M., Wang, H., Wang, G., Liu, Z., & Hu, S. (2020). Factors associated with mental health outcomes among health care workers exposed to coronavirus disease 2019. *JAMA Network, 3*(3), e203976.

Nita, P., Jones, S., Adams, L., & Brown, K. (2020). Pandemics: Risks, impacts, and mitigation. National Library of Medicine

O'Keefe, L., Dellinger, J. T., Mathes, J., Holland, T. L., & Knott, J. (2020). The state of online learning in the Kingdom of Saudi Arabia: A COVID-19 impact study for higher education. Online Learning Consortium.

Philips, R., Anderson, J., Davis, M., & Thompson, S. (2020). *Pandemics influenza risk management for employer* (1–34). Milliman, Inc.

Salama, A. M. (2020). Coronavirus questions that will not go away: Interrogating urban and socio-spatial implications of COVID-19 measures. *Emerald Open Research – Sustainable Cities Gateway, 2*, 14. https://doi.org/10.35241/emeraldopenres.13561.1

Solomon, D. H., Bucala, R., Kaplan, M. J., & Nigrovic, P. A. (2020). The "Infodemic" of COVID-19. DOI: 10.1002/art.41468.

UNESCO. (2020). COVID-19 Educational Disruption and Response. https://www.unesco.org/en/articles/covid-19-educational-disruption-and-response

Vollrath, M., & Torgersen, S. (2002). Who takes health risks? A probe into eight personality types. Personality and Individual Differences, 32, 1185–1197.

Wang, C., Cheng, Z., Yue, X. G., & McAleer, M. (2020). Risk management of COVID-19 by universities in China. *Journal of Risk and Financial Management, 13*, 36.

Wang Porta, G. (2014). The impact of pandemics on global health. *Journal of Epidemiology and Public Health, 25*(3), 345–362.

Wang Shanmugam, H., Juhari, J. A., Nair, P., Ken, C. S., & Guan, N. C. (2020). Impacts of COVID-19 pandemic on mental health in Malaysia: A single thread of hope. *MJP Online, 29*, 78–84.

Wansink, B. (2019). *Mindless eating: Why we eat more than we think.* Hay House.

World Health Organization & Burton, Joan. (2010). WHO healthy workplace framework and model: background and supporting literature and practices. World Health Organization.

World Health Organization. (2023). WHO coronavirus (COVID-19) dashboard.

7 Directions in Gulf Higher Education

Conclusion

John McAlaney and Reynaldo Gacho Segumpan

The chapter in this section has explored reforms in HE in the Gulf region, a process unavoidably shaped by the COVID-19 pandemic. In *Potential Reforms in the GCC Higher Education Post COVID-19*, the authors acknowledge that the pandemic created a space in which to consider and re-design HE in the Gulf. As they note, many institutions were forced to adopt remote education during this time, an impact that remains to be evident through hybrid learning strategies. This raises questions on how we ensure such strategies are appropriate and sustainable. The authors propose that national policies can aide in this, including through the incorporation of resilience plans for remote education in times of crisis. The Design Thinking Model and Delphi Protocol are used to identify the challenges of remote education that arose during the COVID-19 pandemic, such as lack of technological literacy, cultural opposition to change, and online education awareness and training amongst both students and educators. The authors call for policy approaches that incorporate resilience to external threats and which are sustainable. This theme of learning from the challenges of the COVID-19 pandemic is one which is raised by the authors throughout this section.

These topics of opportunities and challenges are further discussed in *Pandemic Upsurge: Insights from higher education reforms in Gulf.* The authors consider how the unique national culture of different Gulf countries can influence how these challenges and opportunities are experienced and addressed. Through qualitative interviews with educators and students in Gulf countries, the authors observe that HE provides students with not only knowledge but also interpersonal skills. This an aspect of the COVID-19 pandemic that needs consideration as students continue to move through their education. It will be several years before there is a generation of students who did not experience some type of online teaching, either at university or earlier in their youth at school, and of course another pandemic or similarly disruptive event cannot be ruled out. Educators who taught online during the COVID-19 pandemic will have likely experienced the situation of lecturing to a screen of black squares, given the reluctance of students during this period to switch on their webcams unless directly instructed to do so. The impact of the pandemic on how people

DOI: 10.4324/9781003457299-9

communicate with each other is something that may take time to determine, but it is an important question for research to answer.

The need for sustainable change in HE is expanded on in *Post Pandemic Quality of Higher Education: 'NFCFFE Model' for Higher Education Quality Improvement and Assurance.* The authors apply a six-layered quality assurance (QA) model built upon 'Need', 'Focus', 'Culture', 'Framework', 'Feedback' and 'Essentials'. Data is collected and analysed from India, Bangladesh, Oman, and the United Arab Emirates. This model aims to support Quality Improvement and Assurance (QIA) by providing a clear and replicable strategy that HEIs can apply to their own courses. The authors call for further application and testing of the model. This proposed approach is interesting as it potentially provides a consistency in HE provision across the Gulf, whilst still accommodating the unique aspects of country- and course-specific requirements through the individual components of the model, such as culture.

The COVID-19 pandemic prompted us to fundamentally question how we operate as a society. In *Pandemic Challenges of Higher Education: Reconsidering Core Values*, the author identifies three major challenges that were encountered by GCC countries during the pandemic – (i) quality of education, (ii) the criteria for university rankings, and (iii) the validity of credentials. Educators are accustomed to the need to consider university rankings and the importance of credentials. They are similarly familiar with the conflicting demands that can arise when trying to deliver quality education whilst ensuring that these expectations around rankings and credentials are met. Given these pressures, it is not surprising that HEIs engage in strategies to ensure that their ranking is as high as possible, which may create further dilemmas for educators. The author of this chapter notes how the COVID-19 pandemic has widened the divide between more prestigious universities that had the resources to quickly switch to online classes during the pandemic, whilst other HEIs lacked the ability to do so. This creates discrepancies in the quality of education offered by HEIs, and in turn the experience of students and their subsequent career prospects. This may worsen the situation of students who are coming from disadvantaged backgrounds, who already face greater difficulty in accessing high-quality HE education. The continued use of online education by prestigious universities may also influence how online education is viewed, and prompt questions amongst students and prospective student how important the traditional, on-campus experience is. This relates to the earlier point on how the move to online teaching may impact on the interpersonal skills.

The role of information and communication technology (ICT) is further explored in *Higher Education in the COVID-19 Environment: ICT-based perspective for GCC Countries.* The authors report the results of a study in the use of ICT tools by faculty members and students. The found that students identified several problems with learning during the pandemic, including time management, accessibility to course materials, lack of resources, and information technology skills. These results highlight the important differences in student

Directions in Gulf Higher Education 103

populations compared to previous decades, which is that students can use ICT to share their experiences and opinions far more freely than in previous generations. This invokes the complaints that <u>are</u> frequently brought up in HE that students are increasingly considered to be akin to customers paying for a service. Regardless of the merits of this concept, it is important that students can communicate their needs and challenges. The authors also note that staff at HEIs experienced similar problems with ICT during the pandemic, namely a lack of training and technical support, and the time commitment required to make use of these technologies. They argue that both students and faculty members would benefit from proper training and full integration of ICT into learning and teaching systems. Doing so would increase the resilience of HE to future pandemics and other globally disruptive events, as discussed previously.

Finally, the authors of *Application of Risk Management on COVID-19 by Universities in the Gulf Cooperation Council (GCC)* examine the coping strategies of HEIs in the Gulf from a risk management perspective. This recognises that, in our increasingly interconnected world, events such as the COVID-19 pandemic will be increasingly common. Putting mitigation plans into place will help reduce the impact of any such events, in keeping with the adage in healthcare that prevention is better than cure. The authors propose that HEIs should engage with governments to determine how best to ensure the health and safety of their staff and students, with a focus on the unique roles and risks of these individuals. It is of course impossible to eliminate all risks, but through consideration of possible risks steps can be taken to prevent or at least mitigate many risks. This approach is commonly used in business outside of HE, where for example a risk register – which aims to identify, analyse, and solve risks before they become problems – is a standing item on the agenda of management meetings.

The chapters in this section raise several questions and opportunities. The COVID-19 pandemic had an undeniable impact on society and was the cause of not only loss of life but wider detriments on the well-being and professional development of many people. This included widening the divide between those with easy access to technology and those without, something that is especially relevant to HEIs where differences in ICT availability and skills can have substantive impacts on learning and teaching. However, HE is and always has been characterised by a culture of innovation and problem solving. There are many examples of HEIs in the Gulf adapting their practices during the pandemic to ensure that students continued to receive quality education. Whilst perhaps not planned, the strategies developed during this time can continue to be used to improve the quality of education at HEIs. Overall, the pandemic has demonstrated how we should not be complacent about the delivery of education in HE; we cannot assume that the situation today will be the same as tomorrow. Nevertheless, we have also learned how we can adapt to external threats, and that within HE we are more capable of finding ways to ensure the success of our students than we may have previously realised.

Part II

Reframing Higher Education Reforms

8 An Empirical Analysis of Oman's Public and Private HEIs Student's Behavioural Intention (BI) in Using E-Learning during COVID-19

Mohit Kukreti, Amitabh Mishra, and Vishal Jain

Introduction

This chapter is structured in the following parts: introduction, literature review, development of hypotheses, conceptualised model, research methodology, data analysis, results and discussions, conclusion, limitations, future and managerial implications, and conflict of interest statement.

In the year 2019, the disastrous pandemic COVID-19 spread to the rest of the world resulting in stopping of all the economic, social, and cultural activities. The pandemic gave rise to learning losses and thereby resulted in the rise of inequality. Since travel between the countries stopped, education sector also bore the brunt of the situation. According to Donnelly et al. (2021), pandemic during its peak forced more than 45 European and Central Asian countries to close higher education institutions (HEIs), impacting 185 million students. The educational institutions globally were closed to prevent the spread of the pandemic (Hammerstein et al., 2021; Litvinova et al., 2019). Therefore, HEIs worldwide were forced to adopt makeshift remote teaching and online learning with the help of internet-based platform such as Blackboard, DingTalk, Google Hangouts Meet, Ms Teams, Skype calling, WeChat Work for Chinese, WhatsApp, and Zoom app. (UNESCO, 2020).

The pandemic forced the HEIs to modify the mode of educational from classroom to online instruction (Strielkowski, 2020).With the help of online education platforms, information was provided to the students and classroom activities were coordinated (Martín-Blas & Serrano-Fernández, 2009). Online education and e-learning have impacted both the students and teachers equally and they both hold positive views about this mode of education (Kulal & Nayak, 2020). Several research have been conducted regarding the impacts of online teaching and e-learning on students (Abbasi et al., 2020; Al Manthari et al., 2020). Mohamed et al. (2021) examined the recognition of distance learning amongst Omani HEI's students during the lockdown. However, there existed a gap as no research studied the COVID-19 impacts

DOI: 10.4324/9781003457299-11

on the behavioural intentions (BIs) of the both private and public sector HEI students' acceptance of e-learning. Therefore, this research is an attempt to study the COVID-19 impacts on BIs of both public and private sector HEIs in using e-learning.

The global spread of the COVID-19 virus took the shape of pandemic. According to UNICEF cited in Mseleku (2020), this pandemic is also referred to as COVID-19. Many different variants of Coronavirus have disturbed the general economic climate (Shang et al., 2021) not only in the developing nations but across the entire world (Johnson et al., 2020; Wargadinata et al., 2020). Coronavirus compelled the HEIs to stop face-to-face teaching and learning process. Due to closure of the HEIs, e-learning emerged as an effective tool that utilises internet, computers, and smart phones in imparting education. It became a part of a contemporary educational process in the HEIs enabling students to gain knowledge anytime and anywhere.

There are various published works on COVID-19; however, not many research studies address the e-learning issues faced by the students of private and public sector HEIs during the pandemic. According to Liguori and Winkler (2020), the steady eruption of COVID-19 created major hurdles to education landscape and institutions forcefully closed their doors and looked for substitute teaching approaches. Consequently, globally many educational institutions adopted online teaching technology to impart education during the pandemic (Kerres, 2020; Wang et al., 2020). Globally, HEIs either postponed or cancelled all campus academic and co-curricular events and activities (Liguori & Winkler, 2020; Sahu, 2020). Similarly, in the Sultanate of Oman HEIs regular classes, seminars, conferences, industrial visits, practical internships, etc. were also initially suspended and subsequently conducted through the online and e-learning mode (Kukreti & Mishra, 2021).

During the COVID-19 period, the Sultanate of Oman's government, like that of other nations, imposed a partial lockdown resulting in HEIs having to shift the educational process from class room lecture to an on line e-learning mode. This shift has greatly influenced the students and the BIs towards teaching and learning process via online medium. Many previous studies investigated student's attitude towards online learning such as in Turkey (Isik et al., 2010) and in Oman (Al Manthari et al., 2020). Previous researchers established the positive association between usefulness and ease of use in deciding the student's behaviour towards online learning (Chiu et al., 2005; Shin, 2006). Although several research have been done on the impact of e-learning on HEIs, no literature is available on the study of BIs of both the public sector HEI's students and private sector HEI's students in Oman towards e-learning. This is a significant research gap. Al-Adwan et al. (2013) examined the students' BI to use e-learning in Jordanian Universities by using the Technology Acceptance Model (TAM) to measure perceived ease of use (PEOU), perceived usefulness (PU), and attitude towards use and its influence on students' intention to use e-learning system. Therefore, the present study also uses TAM to hypothetically test the PU, perceived self-efficacy (PSE), PEOU, environment readiness

(ER), and their relation to BI in acceptance towards e-learning amongst the students of Oman studying in public and private sector HEIs in Oman.

An online survey using Google platform was administered to conduct the research and collect data from the students in Oman. Collected data was analysed using the IBA SPSS AMOS software.

The present research focusses on application of TAM on studying the COVID-19 impacts on the BIs of both public and private sector HEI's students towards usage of e-learning.

Objectives of the Chapter

This chapter aims to explore the link between the PU and BI of public and private sector HEI's students to utilise e-learning and examine the association between PEOU and BI of public and private sector HEI's students towards using e-learning. It also explores the association between PEOU and PU of e-learning of public and private sector HEI's students; between PSE and PU of e-learning of public and private sector HEI's students; between ER and PU of e-learning of public and private sector HEI's students; between self-efficacy (SE) and PEOU of e-learning of public and private sector HEI's students; and between ER and PEOU of e-learning of public and private sector HEI's students.

Technology adoption and use are explained by the TAM. According to Davis (1989), TAM is valuable to study the prediction of attitude and behaviour in the acceptance of new technology. TAM has grown to rank among the models that are most frequently employed to analyse how users interact with technology. The behavioural intention (BI) is affected by the users' beliefs, namely PU and PEOU (Venkatesh & Davis, 2000). The TAM model uses PU and PEOU as its two key determinants (Jain & Jain, 2022). The degree to which a user believes that technology will assist them in carrying out their work or achieving their objectives is referred to as PU. Contrarily, perceived ease of use refers to how much a user thinks technology is simple to use. Users' attitudes regarding technology are directly influenced by PU and PEOU, which in turn affects their intents to use it. The TAM is a valuable framework for comprehending user behaviour in relation to the adoption and usage of technology overall. It has been used in a variety of settings, including online learning, e-commerce, and healthcare, among others.

Perceived Usefulness and Intentions of Using E-learning

Previously under the normal conditions, TAM has been applied only to research e-learning in HEIs (Mohammadi, 2015; Ramírez-Correa et al., 2015), but in this chapter, TAM was utilised to examine the PU, PSE, PEOU, ER, and their relation to BI in acceptance towards e-learning amongst the students of public and private sector HEIs in the Sultanate of Oman during COVID-19 pandemic. According to Sabherwal et al. (2006), "Perceived usefulness" (PU) refers to an individual's willingness to increase a user's performance.

Many previous researchers such as Ramírez-Correa et al. (2015) and Teo (2009) indicated that BIs were significantly correlated to the use of e-learning technology. Sukendro et al. (2020) used TAM to understand students' PU of e-learning during COVID-19.

Self-Efficacy and Behavioural Intention of Using E-learning

According to Kukreti and Mishra (2021), SE can be defined as the degree to which a person considers his capability to execute a specific task/job using the e-learning. (Latip et al. (2020), Thakkar and Joshi (2018) and Yilmaz (2016) explored the effects of self-efficacy and intention to use e-learning. The previous research studies recognised a relationship between PSE and BI of using e-learning by using the TAM model (Adewole-Odeshi, 2014; Revythi and Tselios (2017). The TAM model is applied to study the self-efficacy and BI of Oman's public and private HEI students towards e-learning during the COVID-19.

Perceived Ease of Use and Behavioural Intention of Using E-learning

As mentioned by Kukreti and Mishra (2021), PEOU is how a person considers that information technology is easy to comprehend (Davis, 1989). Mohammadi (2015) and Ramírez-Correa et al. (2015) proved a strong correlation between perceived ease of use and BI to use e-learning. The perceived ease of use variable in the original TAM is defined as the degree to which public and private HEI's students in Oman feel that e-learning would be simple to use during the COVID-19 phase. Consequently, it was estimated that PU correlates favourably with the BI to utilise e-learning.

Environmental Readiness and Behavioural Intention of Using E-learning

Environment factors refer to the users' external environment impacting their capacity to execute a task. E-learning is accessible to be applied in any setting and at any time, and this feature has been reported to be one of the most significant reasons for users to accept internet-based environments for learning (Salehi et al., 2015). Al-Rahmi et al. (2018) employed TAM to study BI of students towards using e-learning in a stable environment. From the review of the literature, perceived ER is hypothesised to be positively related to the BI of using e-learning.

Behavioural Intention Towards E-learning

BI refers to the degree to which an individual has framed cognisant plans regarding whether to perform a definite future behaviour. Kabra et al. (2017) and Khalilzadeh et al. (2017) combined UTAUT model to assess the elements that stimulate users' BIs to use information technology. As shown in Figure 8.1 ("TAM model"), BI is the dependent variable with two predictors:

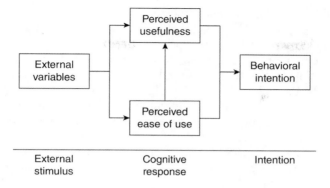

Figure 8.1 TAM model.
Source: Davis (1989).

PU and PEOU. Moreover, two external variables SE and ER have been added in the current study.

In connection with the vast empirical literature on COVID-19 pandemic, BI of students towards acceptance of e-learning and itsPU self-efficacy, ease of use, and ER, the following hypotheses were formulated:

- H1: PU is positively related to the BI of using e-learning.
- H2: The perceived ease of use of e-learning is positively related to the BI of using e-learning.
- H3: The perceived ease of use of e-learning is positively related to the PU of using e-learning.
- H4: PSE is positively related to the PU of using e-learning.
- H5: PSE is positively related to the perceived ease of use of e-learning.
- H6: ER is positively related to the PU of using e-learning.
- H7: ER is positively related to the perceived ease of use of e-learning.

Methods and Analytical Frame

Data were collected from the public and private sector HEI's students in Oman who adopted e-learning for educational purpose during the COVID-19 era. The data were collected from the public and private HEIs of the six cities: Sohar, Ibri, Rustaq, Nizwa, Salalahm, and Muscat. Due to online data collection, the public and private HEI's students were approached based on the availability and readiness of the respondents. The data were collected from May 2022 to June 2022. A structured questionnaire was constructed and pretested to ensure adequate and authentic collection of relevant data, entry, and analysis. The students were given the structured questionnaire via Google form link on MS Teams and WhatsApp and were asked to circulate the same among their friends. The questionnaire consisted of two parts: Section A included the information regarding the demographics of the students and section B was used to measure the ER, perception, and BI towards e-learning. The objective

112   *Mohit Kukreti, Amitabh Mishra, and Vishal Jain*

of the study was well explained to the respondents. The required permissions were obtained from the University of Technology and Applied Sciences – CAS Ibri, Dean's office, and the Scientific Research Department. All the ethical protocols were followed. A tootal of 96 complete questionnaires were received framing the final sample for the research. According to Duponchel (2016), a minimum of 84 sample size is good for PLS analysis.

The pilot research was conducted to validate the questionnaire and make sure that the respondents are able to infer the true connotation of the statements. The pilot research included a questionnaire being distributed to 40 students (Sheatsley, 1983). The specialists and faculty member examined the questionnaire to make sure that the statements were clear and readable.

Measurements

For measuring the constructs, namely, PU, PSE, perceived ease of use, and BI, well-established scales were adopted from Khan et al. (2021) since PU is a key determinant of BI in using e-learning platforms. However, understanding

Table 8.1 Rotated component matrix

	Rotated component matrix				
	Component				
	PE	*PU*	*ER*	*BI*	*SE*
V15	.765				
V11	.753				
V17	.670				
V13	.667				
V14	.659				
V16	.644				
V12	.602				
V24		.795			
V23		.733			
V22		.664			
V21		.525			
V33			.769		
V32			.710		
V31			.624		
V41				.838	
V44				.636	
V42				.547	
V43				.544	
V52					.816
V51					.790
V53					.606

Notes:
Extraction method: Principal component analysis.
Rotation method: Varimax with Kaiser normalization.
Rotation converged in six iterations. PEOU, PU, ER, behavioural intention (BI), SE

the factors that contribute to the PU of e-learning is crucial in designing effective e-learning systems and enhancing student engagement. The PU of e-learning (PU) was calculated using four items. The PU of e-learning (PU) was measured with **four** items. The sample PU items includes "Studying through e-learning mode provided the flexibility to the study at the time convenient to the learner."; "Enabled students to study irrespective of location"; "Enabled to take assessment electronically"; and "E-learning enabled interactive communication between instructor and student without meeting face-to-face".

PSE in e-learning within the TAM is typically related to the individual's confidence in their ability to successfully complete e-learning tasks, their perceived competence in using the technology required for e-learning, and their level of comfort in engaging with e-learning materials. PSE was calculated using three items. The sample SE item includes "I feel confident while using e-learning system; feel confident while operating e-learning systems; feel confident with the usage of e-learning contents."

PEOU was calculated using seven items. The sample PE item includes "I believe e-learning platforms are user friendly; easy to find the necessary information; e-learning service can simplify the e-learning process; compatibility of e-learning service with the learning style, etc."

BI was calculated using four items. The sample BI item includes "I intend to use e-learning to assist my learning; intend to use e-learning to get updated and amended subject knowledge; intend to use e-learning as an autonomous (free) learning tool". ER of the students was measured with the optimism dimension of the well-developed technology readiness index developed by Parasuraman (**2000**). The ER scale consists of various items such as "I am connected to the internet with a fairly fast, reliable connection; comfortable with things like installing software and changing the configuration settings; comfortable with things like doing searches, setting bookmarks, and downloading files; comfortable with submission and assessments and time allotted; satisfactory online participation". Most of the scores are above 0.600. All construct items were collected on a 1–5 range on Likert scale (1 = "strongly disagree" to 5 = "strongly agree"). As mentioned previously, the same scale has been used by the authors, and moreover the students can easily understand it. The analysis of data was executed in two parts: descriptive statistics and structural modelling. IBM SPSS AMOS software was used for reporting descriptive statistics. The structural modelling was performed using AMOS software.

Findings and Discussion

The descriptive analysis of the sample data is given in Table 8.2. The percentage analysis shows that around 79% of the students were female, and 20.8% were male.

The sample data was collected from the students of various cohorts from public and private HEIs (refer to Table 8.3) out of which maximum responses (24%) were collected from 2016 cohort followed by 19.8% from 2021 cohort and 16.7% from 2019 cohort, respectively.

114　*Mohit Kukreti, Amitabh Mishra, and Vishal Jain*

Table 8.2 Demographic profile by gender

		Gender			
		Frequency	Percent	Valid percent	Cumulative percent
Valid	Female	76	79.2	79.2	79.2
	Male	20	20.8	20.8	100.0
	Total	96	100.0	100.0	

Note:
Demographic profile of the respondents

Table 8.3 Students' cohort

		Cohort			
		Frequency	Percent	Valid percent	Cumulative percent
Valid	2016	23	24.0	24.0	24.0
	2017	13	13.5	13.5	37.5
	2018	13	13.5	13.5	51.0
	2019	16	16.7	16.7	67.7
	2020	12	12.5	12.5	80.2
	2021	19	19.8	19.8	100.0
	Total	96	100.0	100.0	

Table 8.4 Respondents' programme and specialisation

		Programme			
		Frequency	Percent	Valid percent	Cumulative percent
Valid	Accounting	1	1.0	1.0	1.0
	Business Administration & Management	63	65.6	65.6	66.7
	Engineering	7	7.3	7.3	74.0
	Information Technology & Computers	25	26.0	26.0	100.0
	Total	96	100.0	100.0	

Note:
The response students of various cohorts from public and private HEIs

Majority of the respondents (65%) were from Business Administration and Management specialisation followed by those from the Information Technology and Computer fields (26%).

Table 8.5 reflects that for the sample data collected from the public and private HEIs majority of the responses (44%) were from HEIs of Muscat, followed by 31% from Sohar and 11% from Salalah.

Table 8.6 shows that that from the sample data it is quite evident that the WiFi was the main source of internet for the students during the pandemic.

Oman's Public and Private HEIs Student's Behavioural Intention   115

Table 8.5 Location of public and private HEIs

		Frequency	*Percent*	*Valid percent*	*Cumulative percent*	
Valid	Bahla	1	1.0	1.0	1.0	
	Muscat	43	44.8	44.8	45.8	
	Musanna	1	1.0	1.0	46.9	
	Ibri	2	2.1	2.1	49.0	
	Nizwa	7	7.3	7.3	56.3	
	Sohar	30	31.3	31.3	87.5	
	Rustaq	1	1.0	1.0	88.5	
	Salalah	11	11.5	11.5	100.0	
	Total	96	100.0	100.0		

Note:
The sample data collected from the locations of public and private HEIs

Table 8.6 Source of internet

		Frequency	*Percent*	*Valid percent*	*Cumulative percent*
Valid	Mobile Data	9	9.4	9.4	9.4
	Optic Fiber	3	3.1	3.1	12.5
	WiFi	84	87.5	87.5	100.0
	Total	96	100.0	100.0	

Note:
The main source of internet for the students during the pandemic

KMO and Bartlett's Test

The KMO value varies between 0 and 1. KMO value of 0 implies diffusion in the pattern of the correlations and therefore factor analysis stands unsuitable and KMO value near to 1 specifies that the factor analysis is different and dependable. Kaiser (1974) endorses KMO values greater than 0.5 as acceptable; KMO values between 0.5 and 0.7 are mediocre; between 0.7 and 0.8 are good; between 0.8 and 0.9 are very good; and above 0.9 are excellent. From Table 8.7, its

Table 8.7 KMO and Bartlett's test

KMO and Bartlett's test		
Kaiser-Meyer-Olkin Measure of Sampling Adequacy.		.885
Bartlett's Test of Sphericity	Approx. Chi-Square	1279.333
	df	210
	Sig.	.000

Note:
The value of KMO is .885, hence, reliable for factor analysis

116 Mohit Kukreti, Amitabh Mishra, and Vishal Jain

Table 8.8 Total variance

	Total variance explained					
Component	Extraction sums of squared loadings			Rotation sums of squared loadings		
	Total	% of Variance	Cumulative %	Total	% of Variance	Cumulative %
PE	9.727	46.320	46.320	4.138	19.703	19.703
PU	1.669	7.947	54.267	3.178	15.135	34.838
ER	1.282	6.103	60.370	2.788	13.275	48.113
BI	1.122	5.344	65.714	2.412	11.488	59.601
SE	1.002	4.773	70.487	2.286	10.885	70.487

Note:
Extraction Method: Principal Component Analysis.

reflected that the value of KMO is .885 which indicates that the factor analysis is reliable, and the Bartlett's test of Sphericity is highly significant at p<0.000, which reflects that the factor analysis is appropriate for the data set.

For the Principal Component Analysis and Varimax rotation method, the variance explained by the particular linear component and SPSS displays the eigen values in terms of the percentage of variance explained; therefore, PE 19.703%, PU 15.135%, ER 13.275%, BI 11.488%, and SE explains 10.885% of the total variance. The eigen values in this part of the table are similar to the values before extraction, and only the values for the discarded factors are disregarded. In the final part of the eigen value table, Rotation Sums of Squared Loadings are displayed as PE (46.320%), PU (7.947%), ER (6.103%), BI (5.344%), and SE (4.773%) and total 70.487% variance.

Model Reliability and Fit Measures

The criteria recommended by Fornell and Larcker were used for discriminant validity (Fornell & Larcker, 1981). Since all the values of inter-correlation among the constructs are less than the square roots of the Average Variance Extracted values of individual construct, discriminant validity was established.

Following the recommendations of Bollen and Long (1993) to report multiple fit indices of the structural model (Figure 8.2), the study includes the chi-square

Table 8.9 Model reliability and fit measures

	PE	PU	ER	BI	SE
PE	0.900				
PU	0.784***	0.863			
ER	0.675***	0.776***	0.775		
BI	0.786***	0.832***	0.817***	0.809	
SE	0.546***	0.667***	0.736***	0.593**	0.756

Note:
CMIN/DF= 1.68, CFI= 0.90, SRMR= 0.07, RMSEA= 0.08

Oman's Public and Private HEIs Student's Behavioural Intention 117

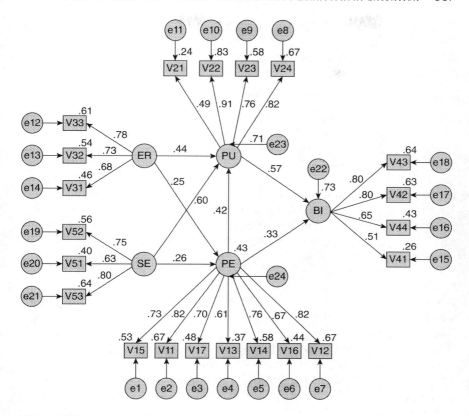

Figure 8.2 Structural model.

fit test (CMIN/DF = 1.68), comparative fit index (CFI = 0.90), and standardised root mean square residual (SRMR = 0.07) that indicate acceptable model fit.

Standardised Regression Weights

The outcomes of regression analysis for hypothesis testing are presented in Table 8.10. These results indicate that ER (p<.001) and SE (p<.05) are

Table 8.10 Regression analysis for hypothesis testing

			Estimate	S.E.	C.R.	P	Hypothesis
PE	←	ER	.596	.147	3.853	***	Accepted
PE	←	SE	.264	.112	2.002	.045	Accepted
PU	←	PE	.424	.126	3.437	***	Accepted
PU	←	ER	.439	.133	3.208	.001	Accepted
PU	←	SE	.250	.097	2.261	.024	Accepted
BI	←	PU	.575	.131	3.324	***	Accepted
BI	←	PE	.331	.119	2.155	.031	Accepted

Note:
The outcomes of regression analysis for hypothesis testing

118 *Mohit Kukreti, Amitabh Mishra, and Vishal Jain*

significantly related to PE. Similarly, PE ($p<.01$), ER ($p<.001$), and SE ($p<.05$) are significantly related to PU. On the other hand, PU ($p<.001$) and PE ($p<.05$) are significantly related to BI.

Conclusion and Recommendations

During the pandemic, e-learning has brought a remarkable shift in Gulf HEIs as regards educational pedagogy in Oman. This shift from physical classroom teaching method to the digital online world is a new phenomenon for the students as well as for the faculty. This chapter shows different variables such as ER and SE which are significantly related to PEOU. Similarly, PEOU, ER, and SE are significantly related to PU. On the other hand, PU and PE are significantly related to behavioural intention (BI) of students in both public and private HEIs towards adopting e-learning. It can be concluded that the PU, SE, PEOU, ER are found to be positively correlated with the behavioural intention (BI) towards using e-learning and hypothetically tested and accepted with the help of TAM.

TAM is an ideal model for assessing technology adoption, which works in different situations including COVID-19 pandemic. It is shown in this chapter that both SE and ER are important for the usefulness and easiness of e-learning. The objectives of the research were well hypothesised and tested using the TAM as an appropriate tool. The findings of this study may be of interest to academia in GCC and serve as bases for further research and policy making on e-learning experience models, particularly in terms of understanding students' perceptions and expectations about e-learning. The e-learning has become a new norm during COVID-19 pandemic era which will always complement the physical classroom teaching process.

In practice, the research findings could pave the following ways to improve the e-learning experience of the students in both public and private HEIs. The e-learning curriculum developers can design courses that include a variety of learning activities to cater to different learning preferences. A course could include pre-recorded lectures, live virtual classes, discussion forums, and interactive quizzes. The study found that students preferred e-learning platforms that were easy to use and provided clear instructions. Therefore, institutions that provide e-learning should carefully choose the technology platforms they use, ensuring that they are user-friendly and provide clear instructions for students. The study found that students valued instructor availability and responsiveness. Therefore, institutions that provide e-learning should invest in instructor training to help them become more responsive and available to students. The students experienced technical difficulties and wanted more support from technical staff. Thus, institutions that provide e-learning should offer adequate technical support to students. They could provide online resources such as FAQs and troubleshooting guides as well as a helpdesk to assist students with technical difficulties. In order to implement

Oman's Public and Private HEIs Student's Behavioural Intention 119

effective e-learning environment in HEIs, it is further recommended to prepare the students for technology acceptance. It is also recommended that HEIs provide e-learning infrastructure, internet access to all the students, contemporary e-learning techniques, and training to the teachers and the students.

Limitations and Future Implications

This chapter presented a study which was cross-sectional in nature and conducted within a short span of time. With the passage of time and accumulation of enhanced knowledge, the Omani students' perceptions of SE, PEOU, PU, ER, and BI towards e-learning might change. Therefore, future longitudinal studies are highly recommended.

One of the implications of the study presented in this chapter is that the public and private universities need to create deeper awareness among its students on the use and benefits of e-learning to facilitate better adaptability. This will further facilitate enhanced adaptability of e-learning environment. This is equally applicable to other GCC students as many of them are currently studying in various HEIs in Oman. Academic staff also need training on e-learning tools so that they will be more creative and interactive. Therefore, more advanced infrastructure and facilities to support e-learning environment need to be provided by the HEIs. Regular students' feedback will help the HEIs in enhancing the e-learning educational experience. The above lessons and insights from this study could be taken into account when designing and implementing policies and guidelines for both the public and private HEIs. These measures can contribute to further improving and enhancing e-learning in Oman.

The COVID-19 pandemic has had a significant impact on higher education in the Gulf region. However, universities have also demonstrated resilience and adaptability in responding to the challenges posed by the pandemic. In response to the pandemic, many universities in the Gulf region have had to shift to online learning. This has been a significant challenge for some institutions that were not fully prepared for such a shift. However, it has also presented an opportunity for universities to develop their online learning capabilities and explore new ways of delivering education. The pandemic has caused significant disruptions to the student's enrolment in the Gulf region. Travel restrictions and permission delays have made it difficult for the students to travel to the campus for admission, enrolment, and other issues and this has financially impacted the revenue of the private HEIs. The pandemic has caused financial challenges for the private HEIs in the Gulf region and also had an impact on research in the Gulf region. Many research projects have been disrupted or postponed due to restrictions on travel and access to laboratories and research facilities. As a result, the generation of new knowledge and contribution of research to the global research community suffered. The pandemic has had a significant impact on the mental health and well-being of students and staff in the Gulf region. The shift to online learning, social isolation, and anxiety about the pandemic have all contributed to increased levels of stress among the students and staff. The COVID-19 pandemic has had a significant ramification on both public and private HEIs in the Gulf region, including Oman.

Statement About Conflict of Interest

The authors declare that the present study in this chapter was not sponsored or financed by any organisation and there is no potential conflict of interest.

References

Abbasi, S., Ayoob, T., Malik, A., & Memon, S. I. (2020). Perceptions of students regarding Elearning during Covid-19 at a private medical college. *Pakistan Journal of Medical Sciences, 36* (COVID19-S4), S57–S61.

Adewole-Odeshi, E. (2014). Attitude of students towards E-learning in south-west Nigerian universities: An application of technology acceptance model. *Library Philosophy and Practice (e-journal)*. https://digitalcommons.unl.edu/cgi/viewcontent.cgi?Referrer=https://www.google.com/&httpsredir=1&article=2504&context=libphilprac

Al-Adwan, A., Al-Adwan, A., & Smedley, J. (2013). Exploring students' acceptance of e-learning using technology acceptance model in Jordanian universities. *International Journal of Education and Development Using Information and Communication Technology, 9*(2), 4–18.

Al Manthari, A., Maulina, S., & Bruce, S. (2020). Secondary school mathematics teachers' views on E-learning implementation barriers during the COVID-19 pandemic: The case of Indonesia. *Eurasia Journal of Mathematics, Science and Technology Education, 16*(7), em186.

Al-Rahmi, W. M., Alias, N., Othman, M. S., Alzahrani, A. I., Alfarraj, O., Saged, A. A., & Rahman, N. S. A. (2018). Use of e-learning by university students in Malaysian higher educational institutions: A case in Universiti Teknologi Malaysia. *IEEE Access, 6*, 14268–14276.

Bollen, K. A., & Long, J. S. (1993). *Testing structural equation models* (Vol. 154). Sage.

Chiu, C. M., Hsu, M. H., Sun, S. Y., Lin, T. C., & Sun, P. C. (2005). Usability, quality, value and e-learning continuance decisions. *Computers & Education, 45*, 399–416.

Davis, F. D. (1989). Perceived usefulness, perceived ease of use, and user acceptance of information technology. *MIS Quarterly, 13*(3), 319–340.

Donnelly, R., Patrinos, H. A., & Gresham, J. (2021, April 2). *The impact of COVID-19 on education–Recommendations and opportunities for Ukraine*. The World Bank Group. https://www.worldbank.org/en/news/opinion/2021/04/02/the-impact-of-covid-19-on-education-recommendations-and-opportunities-for-ukraine

Oman's Public and Private HEIs Student's Behavioural Intention 121

Duponchel, L. (2016). Re: What is the minimum sample size required for Partial Least Squares (PLS) analysis?. https://www.researchgate.net/post/What-is-the-minimum-sample-size-required-for-Partial-Least-Squares-PLS-analysis/56f8ed09cbd5c2ceaa548dc1/citation/download

Fornell, C. & Larcker, D.F. (1981). Evaluating structural equation models with unobservable variables and measurement error. *Journal of Marketing Research*, *18*, 39–50. https://doi.org/10.2307/3151312

Hammerstein, S., König, C., Dreisörner, T., & Frey, A. (2021). Effects of COVID-19-related school closures on student achievement-a systematic review. *Frontiers in Psychology*, *12*, 746289. https://doi.org/10.3389/fpsyg.2021.746289

Isik, A. H., Karakis, R., & Güler, G. (2010). Postgraduate students' attitudes towards distance learning (The case study of Gazi University). *Procedia-Social and Behavioral Sciences*, *9*, 218–222. https://doi.org/10.1016/j.sbspro.2010.12.139

Jain, V., & Jain, P. (2022). From industry 4.0 to education 4.0: Acceptance and use of videoconferencing applications in higher education of Oman. *Journal of Applied Research in Higher Education*, *14*(3), 1079–1098. https://doi.org/10.1108/JARHE-10-2020-0378

Johnson, N., Veletsianos, G., & Seaman, J. (2020). US faculty and administrators' experiences and approaches in the early weeks of the COVID-19 pandemic. *Online Learning*, *24*(2), 6–21.

Kabra, G., Ramesh, A., Akhtar, P., & Dash, M. K. (2017). Understanding behavioural intention to use information technology: Insights from humanitarian practitioners. *Telematics and Informatics*, *34*(7), 1250–1261. https://doi.org/10.1016/j.tele.2017.05.010

Kaiser, H. F. (1974). An index of factorial simplicity. *Psychometrika*, *39*, 31–36.

Kerres, M. (2020). Against all odds: Education in Germany coping with Covid-19. *Postdigital Science and Education*, *2*(3), 690–694.

Khalilzadeh, J., Ozturk, A. B., & Bilgihan, A. (2017). Security-related factors in extended UTAUT model for NFC based mobile payment in the restaurant industry. *Computers in Human Behavior*, *70*, 460–474. https://doi.org/10.1016/j.chb.2017.01.001

Khan, M. A., Vivek, Nabi, M. K., Khojah, M., & Tahir, M. (2021). Students' perception towards E-learning during COVID-19 pandemic in India: An empirical study. *Sustainability*, *13*, 57, https://doi.org/10.3390/su13010057

Kukreti, M., & Mishra, A. (2021). Examining antecedents of tourism students' behavioral intention towards E-learning during COVID-19 pandemic in Oman. *Journal of Tourism*, *XXII*(2), 27–39.

Kulal, A., & Nayak, A. (2020). A study on perception of teachers and students toward online classes in Dakshina Kannada and Udupi District. *Asian Association of Open Universities Journal*, *15*, 285–296. https://doi.org/10.1108/aaouj-07-2020-0047

Latip, M. S. A., Noh, I., Tamrin, M., & Latip, S. N. N. A. (2020). Students' acceptance for e-learning and the effects of self-efficacy in Malaysia. *International Journal of Academic Research in Business and Social Sciences*, *10*(5), 658–674.

Liguori, E., & Winkler, C. (2020). From offline to online: challenges and opportunities for entrepreneurship education following the covid-19 pandemic. *Entrepreneurship Education and Pedagogy*, *3*(4), 346–351. https://doi.org/10.1177/2515127420916738

Litvinova, M., Liu, Q. H., Kulikov, E. S., & Ajelli, M. (2019). Reactive school closure weakens the network of social interactions and reduces the spread of influenza. *Proceedings of the National Academy of Sciences of the U S A, 116*(27), 13174–13181. https://doi.org/10.1073/pnas.1821298116

Martin-Blas, T., & Serrano-Fernandez, A. (2009). The role of new technologies in the learning process: Moodle as a teaching tool in physics. *Computers & Education, 52,* 35–44. https://doi.org/10.1016/j.compedu.2008.06.005

Mohamed, A. H. H. M., Abdel Fattah, F. A. M., Bashir, M. I. A., Alhajri, M., Khanan, A., & Abbas, Z. (2021). Investigating the acceptance of distance learning amongst Omani students: a case study from Oman. *Global Knowledge, Memory and Communication, 71*(6/7), 529–545. https://doi.org/10.1108/GKMC-02-2021-0021

Mohammadi, H. (2015). Investigating users' perspectives on e-learning: An integration of TAM and IS success model. *Computers in Human Behaviour, 45,* 359–374.

Mseleku, Z. (2020). A literature review of E-learning and E-teaching in the era of Covid-19 pandemic. *International Journal of Innovative Science and Research Technology, 5*(10), 588–597.

Parasuraman, A. (2000). Technology readiness index (TRI): A multiple-item scale to measure readiness to embrace new technologies. *Journal of Service Research, 2*(4), 307–320.

Ramírez-Correa, P. E., Arenas-Gaitan, J., & Rondan-Cataluna, F. J. (2015). Gender and acceptance of e-learning: A multi-group analysis based on A structural equation model among college students in Chile and Spain. *PLoS One, 10*(10), e014046.

Revythi, A., & Tselios, N. (2017). Extension of technology acceptance model by using system usability scale to assess behavioral intention to use e-learning. *Education and Information Technology, 24,* 2341–2355.

Sabherwal, R., Jeyaraj, A., & Chowa, C. (2006). Information system success: Individual and organizational determinants. *Management Science, 52*(11), 1849–1864.

Sahu, P. (2020). Closure of universities due to coronavirus disease 2019 (COVID-19): Impact on education and mental health of students and academic staff. *Cureus, 12*(4), e7541.

Salehi, H., Shojaee, M., & Sattar, S. (2015). Using E-learning and ICT courses in educational environment: A review. *English Language Teaching, 8*(1), 63–70.

Shang, Y., Li, H., & Zhang, R. (2021). Effects of pandemic outbreak on economies: Evidence from business history context. *Frontiers in Public Health, 9,* 146. https://doi.org/10.3389/fpubh.2021.632043

Sheatsley, P. B. (1983). Questionnaire construction and item writing. In P. Rossi et al. (Eds.), *Handbook of survey research.* Academic Press.

Shin, N. (2006). Online learner's 'flow' experience: An empirical study. *British Journal of Educational Technology, 37*(5), 705–720.

Strielkowski, W. (2020). COVID-19 pandemic and the digital revolution in academia and higher education. *Preprints 2020,* 2020040290. https://doi.org/10.20944/preprints202004.0290.v1

Sukendro, S., Habibi, A., Khaeruddin, K., Indrayana, B., Syahruddin, S., Makadada, A. F., & Hakim, H. (2020). Using an extended technology acceptance model to understand students' use of e-learning during Covid-19: Indonesian sports science education context. *Heliyon, 6*(11), e05410.

Teo, T. (2009). Is there an attitude problem? Reconsidering the role of attitude in the TAM. *British Journal of Education Technology, 40*(6), 1139–1141.

Thakkar, S. R., & Joshi, H. D. (2018). Impact of technology availability and self-efficacy on e-learning usage. *International Journal for Research in Applied Science & Engineering Technology*, 6(4), 2956–2960.

UNESCO. (2020). *Distance learning tools.* https://en.unesco.org/covid19/educationresponse/support (accessed May 9, 2022).

Venkatesh, V., & Davis, F. D. (2000). A theoretical extension of the technology acceptance model: Four longitudinal field studies. *Management Science*, 46(2), 186–204.

Wang, C., Cheng, Z., Yue, X.-G., & McAleer, M. (2020). Risk management of COVID-19 by universities in China. *Journal of Risk and Financial Management*, 13(2), 36.

Wargadinata, W., Maimunah, I., Febriani, S. R., & Humaira, L. (2020). Mediated Arabic language learning for higher education in COVID-19 situation. *Izdihar: Journal of Arabic Language Teaching, Linguistics, and Literature*, 3(1), 59–78.

Yilmaz, R. (2016). Knowledge sharing behaviors in e-learning community: Exploring the role of academic self-efficacy and sense of community. *Computers in Human Behavior*, 63, 373–382.

9 Transforming Online Teaching of a First-year Business Course

An Autoethnographic Reflection of Managing Teaching and Learning Amidst the Pandemic in the Gulf Region

Mary Precy P. Aguilar and Reynaldo Gacho Segumpan

Setting the Stage

Transitioning to higher education is considered to be a significant and complex phase involving a myriad of adjustments for students, particularly in their academic and personal lives. Academic institutions around the world have given attention to finding plausible solutions and recommending possible best practices to support the first-year experience. There has been a significant body of research solely dedicated to the First Year Higher Education (or FYHE) experience. A large body of research exists on the range of recommended programmes and practices particularly focusing on a curriculum that is engaging, challenging and supportive (Nelson, 2014, p. 9).

Attention to the first-year higher education experience has been in existence for more than 40 years focusing on empirical research outcomes and programmes to enhance and promote first-year student success (Nelson, 2014). First and foremost is the emphasis on an effective curriculum design for FYHE. Nelson (2014) highlighted the need to have an 'effective curriculum design, assessments, pedagogies and teaching practices that engage students in learning' (Nelson, 2014, p. 9). Hence, the concept of a 'Transition Pedagogy' has been a significant reform underpinning the framework of the first-year curriculum (Kift & Nelson, 2005). Second, is the understanding of various first-year student needs and the recognition of the different elements critical for student success which includes a sense of connectedness, capability, resourcefulness, purpose and culture (Lizzio & Wilson, 2010; Nelson, 2014). The third aspect is the academic institutional conditions that must be present to support the first-year experience, such as the major role of the classroom (may it be virtual or physical) as an avenue of FYE endeavours and initiatives; the use of assessments as a tool for student learning and vice versa for staff to identify student learning; the importance of setting the social context in promoting interactions among students and staff; and lastly, the support of the institutions in

DOI: 10.4324/9781003457299-12

Transforming Online Teaching of a First-year Business Course   125

setting expectations which are focused on the first-year success (Tinto, 2012). These are some of the major empirical research outcomes which have played significant contribution in guiding FYHE practices to date. Yet with all these studies built on over the years, no one came prepared to face the major disruption brought about by the COVID-19 pandemic as it hit higher education in the later part of 2019.

This chapter presents an autoethnographic reflection of one of the authors' personal experiences in managing the teaching and learning of a first-year business course during the pandemic. An autoethnography details the personal or professional experiences of the researcher in expanding his or her understanding of a phenomenon as well as voicing his or her concerns, and making sense of that experience within a particular context (Kim & Reichmuth, 2021; Lee, 2020). The chapter focuses on the process of self-reflection and, thus, encourages a much deeper understanding of the range of issues in unique sociocultural contexts (Lee, 2020). Such type of research is known to be rare in higher education, particularly on topics related to the experiences and understanding of teaching and learning (Trahar, 2013). According to Trahar (2013), autoethnography encourages one to reflect on their first-hand experience in teaching and learning, not only on theories and ideas from past experiences but also on reverting one's focus to existing practices that may have been unconsciously overlooked (Trahar, 2013).

The narratives which echo the journey of one of the authors are expressed in the first-person pronoun 'I' in order to reflect an embodiment of the meanings in each shared personal experience.

I shared the beliefs of Trahar (2013) as I found autoethnography a 'powerful' methodology to express my views and reflections on teaching as it narrates my personal real-life experiences. It also documents the many years I have been engaged in this profession and shares some valuable insights about FYHE teaching and learning (Trahar, 2013, p. 369). Admittedly, this methodology may have some major risks for researchers like me, as I would be highly vulnerable to scrutiny and judgement and may render myself open to criticism. However, I believe that an autoethnographic approach is best suited for my aim to share my personal experience and reflections during the most challenging time of my teaching career with my documentation of my students' perceptions of learning and, consequently, my views on teaching (Trahar, 2013).

A Glimpse About Myself and My Pedagogical Practice

My more than twenty-five (25) years of teaching had not entirely prepared me for this pandemic—and from the looks of it, no one was. Modesty aside, I consider myself a good teacher. With my years of experience in higher education, I think I can readily say, I am a well-experienced and effective teacher. I always make it a priority to develop and enhance my teaching skills, particularly on current and effective educational technologies. Teaching business courses to second-language learners—first-year learners to be exact, has been my field of expertise and the area I am passionate about. As I find myself standing in a classroom, surrounded by my first-year students' questioning gazes as if asking 'what is in store for me' does not scare me at all. This, I considered, is not an unusual scenario. In fact, this is something I believe I can readily handle. In such a situation, I would return their gazes with a reassuring look, and with utmost confidence, I would smile and say: 'You have come to the right class and are in good hands!'.

I was born in a Southeast Asian country where Christianity is practised by the majority and the culture is partly influenced by the Spaniards. Furthermore, I was educated in an American system throughout my tertiary studies. I started my teaching career in a Southeast Asian country where Buddhism is the belief of many. I have lived in this country for more than 15 years and was employed in some of the most reputable government-owned universities. Most of my teaching career was spent at offshore campuses of Australian universities. It is also through the Australian educational system that I was able to complete my PhD and teacher training. Given this background, the wide array of cultural settings in which I have been immersed has had the most impact on my approach to both teaching and learning. My educational background is mostly rooted in my Western training coupled with the social and cultural influences of the Filipino, Vietnamese and Thai cultures.

In the span of my teaching career, I have always been a believer of Ramsden's model of student learning (1992, p 83). The model has shaped my practice all these years and I found it to be an effective tool for understanding my students' learning needs. I also use Bigg's constructive alignment theory as a guide in my pedagogy such as in my choice of teaching techniques and activities, and the various suitable and effective assessments (Biggs, 1996). The model also keeps me informed to focus on my students' engagement in learning and, in particular, ensuring they achieve deep learning (Biggs, 1996). Moreover, I also use Bloom's taxonomy to guide me in conceptualising the most effective learning activities and assessments (Bloom, 1956). In the main, these three (3) major and known concepts have shaped my teaching and learning philosophy and had significantly contributed to my being recognised as a highly commendable teacher.

Pandemic Anxiety

It was on March 11, 2020, when the World Health Organisation announced the existence of this highly contagious COVID-19 virus as a global pandemic (Rashid & Yadav, 2020). As I discovered more about this pandemic, I realised it is not a typical one. COVID-19 has an unclear pathogenic mechanism and mainly it lacks a specific cure which made this a serious threat to public health. To prevent the spread of the virus, higher education particularly in the Gulf region had to halt face-to-face learning on campus and resort to a fully online mode of teaching. That very day, when the announcement was made, everyone had very limited time to prepare. A decision was made to immediately implement the use of the online learning management system (LMS) Blackboard for all course delivery.

From that moment on, I felt out of my comfort zone. I began to doubt and question my capabilities in doing a fully online class although I have used the online portal many times to support my teaching for years. I do consider myself competent in using Blackboard but at the onset of the pandemic, I began to feel worried and anxious. The pandemic was a wake-up call and has made me reflect on the many facets of my teaching—something I have not done in years. I was challenged in ways I never would have predicted. I went through a process of personal reflections and numerous self-talk on 'my selves' to come up with ways to adjust and transform my teaching with the student's welfare at the top of the list amidst the disruptions.

Online 'shock': Teaching Shock and Learning Shock

Teaching Shock

I would have to admit that I am not a fan of a fully online classroom. My strength as a teacher is predominantly in the personal connections and interactions I make with my students. I connect well with them when they are physically present as I rely on getting cues and hints of their capabilities, skills and learning through eye contact, facial expressions and bodily movements. To me, that connection has the power to radiate energy and inspires me to exert efforts in making my class lively and interactive.

For years, I use the LMS like Blackboard or Canvas as a tool to support learning. I mainly use it as a depository of course materials and as a portal for submissions of assessments or outputs. I have yet to use the LMS in delivering a fully online class—ever! With the onset of the pandemic—this all came as sudden and overwhelming, perhaps similar to a bout of 'shock'.

Shock? A word that has resonated several times in my mind. Is it possible that I (and even my students) were in a state of shock? I pondered on the word 'shock' and examine its close similarities to the phenomenon known as culture shock. Culture shock is a construct that has long been used in academic studies (Oberg, 1960). It refers to the feeling of anxiety when one is immersed in an unfamiliar culture with different social conventions, values and norms (Griffiths et al., 2005; Oberg, 1960). An individual experiencing culture shock is believed to experience an array of emotional reactions towards that 'new culture' accompanied by intense disorientation, a feeling of confusion and anxiety. I could vividly remember that when we were informed to shift to a fully online class, I felt that sense of confusion. There were so many questions and uncertainties. Although I have used the online portal many times in the past, relying on the full use of LMS in teaching led me to feel disoriented and anxious. I felt that my efforts were insufficient and my teaching activities were ineffective as I struggled in getting my content across. I found it a challenge to encourage my students to interact and sustain their attention throughout the session.

I felt somewhat on the verge of helplessness in trying to find ways and means to make things work similar to how I deliver my classes in a face-to-face mode. I even felt irritable at times, yet holding on to it, as I felt I had to make things work no matter what. Without a doubt, I realised that these emotional responses are clear indications of 'culture shock'(Adler, 1975).

Before the pandemic, I thought about good teaching as bounded by physical space and time. I used to think of effective teaching as seeing and meeting my students in every class session. I tend to focus more on physical interactions as a non-negotiable element in my teaching and, hence, in students' learning. Yet, I found myself displaced and adrift in a new approach contradictory to what has been my strength over the years. This moment has got me thinking earnestly. I recall the story of Alice in Wonderland, just as how confused Alice was when she stumbled into that rabbit hole surrounded by newness and uncertainties, like her, would I be able to survive?

I would have to agree with Adler's. I realised with all this emotional chaos, I am experiencing a state of 'culture shock' not in terms of culture but in the context of teaching (Adler, 1975). With that, I can readily call it a state of 'teaching shock'. Since this concept is similar to culture shock, 'teaching shock' can be defined as a variety of emotional reactions of intense disorientation, confusion and anxiety associated with teaching in a new and unfamiliar setting. The delivery of courses in a fully online format is a new and unfamiliar sphere that triggered those emotional responses.

Learning Shock

After those episodes of discovering and reflecting on myself and the impact of the pandemic, I shifted my focus towards the plight of my students. Then I began to ponder: 'If I, for one, felt those emotional reactions, could it be possible that students may experience a similar state? Could they be suffering from "learning shock"?'

The concept of learning shock is not new in studies associated with teaching and learning. It was first presented by Griffiths et al. (2005). This phenomenon embodies powerful emotions associated with learning which include acute frustrations, confusion and anxiety. The abrupt shift to a fully online class is a new approach to learning and may seem unfamiliar to students which, consequently, may lead them to experience a range of emotional responses (Griffiths et al., 2005).

In the case of first-year learners, they have had their own set of expectations before admission to higher education particularly the expectation of on-campus study (Kift, 2014). Sadly, such expectation is not possible during the pandemic. Gone were those days when they physically interact and enjoy the presence of their teachers and classmates in a physical classroom. Students in my classes have constantly asked: 'When can we have face-to-face classes, Dr (to the teacher)?'. That remark gave me insight into the effects of online learning on students and to reexamine possible reasons that prompted that question.

Transforming Online Teaching of a First-year Business Course 129

That same question tends to illustrate a student's emotional reaction to an unfamiliar learning and teaching method. With that said, can that be an indicator of 'learning shock'? (Griffiths et al., 2005).

As I began to delve deeper into the different scenarios in my online classes, I recall that during the first few months of the pandemic, many students have expressly conveyed their delight with online classes. They were glad they just have to stay home! They believed taking courses online saves them considerable time on travel and preparation. They felt most at ease studying at home, where they could do so in any part of their home and spend extra time with their families. Some shared that they have more leisure time on online entertainment or online games. Others even remarked that they have gained weight from indulging in the food they love at home. To put it plainly, it seems like an excellent decision to study online and stay at home.

As the pandemic progresses and took longer than expected, online learning persisted and a few realisations emerged. I noticed that students began to feel the monotony of online classes. In a number of our online sessions, many students have expressed their desire to return to face-to-face learning, citing the repetitive nature of online classes. At some point, they reflect on what might have transpired had they returned to campus.

It was a challenge to sustain students' interest in my synchronous class sessions. I noticed their lack of engagement during times when I elicit discussions. In almost every session, I had to call on and remind every one of them to participate. Some had expressed their difficulty in catching up with the topic as well as in submissions of assessments. Even with the recorded lecture posted in the learning portal, several students would miss the due dates of their assessments. Others have voiced their concerns about the feeling of being lost or confused, particularly, in having difficulty with concepts that are new to them. Some were overwhelmed and confused even though the information was recorded and posted in the online portal. There were a few who expressed that they had to double their efforts in understanding their lessons as compared to when they were face-to-face. In the main, it is evident that there exist a series of 'emotional reactions' as being observed and at the same time narrated by students. Some have also experienced 'unexpected and disorienting cues'. Others experience being 'ambiguous' and face conflicting expectations. As a whole, these affective cues or responses correspond to the definition of learning shock (Griffiths et al., 2005, p. 276).

I believe that experiencing learning shock influenced students on what and how they learn (Griffiths et al., 2005). It has the potential to affect how students view their classmates, instructors, and the classroom, or in this case, the virtual classroom. Learning shock can also hinder learning by paralysing critical elements in the learning process, but at some point, the opposite could also be true: that learning could be facilitated and new avenues for learning could be possible. Indeed, learning shock is inherent to the most transformative forms of education, those that call for a rewiring of one's identity, worldview and set of values (Griffiths et al., 2005).

Beyond Survival: the Transformation Process

The unplanned shift to online learning in the early part of the pandemic made teaching and learning a challenge for higher education students and with a greater impact felt, in particular, by first-year learners. In the words of Kift (2014), 'Starting the first year at university can be a daunting experience and a big adjustment for new students'(Kift, 2014, p. 1). While the first-year learners struggled as part of their transition to higher education and getting accustomed to university life, they also have to cope with and adjust to the new mode of learning and overcome 'learning shock'.

As I looked back and recall how I was able to transform my teaching of a first-year online course, I remembered at that moment I had to resort to 'bracketing'—a method that is commonly used in qualitative research to temporarily detach our 'selves', open our minds to the way we see things and reflect on (Creswell, 2009; Vagle, 2018). I was able to set aside my thoughts and experiences during the pandemic which include the psychological and emotional circumstances I was in; the 'teaching shock' I was going through; the challenges associated with juggling work and family as well as the feeling of isolation. Bracketing taught me to focus and reflect on some of the most important aspects of my teaching and learning strategies.

Let me walk you through the process of developing and improving my teaching strategies. At the onset, I revisited the FYHE concepts about what works for this particular group of learners, their characteristics and learning. In reflecting on what works best, I came up with highlighting these areas in all my online classes:

Enhancing online engagement

As mentioned previously, 'online learning has been used as an alternative to support on-campus learning for years' (Palmer & Holt, 2009). All these have changed during the pandemic. I was accustomed to delivering my classes in a face-to-face format and having a fully online class has far more disadvantages, particularly in engaging students. I also consider the online method of teaching tends to offer a 'one-size-fits-all' approach. Teaching is mainly focused on lecturing which is a one-way approach and overlooking the diversity of students' needs and characteristics and, hence, their learning needs. Furthermore, in the Gulf region, some countries have a stringent stance on the use of video or any conferencing facilities as it is not mandatory and even restricted. As a result, teaching has become more challenging as facilitators are compelled to find new and effective ways to address such shortcomings.

The *'sense of belonging'* and *'personal connections to learning'* have been highly valued to enhance online engagement for first-year learners (Trahar, 2013). In my online class, I focused on building rapport with my students. I would always ask them to post 'emojis' to show how they

Transforming Online Teaching of a First-year Business Course   131

feel from time to time as reminders that they belong to the group and that their existence is highly valued. As simple as this may seem to be, it has promoted a relaxed atmosphere where students can be themselves. In addition, our online synchronous sessions emphasised collaboration such as the sharing of ideas, opinions and examples using the whiteboard feature of Blackboard in group-wide activities such as 'brainstorming' where each student is free to express his or her ideas. This activity has allowed students to actively participate and encourage them to engage and learn from others. I also use small group dynamics in engaging students while ensuring that activities are short and relatable for first-year learners. Generally, activities should be fun and interesting. Students are divided into small groups of three to five so there is maximum use of time and optimum participation among individual members. Each group should be given an equal chance to share outputs or findings during the whole class session. I would have to admit that, in the planning and preparation of such activities, I have noticed my workload has increased twofold. In the main, to make this work, I realised that I have to be actively involved in each step of the learning process—from the preparation to the actual teaching and, in the midst of it all, in encouraging engagement in every online session with my students.

Variety is the key. In my opinion, achieving increased or active engagement results from the diversity of techniques or activities executed throughout the course. At times, we should initiate group work or activities while some days we should require individual outputs. There were some instances when I used the 'flipped classroom' approach while at times I simply asked them to post their ideas and thoughts using the Discussion feature of Blackboard. Also, I made use of videos, and elicit feedback from the group or at times I introduced new concepts through the use of brainstorming techniques or mind-mapping. In using a variety of techniques, constant real-time feedback is conveyed to students which then serves as a reassurance that they are learning. Mainly, through varied activities, I am confident that students are learning by giving them a chance to talk, to see, to hear and most importantly there is ample time for processing the content or simply a time to 'think'.

Effective online assessments tasks

I view assessments as an integral part of teaching and learning. It is through assessments that we gauge our student's performance in the course and determine how well they are attaining our learning goals. As Taylor puts it, assessments drive students' academic experience and, hence, their learning (Taylor, 2008). In this sphere, I do agree with the significance of a well-thought and planned assessment, particularly for students transitioning to university studies—the first-year learners.

132 *Mary Precy P. Aguilar and Reynaldo Gacho Segumpan*

During the pandemic, I had to rethink and modify the online assessment tasks in my first-year business course relevant to the needs of first-year learners. In the Gulf region, universities have a set of course assessments prescribed by the College depending on the academic discipline. These assessments are approved by the university council and in adherence to the policies of their respective Ministry of Education of the country. With that, as a teacher-in-charge of a course, I can only redesign or modify the assessment tasks and which in this paper—I refer to as 'assessments'. In doing so, I had to consider factors I believe to be effective based on research findings in higher education and to whom the assessments are directed, in this case, those FYHE students. Hence, assessments should be appropriately designed to drive students learning (Taylor, 2008). In the process of reviewing my current assessments, in particular online assessment tasks, I revisited the model developed by Taylor (2008) on assessments for students in transition to universities (2008). According to Taylor (2008), 'the model promotes for continuous assessment to regularly engage students and/or allow them to monitor their understanding and progress' (Taylor, 2008, p. 23). These assessments during the semester involve three (3) overlapping phases: assessments for transition; assessments for development and assessment for achievements. Allow me to clearly outline how I applied this in my first-year course:

a Assessments for transition refer to low contribution to final grades, reflective type of activities mostly administered at the beginning of the term (Taylor, 2008). I mainly use the Discussion board to check their understanding of earlier topics. Some of the examples for this type of assessment include posting photos or noting down their observations about their surroundings and relating that to the use of a particular subject or concept. These observations were posted on discussion boards. This type of task encourages other students to provide feedback or initiate discussions. Other transition activities include short and brief early feedback activities usually given in the first three (3) weeks, a study plan, a self-development contract, and a short reflection on the relevance of the course or a particular topic.

b Assessments for developments are activities happening in the middle part of the semester. These refer to 'the heart of the course's assessment scheme and can feed forward into assessment for achievement. These assessments allow for significant feedback and have low to middle contributions to the final grade' (Taylor, 2008, pp. 22–23). The assessment tasks I created included the submission of a part of a draft of the e-portfolio, parts of an e-diary, group discussion outcomes posted on the Discussion board, and a group mini-analysis related to a short case or concepts or topics they observed in real life.

c Assessments for achievement are known as summative assessments or those assessments which contribute a significant amount of weight to

Transforming Online Teaching of a First-year Business Course 133

the final grades such as the examinations, final projects or final reports (Taylor, 2008). In my case, these are the midterm and final examinations, and these assessments are previously set as part of the curriculum which has been approved by the university council and mandated by the Ministry of Education in the country in the Gulf region. For summative assessments, as a facilitator of a course, I can contextualise the topics and also modify the formats or types of questions. In my course, the midterm examinations are administered in a fully online format. I designed the examinations using fewer multiple-choice questions and a majority of the percentage are allocated for short essays or essay questions. In setting the marking criteria, I allocate a higher percentage of the total marks on examples or scenarios relevant to the concept or topic being asked in examinations rather than in the identification of theories and concepts. The marking criteria mostly emphasised the depth, quality and clarity of the answers.

Realisations along the Way

During this whole process of modifying and implementing the assessments, I have realised a few major points:

Engaging assessments mean meaningful assessments

For assessments to be engaging, it has to be meaningful and relevant to a particular student group. It has to be authentic in a way that depicts the real context of the concept or topic in the workplace. This means assessment tasks are focused on practical applications in business. In addition to that, for an assessment to be meaningful it has to be fun, interesting and engaging for first-year learners. With that in mind, I had to put myself in their shoes and reflect on the following: 'Will this make me (the student) understand the concept better?'; 'Will this be useful for me (student) in my life or the workplace?'; 'Will I (student) enjoy this type of activity?'. Meaningful assessments should be carefully thought of and consequently needs a great deal of planning, preparation and execution from the facilitator's or teachers' side. I usually take time to prepare visual activities such as preparing PowerPoint presentations with clear illustrations or animations to demonstrate examples then followed by short case studies intended for small group discussion. Along these lines, I have learned that the tasks I used for face-to-face or campus teaching have to be modified to suit online teaching. Hence, online teaching is not face-to-face teaching. With that limitation in mind, I think we, facilitators, have to learn or re-learn new competencies or skills in our pursuit of designing meaningful and engaging assessment tasks for our students to learn from. We should invest in ourselves to learn new applications or interactive applications in designing engaging materials for our students.

134   *Mary Precy P. Aguilar and Reynaldo Gacho Segumpan*

Appropriateness of task and timing

The learning shock experienced by first-year learners as a result of their transition to university studies as well as the unforeseen impact of the pandemic on their emotional and psychological well-being should not be overlooked. An important consideration in their success in university studies is dependent on how well they perform the different assessment tasks provided to them. Students should be highly engaged in tasks to learn. Engaging assessment tasks should be appropriately designed based on the intended learning outcome and should consider that the tasks are clear, reasonable and achievable (Biggs, 1996). Students should be able to understand the purpose of a particular assessment task. It is worthwhile to spare some time to go through the tasks and clearly explain the purpose, the process and also the expected outcome, especially to first-year students (Biggs, 1996). In addition, focusing on the time frame given to students in a given task should also be fair and appropriate. The timing or in other words 'when' the task is given should be well-planned and clearly communicated to students at the beginning of the term and even before administering the task. This will enable students to anticipate what is expected of them and also manage their workload.

The outcome

In modifying the assessment tasks, I had to ensure that the general outcome of every activity is relevant and realistic. As it is a business course, relevance means the applicability of the concept to the current times or circumstances in the real world. The main goal, aside from achieving the course's intended learning outcomes, is for assessment tasks to foster engagement and promote deep learning (Biggs, 1996). In doing this, Bigg's theory of constructive alignment and also Bloom's higher-order thinking skills taxonomy will come handy in formulating and designing effective assessment task outcomes leading to deep learning (Biggs, 1996; Bloom, 1956).

The Takeaway

I cannot deny the fact that the pandemic made our role as course facilitators a challenge to a greater extent. The pandemic compelled me to pause and reflect on my understanding of teaching and learning and re-orient my know-how about the nature of first-year learners. Along these lines, it made me reexamine my teaching and learning practices. In a sense, it has allowed me to focus on finding ways and means for the most effective strategies to enhance engagement in my online classes. It has also allowed me to reflect on the 'students' themselves and see beyond who they are —their 'selves' during those difficult times. Mainly, I have learned that the most important consideration during a

Transforming Online Teaching of a First-year Business Course 135

time of major disruptions like this is to look beyond the individual: the 'human' side of every person. Human as we are, we do have our strengths and weaknesses, feelings and thoughts, capabilities and skills, and in the process, acknowledging all these elements in our pursuit of achieving effective and engaging teaching and learning strategies will lead to superior results.

I have also realised this pandemic has impacted both teachers and students alike. The students in transition—the first-year learners, I believe, were the most affected as they had to suffer the adverse effect of the pandemic due to learning shock as well as face the challenging aspects of adjusting to the university. The teachers or facilitators were also vulnerable and were not spared from the impact which as a result led them to experience 'teaching shock'. These realisations have taught me to revisit the theory of Oberg (1960) on culture shock and helped me recognise the vulnerability of the individual's 'human' side during unprecedented times. In the main, these realisations have led me to be more considerate and also to place greater value on the virtue of 'patience' in all my undertakings.

The process of improving my online course for first-year learners here in the Gulf region has not been an easy journey. With that said, my workload has considerably increased as I have to dedicate some time to learning new ways and acquiring new competencies to ensure learning outcomes are achieved successfully in an unfamiliar format. I also have to put every effort into ensuring that in the process of choosing every teaching activity, it should promote a 'sense of belonging' and 'personal connections to learning'. Despite the absence of the video conferencing facility (which has limited use in the Gulf region), I do believe that the fundamental consideration in effective teaching and learning relies on the availability of various teaching techniques and most of all having meaningful assessment tasks. Amidst all these, an important consideration is placing student engagement at the core.

Overall, all these efforts have not come to waste. I appreciate the fact that my efforts have been recognised to a greater extent. All the courses I delivered online, particularly during the later part of the pandemic, have received excellent feedback based on my student evaluations. This simply indicates that despite the challenging circumstances and the negative impact of the pandemic or any major disruptions for that matter, teaching and learning can still be engaging and meaningful for both teachers and students. Indeed, every dark cloud has a silver lining!

The COVID-19 pandemic is a wake-up call for higher education institutions in the Gulf region to look beyond the disruptions and consider what else can be done. It was a time to reflect on whether the higher education sectors in the Gulf region are adequately prepared to confront such challenges, may it be a pandemic or other disruptions that could have a direct impact on their provision of quality education. The unpredictability of those times compelled higher education sectors to find ways and adjust to the changing environment. Simply stated, it has taught everyone resilience. Mainly, the pandemic serves as a valuable lesson: no matter how severe or life-threatening the problem is, there is always a solution.

References

Adler, P. S. (1975). The transitional experience: An alternative view of culture shock. *Journal of Humanistic Psychology*, *15*, 13–23.

Biggs, J. (1996). Enhancing teaching through constructive alignment. *Higher Education*, *32*(3), 347–364.

Bloom, B. S. (1956). *Taxonomy of educational objectives: The classification of educational goals*; Handbook I: Cognitive domain. In M. D. Engelhart, E. J. Furst, W. H. Hill, & D. R. Krathwohl (Eds.). David McKay.

Creswell, J. W. (2009). *Research design: Qualitative and mixed methods approaches*. Sage.

Griffiths, D. S., Winstanley, D., & Gabriel, Y. (2005). Learning shock: The trauma of return to formal learning. *Management Learning*, *36*(3), 275–297.

Kift, S. (2014). Student success: Why first year at uni is a make-or-break experience. *The Conversation*.

Kift, S., & Nelson, K. (2005). Beyond curriculum reform: Embedding the transition experience. In *Proceedings of the 28th HERDSA Annual Conference: Higher Education in a Changing World (HERDSA 2005)*. University of Southern Queensland.

Kim, T., & Reichmuth, H. L. (2021). Exploring cultural logic in becoming a teacher: A collaborative autoethnography on transnational teaching and learning. *Professional Development in Education*, *47*(2–3), 257–272.

Lee, K. (2020). Autoethnography as an authentic learning activity in online doctoral education: An integrated approach to authentic learning. *TechTrends*, *64*(4), 570–580.

Lizzio, A., & Wilson, K. (2010). Assessment in first-year: Beliefs, practices and systems. In *ATN National Assessment Conference*. https://www.Griffith.edu.au/__data/assets/word_doc/0005/525344/11-Lizzio-and-Wilson-First-Year-Students-Appraisal-of-Assessment-paper.docx

Nelson, K. (2014). The first year in higher education-where to from here? *International Journal of the First Year in Higher Education*, *5*(2), 1–20.

Oberg, K. (1960). Cultural shock: Adjustment to new cultural environments. *Practical Anthropology*, *7*(4), 177–182.

Palmer, S. R., & Holt, D. M. (2009). Examining student satisfaction with wholly online learning. *Journal of Computer-Assisted Learning*, *25*(2), 101–113.

Rashid, S., & Yadav, S. S. (2020). Impact of Covid-19 pandemic on higher education and research. *Indian Journal of Human Development*, *14*(2), 340–343.

Taylor, J. A. (2008). Assessment in first year university: A model to manage transition. *Journal of University Teaching and Learning Practice*, *5*(1), 19–33.

Tinto, V. (2012). *Completing college: Rethinking institutional action*. University of Chicago Press.

Trahar, S. (2013). Autoethnographic journeys in learning and teaching in higher education. *European Educational Research Journal*, *12*(3), 367–375.

Vagle, M. D. (2018). *Crafting phenomenological research*. Routledge.

10 University of Buraimi in Oman

Pandemic Lessons and Initiatives for Education Reform from Instructors' Perspectives

Ibrahim Rashid Al Shamsi and Boumedyen Shannaq

Introduction

Undoubtedly, 2020 and 2021 have emerged as a period of re-evaluation of conventional ideas and approaches within the education system. The catalyst for this transformation was the onset of the pandemic, which imposed several new demands on the functioning and operations of universities. The crisis has brought about significant changes in the traditional way of life, influencing various aspects including the dynamics of pursuing higher education. In numerous countries, higher education has evolved into a fundamental social norm and a crucial instrument for driving socio-economic development. The leadership of the Sultanate of Oman system of higher education starts working on rethinking educational models in universities and colleges, which are based on face-to-face communication between an instructor and a student. In such situation, not only an in-depth analysis of the effects on higher education caused by the crisis is relevant but also the development of solutions to mitigate the negative consequences of the pandemic and aimed at ensuring the sustainable development of universities in the new conditions. This work attempts to systematise the key shortages of the domestic system of higher education during the pandemic, and outlines ways to overcome them.

Amidst the COVID-19 period, a multitude of research investigations have been conducted, delving into diverse issues and uncovering the benefits that have emerged from this global pandemic. Osman (2020) explored the impact of COVID-19 pandemic in the education system in the Sultanate of Oman. The author proposed a descriptive analysis methodology to demonstrate the experience of Sultan Qaboos University and how the university responded to the pandemic. The outcomes of his research proposed five learned lessons related to invest in improving the student needs as follows:

- Provide more online environment.
- The online assessment causes a serious challenge to evaluate the student performance.

DOI: 10.4324/9781003457299-13

138   *Ibrahim Rashid Al Shamsi and Boumedyen Shannaq*

- In addition, there should be different methods developed to solve this challenge.
- Efforts should be made to enhance the digital proficiency of both students and instructors.
- A need exists to cultivate new student attributes, including skills such as self-motivation and self-regulation.

Al-Zaabi (2021) introduced and discussed several issues caused by the pandemic on ELT curriculum, teaching methods, and educational growth of teachers. The author concludes that all related entities should go past the urgent online practices and change quality of e-learning. Omanuna (2020) identified different strategies and solutions for several sectors such as initiatives to address the challenges of COVID-19, Education, Health, Voluntary Work, Traveling, Businesses and Investments, Social and Professional Support, and Economy. Al-Saidi (2020), the Minister of Health in Oman, summarised comprehensive and smart reports about the "Sultanate of Oman Preparedness and Response to COVID-19 Pandemic". Many valuable information could be found in this report. The report provided the status and statistical analysis of the response to COVID-19 pandemic, and the main strategies were also introduced in this report.

Mohamed et al. (2021) worked on several statistical methods for analysing the advantages and disadvantages of e-learning and found that e-learning system was accepted by many students and entities. Abdalellah et al. (2020) used "CIPP" evaluation model and collected data from faculty members and students. The analysis results yield a set of recommendations aimed at enhancing the performance of teaching and learning activities during similar circumstances. According to Al-Maskari et al. (2021), students enrolled in higher education institutions (HEIs) in the Sultanate of Oman expressed satisfaction with the support provided by their respective institutions. Key challenges were the insufficient internet connection, quality of recorded videos, and interaction with their instructors as well as large family size which paused the challenges regarding comfortable places at home and availability of computers.

Abushammala et al. (2021) conducted a survey of students in Oman private institutions to identify the approaches accepted by academic organisations in Oman in providing education during the COVID-19 pandemic. Data about 213 students have been collected and analysed, and results showed that only 50% of the students show their satisfaction with the methods of the online education delivery process. A significant number of exams were cancelled and substituted with additional coursework, while, in certain cases, students were evaluated solely based on existing coursework. Additionally, 40% of students faced challenges in paying their instruction fees due to the financial implications brought about by the COVID-19 pandemic.

Mustafa and Javed (2021) analysed 966 students' opinions about the stress caused by the pandemic of COVID-19. The outcome of the study showed that 82.5% had moderate stress and 14.4% with high stress. Al Khalili et al.

University of Buraimi in Oman   139

(2021) found that the health care system at all levels and citizens were aware of the pandemic procedures including the COVID-19 vaccination movement. Many health sectors have been introduced and providing professional technical leadership for improving the health sector services. More information related to the research work available in Mohmmed et al. (2020) and investigated by the authors available in Al Shamsi and Shannaq (2020), Shannaq and Al Shamsi (2020), and Shannaq and Alshamsi (2019).

The key challenges faced were the shortage of the public health company and lack of an ERP for the health care information. The pandemic taught the health sector in Oman the importance of investing on preventive and preparedness strategies.

Objectives of the Chapter

Omani universities hold a significant position as key educational establishments, renowned for their scientific and knowledge-driven nature. They serve as prominent institutions spearheading modernisation and development efforts. Amidst the challenges posed by the pandemic, universities like the University of Buraimi in Oman have strived to confront obstacles impeding the continuity of the learning process. Recognising the importance of rapid advancements in distance education technologies, these institutions have embraced their utilisation in response to the prevailing educational demands.

In light of this shift, it becomes crucial to engage in comprehensive and ongoing evaluation of distance education experiences within the Omani university context. It is essential to identify best practices and undertake research that sheds light on the reality of distance education in Oman universities during the COVID-19 pandemic, specifically from the perspective of faculty members. Understanding their viewpoints will contribute to a deeper comprehension of the successes, challenges, and areas for improvement in the implementation of distance education.

Exploring the current state of distance education in Oman universities under the pandemic involves examining the strategies, tools, and approaches employed to facilitate remote learning. It entails investigating the effectiveness of different instructional methods used in this context and understanding the experiences, perspectives, and feedback of faculty members who have been at the forefront of this transition. Such research will help inform future planning and decision-making processes, ensuring the continuous enhancement of distance education practices in Omani universities. Additionally, studying the reality of distance education during the pandemic necessitates considering the unique needs and challenges faced by students and instructors alike. It involves assessing the readiness of both parties in terms of digital competencies and infrastructure, as well as identifying areas where further support and resources are required. By addressing these aspects, Omani universities can strive to enhance the digital preparedness of students and instructors, fostering a more conducive and effective remote learning environment.

As the educational landscape continues to evolve, Omani universities must remain adaptive and responsive to emerging educational needs and circumstances. Through rigorous research and evaluation of distance education experiences, these institutions can leverage the lessons learned during the pandemic to shape future pedagogical strategies and create resilient and inclusive educational systems for the benefit of all stakeholders involved.

This chapter aims to:

- explore the views of academic staff about distance education during COVID-19 pandemic in Oman universities, in particular, at the University of Buraimi
- compare the effectiveness of teaching-learning processes before and during the pandemic

In particular, this chapter will address the following questions:

- How feasible is the implementation of e-learning in Oman universities during the COVID-19 pandemic based on the perceptions of instructors?
- Are there significant changes in the effectiveness of the educational process from pre-pandemic to during the pandemic, as evidenced by statistical analysis?

Importance of the Study

The primary focus of the chapter is to examine the practicality and viability of e-learning in the context of Oman universities amidst the challenges posed by the COVID-19 pandemic. The perspectives and judgments of instructors were sought to gain insights into the feasibility and effectiveness of the transition to e-learning. Additionally, statistical analysis was conducted to determine if there were notable and statistically significant transformations in the overall efficacy of the educational process when comparing the period before the pandemic with the period during the pandemic. These research questions aimed to provide a comprehensive understanding of the impact and implications of the pandemic on the educational landscape and the adaptability of e-learning in Oman universities.

The significance of the present research work can be attributed to several key factors. Firstly, it aims to address the critical education challenges experienced during the COVID-19 pandemic, thus providing valuable insights into the specific hurdles faced in the field of education. By identifying and developing a comprehensive list of these challenges, the research contributes to a deeper understanding of the impact of the pandemic on the education sector. Secondly, the research endeavours to foster positive attitudes towards distance learning and education among both students and faculty members. By highlighting the benefits and effectiveness of distance education, it seeks to promote a favourable perception and acceptance of remote learning methods. This is crucial in facilitating the successful implementation and adoption of distance education in Oman universities. Thirdly, the research sheds light on the reality of distance education within the context of Oman universities. It examines the current state of distance education, its strengths, limitations, and areas for improvement. By drawing attention to this reality, the research provides an opportunity to reflect on and enhance the existing practices and strategies related to distance education.

Lastly, the findings of the study hold significance beyond the immediate scope. The results can serve as a valuable resource for students, decision-makers, and educational institutions in the Gulf region. By highlighting the importance of distance education during and beyond the COVID-19 pandemic, the research can inform future decision-making processes, emphasising the need to prioritise and invest in distance education initiatives. This can lead to improved educational strategies, enhanced preparedness for future crises, and a more resilient and adaptable educational system overall. In summary, the importance of this chapter lies in its contribution to identifying education challenges during the pandemic, promoting positive attitudes towards distance education, highlighting the reality of distance education in Oman universities, and influencing decision-makers and students in recognising the significance of distance education both during and after the COVID-19 pandemic.

Distance Education Experiences of University of Buraimi and the GCC

The system analysis approach is concerned with evaluating the inputs and outputs of Oman universities, in particular, the University of Buraimi, according to specific indicators and criteria. Evaluating the performance of the internal components and the interaction between them and their external environment ensures that the system achieves its objectives in accordance with pre-defined criteria and indicators.

The collected material is based on dozens of large-scale research, including data from the University of Buraimi and other universities in Oman, meeting and discussion reports, strategic plan, operational plans, quality assurance data, surveys, focus groups and interviews with students, faculty, administrators, and also an extensive review of domestic materials of universities in Oman. The research community consists of all members of the academic institutions in Oman.

The chapter focused on the academic staff of the University of Al-Buraimi and other universities in Oman who were actively involved in teaching during the second semester of the academic year 2020. This period witnessed the implementation of distance education, with a range of courses being offered across different colleges from different universities in Oman. The survey was conducted when the academic staff returned to the university headquarters, aiming to gather their perspectives and satisfaction regarding their experience with distance education. It was important to capture their insights as they had been engaged in distance education for a minimum duration of one year, providing valuable feedback on the effectiveness and outcomes of this educational approach. The selection of participants was done randomly, ensuring a diverse representation. The research questionnaire was

142   Ibrahim Rashid Al Shamsi and Boumedyen Shannaq

Table 10.1 Demographic information about the participants

Female	Male	PHD	Master	Nationalities	Academic experience	Age
111	1003	677	437	> 16	2–17	25–57

distributed to all members of the study sample, and their responses were collected for analysis.

The chapter encompassed the examination of the following variables: Independent variables: gender, qualification, nationality, academic experience, and dependent variable: the perception of faculty members at the University of Al-Buraimi and their satisfaction with e-learning during the Corona pandemic. The study aimed to investigate how specific college affiliation of faculty members influenced their perception and satisfaction with e-learning during the challenging circumstances of the Corona pandemic. By exploring these variables, the research sought to gain valuable insights into the experiences and perspectives of faculty members in relation to the adoption and effectiveness of e-learning during this unprecedented time. The researchers from the College of Business at the University of Buraimi have initiated a survey research project which focused on the perception of academic staff regarding the transformation of the educational process in higher education during the COVID-19 pandemic in Oman.

The participants were requested to take part by completing the questionnaire, and their time and cooperation were sincerely appreciated. Table 10.1 provides an overview of the participants' demographic information.

Secondary Data

There were 53164 academic records related to the University of Buraimi from Fall 2017–2018 to Fall 2021–2022. The data set had 32 attributes. Figures 10.1 and 10.2 show the distribution of academic records in the study sample according to the variables:

```
Current relation
  Relation: Fall2017_2022DB                              Attributes: 32
  Instances: 53164                                       Sum of weights: 53164

DATASET NAME DataSet3 WINDOW=FRONT.
FREQUENCIES VARIABLES=AcademicSemester StudentID Sponsor Major Degree courseTitle scoreDistribution
    classwork_score Midterm_score FinalExamScore Total_100 Grade instructor_name GPA_Before GPA_After
    ENGLISH_LEVEL MATH_LEVEL IT_LEVEL SKILL_LEVEL EN_NATIONALITY GENDER STUDY_MODE
    MARITAL_STATUS PARENT_WORK_STATUS WILAYA HIGH_SCHOOL_CITY HIGH_SCHOOL_BRANCH
    HIGH_SCHOOL_YEAR HIGH_SCHOOL_SCORE CurrentStatus CurrentECH CurrentCGPA
/STATISTICS=STDDEV MINIMUM MAXIMUM SEMEAN
/ORDER=ANALYSIS.
```

Figure 10.1 Secondary data (attributes and instances number).

University of Buraimi in Oman 143

Academic_sem

		Frequency	Percent	Valid Percent	Cumulative Percent
Valid	Fall 2017–2018	4192	7.9	7.9	7.9
	Fall 2018–2019	4441	8.4	8.4	16.2
	Fall 2019–2020	4607	8.7	8.7	24.9
	Fall 2020–2021	4818	9.1	9.1	34.0
	Fall 2021–2022	4895	9.2	9.2	43.2
	Spring 2017–2018	4094	7.7	7.7	50.9
	Spring 2018–2019	4290	8.1	8.1	58.9
	Spring 2019–2020	4302	8.1	8.1	67.0
	Spring 2020–2021	5015	9.4	9.4	76.5
	Spring 2021–2022	4597	8.6	8.6	85.1
	Summer 2017–2018	1614	3.0	3.0	88.2
	Summer 2018–2019	1893	3.6	3.6	91.7
	Summer 2019–2020	2083	3.9	3.9	95.6
	Summer 2020–2021	2323	4.4	4.4	100.0
	Total	53164	100.0	100.0	

Figure 10.2 Secondary data distribution (semester based).

Research Tools

The research tool used in this study was a survey designed to explore the reality of distance education during the COVID-19 pandemic in Oman universities, specifically focusing on the perspectives of instructors. The survey was developed in the form of a Google questionnaire and distributed to the participants. The questionnaire was structured into four main areas to gather comprehensive data and insights. The first area focused on acquiring distance education skills and consisted of six sections. This section aimed to assess the level of proficiency and competence of instructors in utilising distance education tools and techniques. The second area of the questionnaire explored the attitudes of instructors towards distance education. It comprised five sections that aimed to gauge their perceptions, beliefs, and satisfaction regarding the effectiveness and suitability of distance education in the current circumstances.

The third area of inquiry was infrastructure and component availability, consisting of five sections. This section aimed to assess the accessibility and availability of necessary resources, such as internet connectivity, devices, learning platforms, and technical support, to facilitate effective distance education delivery. The fourth and final area of the questionnaire addressed the challenges of distance education. It encompassed six sections that aimed to identify the various obstacles, difficulties, and concerns faced by instructors during the transition to distance education.

To gather responses, a five-point Likert scale was employed, ranging from 1 to 5. The scale allowed participants to indicate their level of agreement

144 *Ibrahim Rashid Al Shamsi and Boumedyen Shannaq*

Table 10.2 Reliability of the research tool

	Variable numbers	Overall Cronbach alpha
Faculty members	22	.824

or disagreement with the statements presented in each section. A higher degree on the scale represented a stronger agreement, while a lower degree represented a stronger disagreement. By utilising this structured questionnaire with its four distinct areas, the research aimed to obtain detailed insights into the experiences, perspectives, and challenges faced by instructors in implementing distance education during the COVID-19 pandemic. The data collected through the survey would provide valuable information for analysing the current state of distance education in Oman universities and formulating effective strategies to address any identified shortcomings or areas for improvement.

To verify the apparent validity of the research tool, it was presented to several qualified and experienced specialists in order to judge the suitability of its content, clarity of language, the appropriateness of their number, and the extent of their representation to measure the reality of distance education during COVID-19 pandemic in Oman universities, among others. Table 10.2 describes the survey data reliability.

All values were acceptable under the significance level of 0.05, which means that there is an acceptable degree of internal consistency in the domain paragraphs on the scale.

The Consistency of the Study

To ensure the reliability and consistency of the research tool, a sample of 133 faculty members was selected. Three weeks after the initial data collection, the reliability coefficient of the survey was re-applied to this examining sample. The Pearson correlation coefficient was calculated to assess the consistency between their estimations. To further validate the stability of the research tool, the internal consistency method using Cronbach's alpha equation was employed, and its reliability coefficient was determined. The stability coefficients are presented in Table 10.3, demonstrating the robustness and consistency of the research tool.

Table 10.3 Survey stability coefficients

	Retest-test	Cronbach's alpha
Overall Faculty Members	0.940	0.957

University of Buraimi in Oman 145

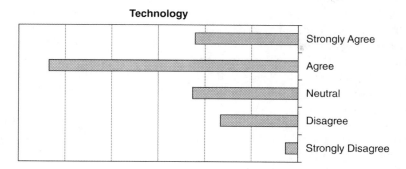

Figure 10.3 Survey results for technology effect.

Distance Education in Oman

This section presents the reality of distance education during COVID-19 pandemic in Oman universities considering the students and instructors' judgment. In Figure 10.3, the conclusion drawn from the study indicates that the use of technology in education is not without challenges. However, the majority of academic staff (84%) expressed agreement and satisfaction with the technological tools used during online learning. This positive perception highlights the effectiveness of the technology in supporting educational processes. On the other hand, a minority of instructors (16%) reported being dissatisfied with the technology. The instructors were given the opportunity to rate their level of satisfaction on a five-point scale, with options ranging from 1 (Strongly Disagree) to 5 (Strongly Agree). These findings emphasise the overall positive sentiment towards technology among academic staff, while acknowledging that there is room for improvement to address the concerns of the dissatisfied minority.

Based on the analysis of the delivery of course contents, shown in Figure 10.4, it was observed that a significant majority of instructors (86%) agreed with the use of course materials and found it easy to manage. This indicates that they

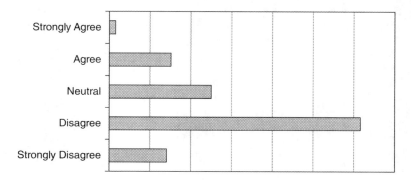

Figure 10.4 Survey results for delivery of course contents.

found the access to course content to be convenient, efficient, secure, and flexible for making changes and updates to the materials. However, a minority of instructors (14%) expressed disagreement with the use of course materials during online learning. These findings highlight the overall positive perception of instructors regarding the accessibility and manageability of course contents, while acknowledging the differing opinions and concerns of a small portion of instructors.

The concluding phase of the survey involved identifying the problems, challenges, and overall perceptions of the instructors regarding online learning amidst the COVID-19 pandemic. The questionnaire incorporated a self-assessment task where instructors were able to gauge their attitudes and level of satisfaction with the online learning experience. The respondents unanimously expressed that teaching online significantly differs from traditional in-person teaching. They highlighted challenges such as effective communication with students, difficulties in conveying information online, limited direct interaction between instructors and students, performance-related concerns, and various other challenges that are distinct to the online learning environment.

Figure 10.5 demonstrates that the participants exhibited a positive outlook regarding their knowledge and skills in utilising online learning during the COVID-19 pandemic, about 22% have very good experience in using online learning, 45% have good experience in using online learning, and 33% have poor experience in using online learning.

Figure 10.6 demonstrates the STD, AVG, and variance using 53164 academic records related to the University of Buraimi from Fall 2017–2018 to Fall 2021–2022.

The obtained results from the secondary data in Figure 10.6 show that the standard deviation for the student performances was smaller than the difference of the AVG (before COVID-19 and during COVID-19) only for the class work assessment. The performance of the students has improved significantly only for the class work assessment and remains stable for the midterm and final exam before and during pandemic. The analysis of the primary data is presented in

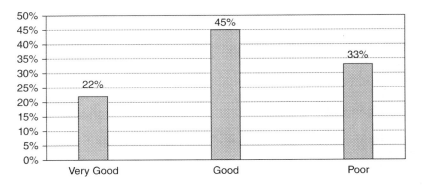

Figure 10.5 Experience of using e-learning tools.

University of Buraimi in Oman 147

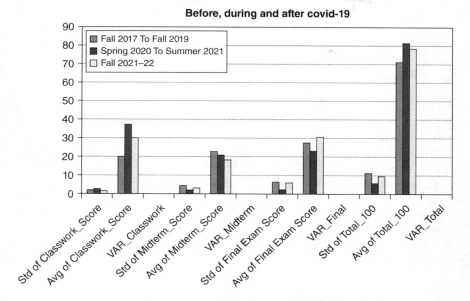

Figure 10.6 Statistical results from Fall 2017–2018 to Fall 2021–2022.

sections 5, 6, and 7. Each section describes the direction of the entity (Student, Instructor, Academic process), the challenges, and the initiatives extracted from the learned lessons before and during the pandemic of COVID-19.

Initiatives to Support Instructors' Development in New Conditions

The development of instructor competencies has become the task of many academic leadership programmes, such as the Qedex project, the Staff Professional Development Committee and research universities, and the instructor education modernisation programme. However, many challenges in this area continue to be relevant, and the weak readiness of instructors to change and work in the digital environment is one of the fundamental ones.

To overcome such challenges, a number of activities were formulated as part of conferences, webinars, workshops, and a survey of decision-makers in Oman universities.. The University of Buraimi has developed a template form specifically designed for every employee of the university. This form is to be completed by each employee at the beginning of each academic year. The form serves as a comprehensive tool for gathering essential information related to personal activities, research endeavours, and the participation in workshops and training sessions aimed at enhancing their expertise in various academic domains. This form enables employees to provide a structured overview of their professional commitments and aspirations, facilitating effective planning and resource allocation within the university. As part of its initiatives for professional development and growth, the University of Buraimi has introduced a mandatory requirement for all academic staff members to enrol in the Qedex programmes. These programmes are specifically designed to enhance their professional skills and provide valuable learning opportunities. As part of their participation, academic staff are encouraged to engage in various workshops and activities organised by the Qedex programme. This proactive approach by the university ensures that faculty members have access to valuable training and developmental opportunities, further contributing to their knowledge and expertise in their respective fields.

The University of Buraimi actively organises both local and international conferences, webinars, and workshops with the aim of gathering diverse experiences from various institutions to address the challenges posed by the pandemic. These events serve as platforms for sharing knowledge, best practices, and innovative solutions to overcome the difficulties faced in the academic community. The instructors' survey results during several months of remote work in the context of the coronavirus pandemic more accurately showed the existing problem areas:

Challenge 1: Unpreparedness/Rejection to Use New Technologies

During the pandemic, one of the most significant shortages is the refusal/unpreparedness of some university/colleges' instructors to use modern educational technologies. These technologies include both e-learning tools and new pedagogical practices, according to National Strategy for Education (2040, 2020).

Figure 10.7 depicts the challenges and unpreparedness/rejection in adopting new technologies among a sample of 12 universities/colleges. The results

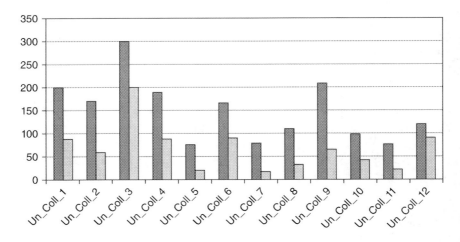

Figure 10.7 Position of use new technologies.

show that 68% of the instructors rarely or never taught or implemented classes in electronic or webinar formats (indicated by the red column). On the other hand, 32% of the instructors were prepared and willing to teach and implement classes in electronic or webinar formats (indicated by the green column).

Challenge 2: Methodological Shortage

The methodological shortage covers the lack of knowledge and practice in incorporating online formats and tools in the implementation of educational courses and programmes. Such an integrated approach requires instructors to both master new technical means and tools, as well as mastering new professional settings. Among them are:

- The ability to organise regular feedback, both during online classes and throughout the course.
- The ability to apply modern methods of online assessment to conduct intermediate and final attestations.
- The use of active learning strategies focused on the practical activities of students along with the acquisition of fundamental knowledge, allowing optimising the number of passive interaction formats focused on "reading" educational material.
- Readiness/Willingness to involve students in interactive activities during online classes, attention management.
- Readiness/Willingness to regularly and systematically update the content of educational programmes. The growth of accessibility for students of new research, publications, and materials in open internet sources also requires the instructor to constantly update the teaching materials of the course.

Challenge 3: Technical and Technological Shortages

Technical and technological shortages are primarily associated with a low level of digital literacy. Some instructors do not know (or do not know enough). Unfamiliarity and non-use of technologies in the following areas can be striking manifestations of such unpreparedness:

- Technologies for organising and conducting online classes using both university learning management system (LMS) and third-party electronic services;
- Technologies for communication, support, and accompaniment of students using instant messengers, social networks, and services for joint work with documents;
- Digital tools for designing and preparing electronic content for interactive online classes and independent work of students.

The lack of online tools' integration in educational programmes is influenced by factors such as outdated course content and the gap between

150 *Ibrahim Rashid Al Shamsi and Boumedyen Shannaq*

research and educational activities, leading to decreased instructor motivation. Survey results show that a significant proportion of students (66%) reported that instructors in their universities/colleges partially or fully translated course materials into the LMS, facilitating remote learning and ensuring accessibility. This integration reflects the commitment of institutions to provide a seamless online learning experience. However, a considerable percentage of instructors (77%) expressed uncertainty about distance learning, attributed to sudden shifts, limited training, and challenges in adapting teaching methods to the virtual environment. To address this, providing professional development opportunities, training workshops, and ongoing guidance is essential to enhance instructor confidence and proficiency in distance learning.

Additionally, a significant number of instructors (39%) believe that the transition to an electronic format contributes to a decline in the quality of higher education. Offering comprehensive training programmes focused on effective online teaching methodologies, instructional design, and interactive technologies can help overcome perceived limitations and ensure high-quality education. Continuous feedback, assessment, and improvement strategies are necessary to enhance online education quality.

While a majority of instructors (74%) express scepticism about most classes being conducted online, it is crucial to acknowledge their concerns and foster dialogue between instructors, administrators, and stakeholders. Implementing a blended learning approach and providing comprehensive training on technology integration can strike a balance between in-person and online instruction, meeting the needs of both instructors and students. Overall, addressing concerns, providing support, and promoting dialogue can empower instructors and ensure a confident and flexible approach to the future of education.

Challenge 4: Instructor Support

At the same time, the experience of the past year has shown that the academic system can still function in a new mode, both in terms of organising the management of universities/colleges and in terms of implementing the educational process. The shortcomings of competencies described above are recognised by the administration and instructors. Universities/colleges have made serious efforts to adapt teaching staff. In total, 53.2% of instructors have completed courses on online learning in recent months, although 87.8% of instructors say that their classes can still improve if carried out face to face.

These efforts have had positive results. Research carried out during the transition to e-learning indicate that many universities\colleges have organised a special support system for instructors. Websites and other ICT tools have been created with specific sections for informing and helping instructors, and online communication with them through instant messengers has been organised. Thus, with a general constructive attitude and the actual possibility of mobilising and introducing digital technologies into the educational process, some instructors remain careful, partly pessimistic.

University of Buraimi in Oman 151

Despite the transition to online teaching, a notable portion of the teaching staff still lacks preparedness for the long-term integration of online tools and technologies into educational programmes. The forced use of e-learning, on the one hand, expands the possibilities updating the higher education system, but, on the other hand, in the event of a decrease in the activity of the regulator and the leadership of universities, it creates risks of a quick rollback of the system or even increased opposition to mastering digital tools and practices.

According to the survey findings, a significant majority of instructors (92%) expressed their satisfaction with the measures implemented by their educational institutions to support the transition to online learning. This indicates that the institutions have made significant efforts to provide the necessary resources, training, and support for instructors to effectively navigate the challenges posed by the transition. The high level of satisfaction suggests that instructors feel adequately equipped to deliver their courses in the online environment. However, it is essential for institutions to continue assessing and addressing the evolving needs of instructors, offering ongoing support, and refining their strategies to ensure a seamless transition to online learning. By consistently evaluating and enhancing their measures, institutions can ensure that instructors have the tools and support required to deliver high-quality education in the online format and maintain student engagement and learning outcomes.

Based on the survey results, a substantial majority of instructors (89%) reported a successful transition to electronic work format during the pandemic. This high percentage suggests that instructors were able to adapt to the challenges brought about by the sudden shift to remote teaching and learning. Their ability to switch to electronic work highlights their resilience, flexibility, and willingness to embrace new technologies and methodologies. This successful transition is a testament to the dedication and efforts of instructors in ensuring the continuity of education amidst unprecedented circumstances. Moving forward, it is crucial for institutions to continue supporting instructors in their ongoing professional development, providing resources and training to further enhance their digital teaching skills. By leveraging the lessons learned from this experience, instructors can continue to deliver effective and engaging electronic work, enabling students to receive a quality education regardless of the circumstances.

Proposed Initiatives and Solutions from Learned Lessons (Instructors)

The past year has delivered university instructors with valuable hands-on experience in e-learning. This transition presents a space of chance to address existing shortages. Strategic and systemic solutions are necessary to consolidate and change the education system in the long term. Decision-making covers both short-term and long-term perspectives at the supervisor and university levels, as well as national regulations. Developing a comprehensive strategic and operational plan is crucial for leveraging lessons learned from the COVID-19 pandemic. This plan should address technological infrastructure, professional development, pedagogical approaches, and student support services. By focusing on these areas, institutions can ensure a smooth transition to online learning and maintain the quality of education (Figure 10.8).

This work is also developing national and Gulf region initiatives in the form of strategic and operational plans based on instructor perspectives. These plans aim to address the challenges posed by the COVID-19 pandemic on the education systems in Oman. By gathering insights and experiences from instructors from the survey, these initiatives seek to provide effective strategies and solutions to overcome the impact of the pandemic on education. The goal is to develop comprehensive plans that can enhance the resilience and adaptability of educational institutions, ensuring the continuity and quality of education in Oman and the wider Gulf region. Figure 10.9 shows the proposed initiatives.

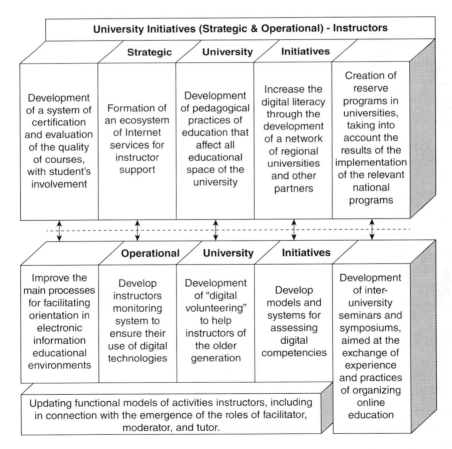

Figure 10.8 Comprehensive strategic and operational plan: Leveraging lessons learned from instructors' perspectives.

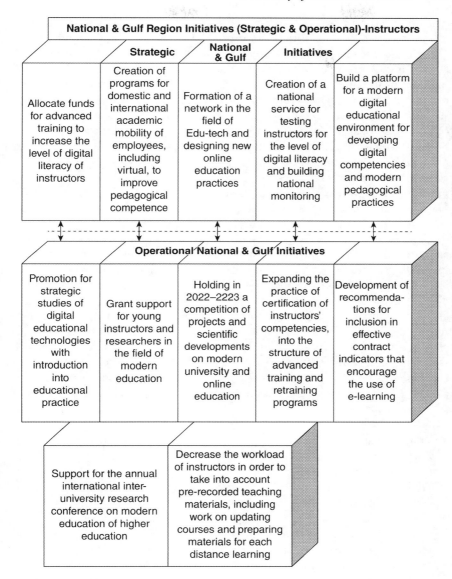

Figure 10.9 National and Gulf region initiatives in the form of strategic and operational plans based on instructor perspectives.

Implications on the Ramifications of COVID-19 Pandemic to Gulf Higher Education

In Oman, e-education has primarily motivated on providing online courses, leading to restricted development in online teaching practices. However, the crisis revealed that existing online courses were insufficient for effective e-learning in universities. This prompted university to transition to online education, which opened up new opportunities for multi-channel pedagogical communication. However, this transition also exposed a shortage of proven unified educational methods in digital pedagogy. University professors had to rely on trial and error or borrow techniques from practitioners in related fields. Traditional methods of attention management, student work organisation, and current control needed significant revision in the online teaching environment. Motivating students became a crucial task for instructors, as it directly impacted the quality of the educational process. The study concludes that universities lack systematic tools to work with student motivation. The pandemic crisis highlighted the barriers and limitations of existing educational models, methodologies, and didactic approaches in universities. Universities need to be more flexible in addressing individual student needs and focusing on competency development rather than knowledge transmission. Additionally, there is a critical need for high-quality content to combat the rapid obsolescence of educational models.

The researchers from the College of Business at the University of Buraimi are currently engaged in developing a smart tool aimed at optimising e-learning systems. The project, currently in its alpha version, is titled TAER-Project and can be accessed via the following link: [https://taerproject.com/]. The TAER-Project is an innovative platform that offers live and intelligent automated services through a web-based academic robot. This cutting-edge technology aims to enhance knowledge transfer and foster innovation in an interactive manner, utilising machine learning algorithms. Users can engage with the platform through text or voice inputs, and the TAER-Project will identify their interests and provide guidance to access the required information.

The TAER-Project holds the potential to address the following key areas of strategic growth:

- Transformation of educational programmes to create an environment conducive to new educational formats and practices that enhance class interactivity and student engagement.
- Development of digital infrastructure, including educational platforms, content, and services for students and staff.
- Focus on personnel development, promoting advanced digital literacy among instructors and incorporating modern educational practices and technologies to facilitate online and blended learning models.
- Implementation of management models that embrace distributed and collective management approaches, such as supervisory and management boards, and flexible project-based methods for university administration.
- Review and revision of regulatory models pertaining to control and supervision activities.
- Support for research and projects focused on the development of digital didactics, encompassing the utilisation of digital tools and technologies, as well as the implementation of new teaching methodologies through integrated models that combine online and offline formats.
- Encouragement of remote research collaborations and communities, including active participation in international interactions, fostering the

integration of domestic researchers into the global academic agenda through joint publications, collaborative projects, and events.

- Establishment of a comprehensive support system for students within the context of blended learning models, aiming to address inequality and enhance the accessibility of education. This includes exploring innovative financial, technical, and methodological approaches to organise the educational process effectively.

Conclusion

The outbreak of the novel coronavirus pandemic has caused a significant upheaval in the higher education system, both in the Sultanate of Oman and in other countries. Virtually, all universities have undergone a rapid transition to a new mode of operation. Notably, the development of new online educational formats has emerged as one of the prominent areas in response to these unprecedented circumstances. Nevertheless, numerous other areas necessitated swift reassessment, including student communication and engagement, research endeavours, collaboration among research teams, campus infrastructure, administrative processes, and overall university management. These aspects of university life underwent rapid transformations, posing a genuine test of efficiency and adaptability for the majority of HEIs. The pandemic has presented an immediate and pressing agenda of challenges for the advancement of all aspects of university life. On the one hand, pre-existing issues have become more apparent, while, on the other hand, tasks that were once perceived as distant future milestones have now become immediate realities. Previously, universities could prioritise operational matters and delay digital, educational, research, and innovative transformations to a later stage. However, during and after the pandemic, there is an undeniable need for comprehensive and systemic change. It is important to emphasise that the list of strategic growth points is not exhaustive and extends beyond the mentioned ones. To effectively implement these directions of systemic development, Gulf higher education systems could establish a comprehensive policy for the advancement of the entire network of higher educational institutions. The potential of such a network has the capability to take a leading role not only in world-class research but also in driving the territorial development of regional economies.

References

Abdalellah O. Mohmmed, Basim A. Khidhir, Abdul Nazeer, & Vigil J. Vijayan. (2020). "Emergency remote teaching during Coronavirus pandemic: the current trend and future directive at Middle East College Oman". *Innovative Infrastructure Solutions*, 5(72). https://doi.org/10.1007/s41062-020-00326-7

Abushammala, M., Qazi, W., & Manchiryal, R. (2021). The impact of COVID-19 on the private higher education system and students in Oman. *Journal of University Teaching & Learning Practice*, *18*(3). https://ro.uow.edu.au/jutlp/vol18/iss3/; https://doi.org/10.53761/1.18.3.13

Al Khalili, S., AlMaani, A., AlWahaibi, A., AlYaquobi, F., Al-Jardani, A., AlHarthi, K., Alqayoudhi, A., Al Manji, A., AlRawahi, B., & Al-Abri, S. (2021). Challenges and opportunities for public health service in Oman from the COVID-19 pandemic: Learning lessons for a better future. *Frontiers in Public Health, 9*, 770946. https://doi.org/10.3389/fpubh.2021.770946

Al-Maskari, A., Al Riyami, T., & Kunjumuhammed, S. (2021). Challenges faced by students during COVID-19 in higher education institutions in the sultanate of Oman. *International Journal of Information Technology and Language Studies, 5*(3), pp. 34–46. https://journals.sfu.ca/ijitls/index.php/ijitls/article/view/259

Al-Saidi, A. (2020). Sultanate of Oman preparedness and response to Covid19 pandemic. https://apps.who.int/gb/COVID-19/pdf_files/11_06/Oman.pdf

Al Shamsi, I., & Shannaq, B. (2020). Predictive management model- the leading business model with the coronavirus (COVID-19) epidemic. *International Journal of Advanced Science and Technology, 29*(3), 14975. http://sersc.org/journals/index.php/IJAST/article/view/31999

Al-Zaabi, H. K. (2021). Covid-19 and education in Oman. *International Journal of English Language Teaching, 9*(3), 35–39. https://www.eajournals.org/wp-content/uploads/COVID-19-and-Education-in-Oman.pdf

Malik, M., & Javed, S. (2021). Perceived stress among university students in Oman during COVID-19-induced eLearning. *Middle East Current Psychiatry, 28*, 49. https://doi.org/10.1186/s43045-021-00131-7

Mohamed, A. H. H. M., Abdel Fattah, F. A. M., Bashir, M. I. A., Alhajri, M., Khanan, A., & Abbas, Z. (2021). Investigating the acceptance of distance learning amongst Omani students: A case study from Oman. *Global Knowledge, Memory and Communication, 71*(6/7), 529–545. https://doi.org/10.1108/GKMC-02-2021-0021

Mohmmed, A. O., Khidhir, B. A., & Nazeer, A. (2020). Emergency remote teaching during coronavirus pandemic: The current trend and future directive at Middle East College Oman. *Innovative Infrastructure Solutions,, 5*, 72. https://doi.org/10.1007/s41062-020-00326-7

Mustafa, Malik M., & Javed S. (2021). Perceived stress among university students in Oman during COVID-19-induced elearning. *Middle East Current Psychiatry, 28*, 49. https://doi.org/10.1186/s43045-021-00131-7

National Strategy for Education 2040. (2020). https://www.educouncil.gov.om/downloads/Ts775SPNmXDQ.pdf

Omanuna. (2020). *Oman portal service.* https://www.oman.om/wps/portal/index/covid19

Osman, M. E. (2020). Global impact of COVID-19 on education systems: The emergency remote teaching at Sultan Qaboos University. *Journal of Education for Teaching, 46*(4), 463–471. https://doi.org/10.1080/02607476.2020.1802583

Shannaq, B., & Al Shamsi, I. (2019). Innovative web service for streaming student tweeting in real-time technology. *International Journal of Innovative Technology and Exploring Engineering (IJITEE), 9*(2), 2278–3075. https://www.ijitee.org/wp-content/uploads/papers/v9i2/B7306129219.pdf

Shannaq, B., & Al Shamsi, I. (2020). Automation the search processing E-learning using relational visual query and associative rules. *International Journal of Advanced Science and Technology, 29*(4), 9778. http://sersc.org/journals/index.php/IJAST/article/view/33003

11 The Role of Internal Crisis Communication on Faculty Members Implementation of Blended Learning Practices in the Gulf

Ridwan Adetunji Raji and Bahtiar Mohamad

Introduction

Immediately COVID-19 was officially pronounced as a pandemic crisis in 2020 and its impact became apparent in every work of life, higher educational learning and teaching soon became virtual and digitalised. In other words, COVID-19 prompted a sudden and broad change in the learning and teaching modalities of higher educational systems. This meant that both instructors and learners had to adopt some forms of digital learning with little preparedness or no digital pedagogical training. Meanwhile, the digitalisation of the learning and teaching process in many Gulf Cooperation Council (GCC) states was particularly complicated. According to Bystrov (2021), educational regulators and administrators across the region had been reluctant towards institutionalising and investing in the full digitalisation of learning systems prior to COVID-19. As such, when digital learning and blended learning (BL) became a do-or-die options during the pandemic, it was not completely surprising that the sudden transition was laden with a series of managerial and organisational challenges. Chiefly among these problems are issues related faculty's readiness and preparedness for teaching, grading, and timely virtual communication with their students (Clyde & Co., 2020). However, as the COVID-19 crisis continues to subside, and social distancing restrictions are being raised in many GCC states, the digitalisation imposed by the pandemic is continually encouraged either in the form of full online learning or BL methods (Oxford Business Group, 2020).

Several studies have revealed that BL positively enhances the teaching process, learning engagement, and environment of both teachers and learners (Anthony, 2021; Anthony et al., 2019; Graham et al., 2013). Additionally, Carbonell et al. (2013) reported that BL is a prudent approach to learning which incorporates flexibility and interactivity in to learning and teaching methods. However, other research findings (Anthony, 2021; Dakduk et al., 2018) have also bemoaned the technical, instructional, and organisational issues related to

DOI: 10.4324/9781003457299-14

158   *Ridwan Adetunji Raji and Bahtiar Mohamad*

BL implementation. On the one hand, the implementation of BL can be challenging, especially considering the monumental changes impacted upon the overall learning environment within the BL modalities. On the other hand, implementing BL requires a bifurcated effort of faculty in both online and offline environments (Carbonell et al., 2013; Graham et al., 2013). There is also a necessitated need for revamping learning contents and activities to suit the BL process. In other words, in addition to the invaluable opportunities that are offered to faculty within BL mode, the implementation of BL comes with added responsibilities for faculty who will have to adjust their teaching styles, materials, and instructional roles to fit the BL environment. As such, faculty members might be naturally unwilling and/or apprehensive about the idea of implementing BL during the COVID-19 pandemic. Thus, creating a gap in the communication behaviour and commitment of faculty members towards BL implementation.

Meanwhile, managing change and crises depends on effective leadership and management initiatives (Black, 2015). As such, implementing an internal crisis communication (ICC) initiative will go a long way to mitigate the communication gap that the sudden change might have caused between university administrators and faculty members and alleviate any form of ambiguity towards the successful implementation of BL during the COVID-19 crisis (Adamu & Mohamad, 2019; Kim, 2018). More so, ICC can also be used to build a positive reaction and favourable outcome towards a crisis (Mazzei et al., 2012). In other words, a successful transition towards digitalisation and BL adoption in GCC's higher educational institutions (HEIs), especially under the lingering COVID-19 circumstance, is heavily dependent on universities' management and educational regulators' understanding of ICC factors in building a positive relationships and effective communication in sustaining faculty's adaptability, allaying their apprehensions, and enhancing their willingness and attitude towards embracing BL (Calonge et al., 2021). However, there is a dearth of study on the parameters of an ICC model that can guide educational administrators and regulators towards communicating the importance of BL and enhancing faculty's commitment and willingness.

Notably, previous studies have also suggested that in the face of a crisis, an effective ICC initiative would not only be crucial to influence employees' perception of an expected coping mechanism and operational changes, but they could also be converted into "change ambassadors" who can be instrumental in successful change implementation (Adamu & Mohamad, 2019; Frandsen & Johansen, 2011; Mazzei & Ravazzani, 2015). To put that in context, there is a possibility of faculty members embracing BL for themselves and becoming self-appraised ambassadors who can encourage and persuade their colleagues and students on the importance of using BL to cope with the COVID-19 situation, when they are properly incorporated within the organisational ICC framework (Sanders et al., 2020). Additionally, Johansen et al. (2012) and Kim (2018) emphasised that managerial communication initiatives are crucial to employees' understanding of ICC dynamism during a given crisis.

The Role of Internal Crisis Communication   159

However, there have been relatively few studies focusing on the factors that can influence faculty members' understanding of university management and regulators' ICC initiative towards implementing BL as the coping mechanism during the COVID-19 crisis (Calonge et al., 2021). In line with the strategic communication prism, this study investigates the factors that enhance ICC and their impact on faculty members' perception and attitude towards implementing BL during the COVID-19 pandemic. Relying on the literature on strategic crisis management and crisis communication, this study examines the factors (university support, technological support, supportive environment, and university management commitment) that ICC of BL. Also, the study examines the influence of ICC on faculty members' crisis perception and their affective commitment towards BL implementation. Therefore, this present study develops a strategic model of ICC of BL implementation among faculty from HEIs in the GCC. This research findings offer significant insights to university administrators and educational regulators in the GCC region towards initiating effective ICC for faculty implementation of BL.

Implementation of BL during Pandemic in the GCC

Undoubtedly, one of the long-lasting impacts of COVID-19 on the global higher educational systems would be the pervasiveness of digital learning. Specifically, in the GCC, virtual learning was widely adopted as a major reaction to the COVID-19 pandemic to reduce the detriment of the COVID-19 on learning progression and ultimately to prevent the spread of the virus in university communities. Many universities in the GCC shifted classes and other educational services to online, in just several days. Meanwhile, more recently, as restrictions are being lifted and the COVID-19 situations appear to be increasingly subsided, there is an increasing interest in the hybrid form of learning and teaching. Partly because the virus was not totally eradicated, thus, the number of attendees at any given social gathering is being monitored and restrictively low. The BL modality is highly encouraged in that, classes with huge numbers of student enrollments and classes that are not practical-oriented are conducted online while some other classes are conducted physically (Ashour, 2021). Thanks to the huge number of investments that were immediately directed towards different learning technologies, there seems to be relatively sufficient technical resources in the gulf for the continuous adoption of BL among HEIs. For example, The Qatar Foundation for Education, Science and Community invested in various learning software and trainings that aided the digitalisation of learning in Qatar. Similarly, the Kuwait Foundation for the Advancement of Sciences also rose to the occasion by providing resources for the successful adoption of BL in Kuwait. In the UAE and specifically in the emirate of Sharjah, an e-platform was quickly established to conduct a series of digital trainings for teachers to carry out digital learning by the Sharjah Private Education Authority. This was in addition to forming a committee for monitoring and evaluating the digital learning transition. The effort of the Saudi Arabian government on the full digitalisation of learning during the COVID-19 was big enough to earn UNESCO commendations (Oxford Business Group, 2020). Ashour (2021), many universities in the UAE and by extension most of the higher educational universities in the GCC are originally equipped with virtual classroom technologies, teleconferencing tools, and virtual exam proctoring resources and thus, capable of anchoring the prompt required digitalisation of learning.

Proposed Theoretical Framework and Hypotheses Development

The proposed model in Figure 11.1 relies on the literature of crisis communication to determine the connection between ICC strategies on faculty members' crisis perception, perceived technological support, university support, and their commitment towards the implementation of BL in the face of the COVID-19 crisis. Specifically, the framework conforms to the situational crisis communication to develop the connections between ICC and faculty members' perception of crisis, supports, and commitment towards the adoption of BL during the COVID-19 crisis. The situational crisis communication theory asserts that during the occurrence of a crisis, the communication strategies adopted by the organisation will impact stakeholders' sense-making, responsibilities, and interactions towards the necessitated operational changes (Coombs, 2007; Coombs & Holladay, 2002; Holdsworth et al., 2014; Mohamad et al., 2022). According to the theoretical proponents of Situational Crisis Communication Theory, university administrators are expected to improve their communication strategies and initiatives with their stakeholders during crisis situations (Arpan & Roskons-Ewoldsen, 2005; Quiroz Flores

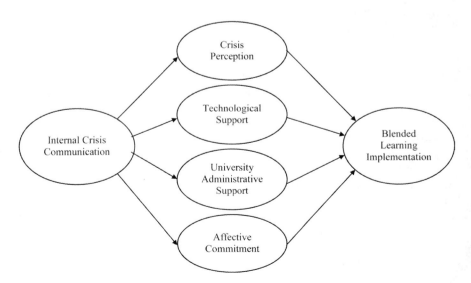

Figure 11.1 Proposed theoretical model.

The Role of Internal Crisis Communication   161

et al., 2021). In order words, communication during a crisis is crucial for managing the detriments of the crisis on the organisation (Coombs, 2015; Huang & DiStaso, 2020; Quiroz Flores et al., 2021). Therefore, the proposed framework examines the relationships between ICC and faculty member's crisis perception, perceived technological support, university administrative support, affective commitment, and BL implementation during the COVID-19 crisis. Other studies have also demonstrated that, the sooner an organisation created a communication pathway for engaging with stakeholders on the strategic management of a crisis, the sooner the situation is perceived a crisis by the stakeholders. Without stakeholders understanding, they are likely not interested in taking immediate strategic management actions (Coombs, 1999; Penrose, 2000). Based on this argument, it is proposed that, ICC during the COVID-19 crisis will justify faculty members understanding of implementing BL as an alternative means of surviving during the COVID-19 crisis.

Hypothesis 1: ICC will significantly influence faculty members' perceived crisis perception

The study conducted by Adamu and Mohamad (2019) among practitioners in the Malaysian oil industry revealed that ICC influences stakeholders' perception of support towards adopting the necessitated changes that come with any given crisis. The implication of their assertion is that employees need to be communicated and clearly informed on the available administrative supports to implement the organizational strategic management of the crisis. A significant level of standard ICC in an organisation will yield an appreciable positive effect on the employees' intentions towards other people and, on the other hand, aid the progress of employees career (Adamu & Mohamad, 2019; Eisenberger et al., 1990). Also, Korn and Einwiller (2013) established that, employees who are very knowledgeable on conditions and circumstances revolving around a crisis will be fully confident in the organisational proposed strategies and approach of managing the situation. According to Adamu and Mohamad (2019), one of the key importance of establishing internal communication during a crisis is to assure employees of the support that organisations are willing to provide towards mitigating the impact of a crisis on organisational performance. As such, university administrators are expected to provide clear and effective communication with faculty members of the available administrative support on BL implementation. Therefore, the following hypothesis is proposed:

Hypothesis 2: ICC will significantly influence faculty members' perceived university administrative support

In the same vein, the university management might be surcharging itself if their investment were not well incorporated within their ICC contents. The digitalization of learning and BL requires a significant level of digital

162   *Ridwan Adetunji Raji and Bahtiar Mohamad*

readiness in the sense of technological availability and digital literacy training for the faculty members. As such, for BL to be successfully implemented, faculty members are expected to have positive perceptions and a considerably high confidence in the feasibility of digital learning modalities (Ahmed & Opoku, 2022). This is because, BL is a platform-based learning, and being that the adoption of BL becomes a rescue for educational learning against the disruption caused by COVID-19. More so, the perception of digital preparedness and digital literacy is expected to affect faculty members' confidence on BL (Doucet et al., 2020; Hillman et al., 2021; Scully et al., 2021). Additionally, Calonge et al. (2021) argued that communication during a crisis like COVID-19 is key for shaping faculty member's perceptions of the availability of enabling technologies such as virtual classrooms, learning management systems, and digital literacy training, faculty members towards the implementation of BL. Therefore, the following hypothesis is proposed:

Hypothesis 3: ICC will significantly influence faculty members perceived technological support

One of the major ways that organisational crisis affects an organisation is by dampening the morale of employees and stakeholders alike (Jin & Pang, 2010). In other words, employees naturally respond to a looming crisis with negative emotions such as anger, anxiety, and apathy towards their job responsibilities. As such, during a crisis as detrimental to employees health and job performance as COVID-19, it is expected that, faculty might lose their sense of commitment and motivation towards continuous teaching and especially implementing a BL modality for teaching. Kim et al. (2019) asserted that when information related to crisis is disseminated in a timely and clear manner, employees' sense of commitment towards crisis response will be significantly influenced. Coombs (2015) also demonstrated that, employee's commitment to crisis response in terms of their duties and job responsibilities is significantly related to their level of understanding of the crisis facing the organisation. Similarly, Adamu and Mohamad (2019) revealed a direct correlation between ICC and the emotional attachment of employees in the petroleum industry. As such, the essence of establishing an effective communication channel during a crisis is not only to provide a basic explanation of the situation and introduce possible changes, but it should also serve as a strategic tool for allaying stakeholder's fears and anxiety towards the future (Heide & Simonsson 2019). As such, the following hypothesis is developed

Hypothesis 4: ICC will significantly influence faculty members perceived affective commitment

Calonge et al. (2021) concluded that the importance of crisis communication during COVID-19 is mainly to communicate and engage stakeholders with empathy, emotional, and clear messages to shape their understanding positively towards the necessitated changes and responses to the crisis. As

The Role of Internal Crisis Communication   163

such, when HEIs have an efficient communication plan to accurately and frequently communicate the complexity revolving around BL implementation, stakeholders and especially faculty members will be better ready and committed towards implementing BL (Sanders et al., 2020). In other words, establishing effective clear communication during the crisis will help enhance faculty members' positive perception and attitude towards implementing BL. Following this, the hypothesis below is developed:

Hypothesis 5: Faculty members perceived crisis perception will significantly influence their BL implementation

Another crucial benefit of crisis communication is to affirm organisational and administrative support among employees (Mohamad et al., 2022). In the context of BL implementation during COVID-19, university administrators are expected to clearly inform and establish communication channel and contents that provide feedbacks and communicative supports that the university have invested in towards implementing BL during COVID-19 (Chesser et al., 2020; Liang & Jiang, 2017). Having faculty members well informed on the available administrative supports is expected to motivate them towards implementing BL. Therefore, the following hypothesis is proposed:

Hypothesis 6: Faculty members perceived university administrative support will significantly influence their BL implementation

Given that the sudden migration towards BL is situationally related to the COVID-19 crisis. This evidently created some unprecedented challenges to both university administers and faculty members who are a significant stakeholder towards the successful adoption of BL (Ferdig et al., 2020; Howard et al., 2020). The challenges revolving around BL can be technological, pedagogical, and psychological (Ahmed & Opoku, 2022). Meanwhile, the adoption of BL relies heavily on digital availability, preparedness, and pedagogical adjustments (Gurley, 2018). Given that, perception shapes the reality. As such, regardless of how much investment or preparedness the university administrators have advanced towards their digital preparedness and digital literacy, faculty members might still feel unready and digitally illiterate towards the implementation of BL during the COVID-19 crisis (Fedynich et al., 2015). Therefore, the following hypothesis is proposed:

Hypothesis 7: Faculty members perceived technological support will significantly influence their BL implementation

Previous studies on ICC have empirically affirmed that, employees respond to crisis cognitively, affectively, and behaviourally (Adamu & Mohamad, 2019; Frandsen & Johansen, 2011). These studies show that commitment as a physiological state is an index of employees' motivation and commitment towards the necessitated operational changes and crisis response (Meyer & Allen, 1991). In this regard, Meyer et al. (2004) stated three perspectives namely, affective, normative and continuance of employees' commitments towards crisis responses. However, Solinger et al. (2008) elaborated that, emotional attachment relates with employees' sense of identification and attachment with organisational changes during crisis. Meyer et al. (2006) also demonstrated that emotional attachment is of a significant influence on employees' workplace behaviour, performance, organisational citizenship, and organisational advocacy. Therefore, when faculty members are committed towards BL as a mechanism for managing teaching during COVID-19, they are expected to implement and advocate BL to their colleagues. As such, the following hypothesis is proposed:

Hypothesis 8: Faculty members perceived affective commitment will significantly influence their BL implementation

Demographic Profile of Respondents

This study was conducted among faculty members in various universities in the GCC including UAE, Saudi Arabia, Kuwait, Qatar, Bahrain, and Oman. According to Lovell et al. (2022), the necessitated shift to BL is at the mercy of faculty members who are the actual implementers of the policies and pedagogical adjustments required for the successful implementation BL. Therefore, the internal crisis communicative factors that affect the implementation are best understood from the perspectives of faculty members. As such, respondents in this study were selected among faculty members who have had to adopt BL as a coping mechanism in various universities and colleges within the GCC countries. The research survey was developed through the Qualtrics XM and distributed using the snowball sampling techniques. In other words, the survey links was distributed through various social groups, LinkedIn, and different social connections. In total, 198 faculty members responded to the research survey. A total of seven surveys were considered unusable due to excessive missing data and those who have not implemented any form of BL were excluded from the study. Regarding the demographic details of the respondents, the majority (72.3%) of them are aged between 41 and 50 years old, 19.9% of them are between the ages of 31 to 40 years old, and only 7.9% are above 51 years old. In terms of the respondents' gender distribution, 56% are male and 44% are female. Unsurprisingly, majority of them (70.7%) hold a PhD degree, followed by 20.9% who are master's degree holders and only 8.4% have only a bachelor's degree as their highest level of education. Finally, the respondent in this study works at different universities across GCC states including, (Zayed University, United Arab Emirates University, Khalifa University, Canadian University, Dubai, American University, UAE, Fujairah University, HCT) from the UAE, (King Fahd University, Hafr Al Batin University) Saudi Arabia, (Bahrain University) Bahrain, Kuwait and (UTAS Ibri-CAS, Military Technology College) Oman.

Measurement and Instrumentation

To measure the variables included in the proposed theoretical framework, measurements were adapted to measure the variables of the study. Specifically, 7 items were adapted from Adamu and Mohamad (2019) to measure ICC. The sample items for the construct include "My university/college management has informed me on implementing blended learning practices during the Covid-19 pandemic"; "I feel it easy to communicate issues related to implementing blended learning to the top management during the Covid-19 pandemic"; and "I understand that my university/college has a crisis management plan for issues related to blended learning practices during the Covid-19 pandemic". Six items were adapted from Kim and Grunig (2011) and Adamu and Mohamad (2019) to measure crisis perception. The sample item samples are "I believe blended learning practices are essential for my university/college to survive teaching during COVID-19 pandemic"; "I believe faculty members in my university/college need to pay more attention to blended learning practices because of the COVID-19 pandemic"; and "I know that the COVID-19 pandemic affects my teaching substantially". As for technological support, 5 items were adapted from Anthony (2021). Items for measuring this variable include "System applications for blended learning course development are provided"; "Collaborative web-based teaching tools and software are provided to implement blended learning"; and "Additional devices needed for implementing blended learning are provided". Additionally, university administrative support was measured with 8 items adapted from Adamu and Mohamad (2019). The sample statements include "My university/college cares about my opinions related to implementing blended learning practices"; "My university/college cares about my comfort regarding the implementation of blended learning"; and "My university/college strongly consider my goals and values in its blended learning policies". Furthermore, affective commitment was measured with seven items adapted from Adamu and Mohamad (2019). The sample statement includes "I enjoy having face-to-face classes at the same time as online classes"; "I feel the problems with blended learning implementation in my university/college as my problem"; and "I think I can enjoy blended learning practices as I enjoy face-to-face teaching". Finally, BL implementation is measured with seven items adapted from Anthony (2021). The items include "I am very committed to using system applications provided for blended learning course development"; "I am willing to implement web-based teaching and software provided for blended learning"; and "I am willing to implement blended learning practices in my course development".

Measurement Model Assessment

The smart PLS 3.0 is used in estimating the measurement and structural models. The specifics of the measurement and structural model are presented in the following sections. The measurement model considers how

166 Ridwan Adetunji Raji and Bahtiar Mohamad

Table 11.1 The results indicating the Cronbach alpha and composite reliability

Variables	Cronbach's alpha	Composite reliability	AVE
Affective Commitment	0.890	0.912	0.567
BL Implementation	0.613	0.782	0.546
Crisis Perception	0.904	0.928	0.685
ICC	0.931	0.944	0.708
Technological Support	0.946	0.959	0.823
University Admin Support	0.891	0.913	0.568

the latent variable and observed variables are related. The model is tested through the evaluation of constructs and elements in the model for validity and reliability (Akanmu et al., 2017). This is to ensure that the validity and reliability of the construct is confirmed prior to the evaluation of the relationships between constructs. As shown in Table 11.1, all constructs have satisfactory Cronbach alpha values ranging from 0.613 to 0.931. But in PLS path models, Cronbach alpha frequently provides a less significant estimation of the internal consistency reliability of latent variables (Henseler et al., 2009).

The composite reliability gives a consideration to interpretation of indicators with different loadings similarly to the Cronbach alpha. According to Table 11.1, with relation to internal consistency, a strong reliability is indicated by the composite reliability. The composite reliability of the constructs has values between 0.782 and 0.959, all of which lie above the necessary threshold value (Nunnally & Bernstein, 1994).

Structural Model Assessment

In order to evaluate the assumptions in Figure 11.1, the structural model is used to assess the causal relationships between latent variables. The predictive relevance of the model (blindfolding) and R^2 value were used to evaluate the general fitness of the model (Hair et al., 2017; Shmueli et al., 2019). Firstly, the Stone-Geisser's Q^2 value (Hair et al., 2017) is considered as a measure of predictive relevance. With an application of the blindfolding method, the Q^2 value of latent variables in the PLS path model is determined. By employing the smart-PLS software in carrying out the blindfolding method, the predictive significance of the model may be assessed. The blindfolding process is created while treating them as missing values for estimating parameters. The blindfolding process results in a production of generic cross validating metrics Q^2. The outcome of the latent variable acquiring the data point prediction is a cross-validated redundancy Q^2. The redundancy communality of all endogenous variables was found to be bigger than zero (Stone, 1974). Table 11.2

The Role of Internal Crisis Communication 167

Table 11.2 The results show the Q^2 values

	Q^2 (=1-SSE/SSO)
Affective Commitment	0.274
BL Implementation	0.049
Crisis Perception	0.207
Tech Support	0.494
Uni Admin Support	0.131

lists the cross-validated redundancy for Faculty members' perception of the crisis, Technological Support, University Administrative Support, Affective Commitment, and BL Implementation as 0.207, 0.494, 0.131, 0.274, and 0.049 respectively. The outcome showed that the model's predictive relevance was respectable. Thus, the structural model is adequate. In addition, the size of the R^2 values is assessed by the researcher as a measure of the precision in prediction. The R^2 value assesses the standard of variables included in the model (Hair et al., 2010). According to Cohen (1988), when the R^2 value is greater than 0.26 is regarded as substantial, 0.13 is regarded as medium while 0.02 is regarded as weak. According to this measure, the values of R^2 for endogenous variables including: Faculty Members' perception of crisis, Technological Support, University Administrative Support, Affective Commitment, and BL Implementation as 0.312, 0.608, 0.240, 0.506, and 0.141 as shown in Table 11.3.

The structural model describes how the latent constructs are related to one another. Testing the structural model, which is a sign of the model's predictive power, involves an estimation of the paths between the constructs. The smart PLS gives the R^2 for the path coefficient and each endogenous construct in the model. The R^2 measures the construct's variance while the path coefficient serves as an index of the strength of linkages among the constructs (Chin, 1998). Before examining the structural modeling, the inner model should be rid of the problem of collinearity. The results of the model's collinearity test yielded a less than five VIF value, which confirms that there is no problem with collinearity (Diamantopoulous & Siguaw, 2006). A less than five VIF value shows that there's no problem with collinearity (Diamantopoulous & Siguaw, 2006). Unlike the VIF value, a significant t-value is required to back

Table 11.3 The results show the R^2 values

Variables	R Square
Affective Commitment	0.506
BL Implementation	0.141
Crisis Perception	0.312
Technological Support	0.608
University Admin Support	0.240

168 *Ridwan Adetunji Raji and Bahtiar Mohamad*

Table 11.4 Hypotheses testing

Hypotheses	Correlation	β	T statistics	P values	Result
H1	ICC → Crisis Perception	0.057	9.774	0.000	Supported
H2	ICC → Tech Support	0.036	21.554	0.000	Supported
H3	ICC → Uni Admin Support	0.079	6.172	0.000	Supported
H4	ICC → Affective Commitment	0.039	18.392	0.000	Supported
H5	Crisis Perception → BL Implementation	0.095	0.555	0.579	Not supported
H6	Tech Support → BL Implementation	0.106	2.533	0.012	Supported
H7	Uni Admin Support → BL Implementation	0.082	3.951	0.000	Supported
H8	Affective Commitment → BL Implementation	0.137	2.082	0.038	Supported

up a hypothesis. Parameter having total t-value above 1.96 shows significance at the level of 0.05. Table 11.4 displays PLS results for hypotheses 1 to 7.

In Table 11.4, H1 is supported by the ICC shown to have a significant influence on crisis perception (β = 0.057, p < 0.00). Based on this result presented in Table 11.4, the H2 is supported (β = 0.036, p < 0.00). The result demonstrates that, ICC has a significant influence on faculty members' perceived technological support. Additionally with regards to H3, the result reveals a significantly positive influence of ICC on university administrative support (β = 0.079, p < 0.00). Also, the findings presented in Table shows that, ICC has a significant influence on affective commitment of faculty members (β = 0.039, p < 0.00). Thus, H4 is supported. However, the result presented in Table 11.4 does not show enough reason to support H5 (β = 0.095, p > 0.00). This shows that, crisis perception does not significantly influence BL implementation. In addition, H6 is supported by the result presented in Table 11.4. As it demonstrates that a significant nexus between technological support and BL implementation (β = 0.106, p < 0.00). The result presented in Table 11.4 shows enough evidence to support H7 (β = 0.82, p < 0.00). The result shows that, the influence of university administrative support is statistically significant. Finally, the result in Table 11.4 shows affective commitment has a statistically significant influence on BL implementation (β = 0.137, p < 0.00).

Discussions and Conclusions

This chapter examines the connections between university administrators' ICC influence on faculty member's crisis perception, perceived technological support, university administrative support, and affective commitment. Also, this chapter reveals important findings on the influence of faculty members' crisis perception, perceived technological support, university administrative support, and affective commitment on BL implementation during the COVID-19 crisis in the GCC. As it appears, the role of ICC in motivating faculty members towards implementing BL during COVID-19 crisis is multifaceted. The result of this study shows that, the most crucial influence of ICC is for shaping faculty members' affective commitment towards BL implementation. According to the findings reported in this study, university administrators should consider investing in communication strategies that can shape a strong sense of attachment and help faculty members build a positive attitude towards the implementation of BL as a responsive mechanism to the COVID-19 disruptions of higher educational learning. This can be done by communicating clearly and passionately and by developing considerate communication policies for the implementation of BL (Calonge et al., 2021).

Additionally, the results reported in this study reiterate the importance of ICC on technological support and university administrative support towards BL implementation. This implies that university administrators and regulators are expected to communicate the available technological support and administrative support to their faculty in a timely manner. This is because the shift towards BL is necessitated by COVID-19 situation and hence a sudden transition, faculty members might be apprehensive about the sudden need for digitalisation of learning. As such, timely and strategic communication contents will go a long way to reassure faculty members and allay their fears towards the implementation of BL. Another important role of crisis communication is to help faculty members develop positive and favorable perception of the COVID-19 crisis which necessitated the sudden shift in teaching styles. The findings reported in this study demonstrated, it is important for university and educational regulators to communicate the essentiality and necessity of implementing BL with their faculty. This will help faculty members have a positive disposition towards the change.

As revealed in this study, failure to communicate honestly and clearly might leave a communication gap that might lead faculty misunderstanding the motive of the university and ultimately develop a negative perception of BL. According to previous crisis communication studies, the success of any organisational ICC initiatives is heavily dependent on crucial factors such as crisis responsibility, leadership role, social media usage, error management, and communication culture are crucial in shaping employee sense-giving and sense-making during crisis and ultimately their preparedness and willingness to embrace necessitated changes within their organisational roles and responsibilities (Heide & Simonsson, 2015; Johansen et al., 2012; Kim, 2018; Kim et al., 2019; Mazzei & Ravazzani, 2011).

Conclusively, the findings of this study suggest that the COVID-19 pandemic has had significant implications for higher education in the Gulf region. As a result of the pandemic, universities and colleges across Gulf countries had to move to remote learning to curb the spread of the virus. This sudden shift exposed the significant challenges facing the higher education sector and institutions had to rapidly adjust their teaching and learning methods, including the adoption of digital technologies, to continue delivering quality education to students. Consequently, the pandemic has accelerated the digital transformation of higher education in the Gulf region, with institutions embracing e-learning and digital technologies to deliver education in the post-pandemic era. However, it is worth noting that the digital divide may exacerbate inequality among faculty, particularly those whose expertise is not IT-related or those who do not have access to the required technology and resources.

Another potential impact of the COVID-19 pandemic on Gulf higher education is the disruption of international student mobility. The Gulf region has been a popular destination for international students from across the world due to the quality of education and opportunities for personal and professional growth. However, the pandemic has opened up possibilities for remote learning, and many international students may prefer to study in Gulf universities remotely. This may further necessitate the implementation of blended/digital learning. Therefore, it is crucial for Gulf-based universities to adopt a holistic approach and aggressively invest in the digitalisation of learning and teaching to mitigate the impact of future disruptions.

References

Adamu, A. A., & Mohamad, B. (2019). Developing a strategic model of internal crisis communication: Empirical evidence from Nigeria. *International Journal of Strategic Communication, 13*(3), 233–254.

Ahmed, V., & Opoku, A. (2022). Technology supported learning and pedagogy in times of crisis: The case of COVID-19 pandemic. *Education and Information Technologies, 27*, 365–405.

Akanmu, M. D., Bahaudin, A.Y. B., & Jamaludin, R. (2017). A partial least square structural equation modelling preliminary analysis on total quality management elements and environmental regulation and policy influencing organisational performance in the food and beverage companies of Malaysia. *International Journal of Productivity and Quality Management, 22*(1), 60–81.

Anthony, B., Kamaludin, A., Romli, A., Raffei, A. F. M., Abdullah, A., Ming, G. L., Nurbiha, A. S., Shukri, M., & Baba, S. (2019). Exploring the role of blended learning for teaching and learning effectiveness in institutions of higher learning: An empirical investigation. *Education and Information Technologies, 24*(6), 3433–3466.

Anthony, J. B. (2021). Institutional factors for faculty members' implementation of blended learning in higher education. *Education + Training, 63*(5), 701–719.

Arpan, L. M., & Roskos-Ewoldsen, D. R. (2005). Stealing thunder: Analysis of the effects of proactive disclosure of crisis information. *Public Relations Review, 31*(3), 425–433.

Ashour, S. (2021). How COVID-19 is reshaping The role and modes of higher education whilst moving towards a knowledge society: The case of the UAE. *Open Learning: The Journal of Open, Distance and e-Learning.* https://doi.org/10.1080/026 80513.2021.1930526

Black, S. A. (2015). Qualities of effective leadership in higher education. *Open Journal of Leadership, 4*(2), 54. https://doi.org/10.4236/ojl.2015.42006

Bystrov, I. (2021). COVID-19 outbreak: Impact on higher education in GCC. *Higher Education Digest.* https://www.highereducationdigest.com/covid-19-outbreak-impact-on-higher-education-in-gcc/

The Role of Internal Crisis Communication   171

Calonge, D. S., Aguerrebere, P. M., Hultberg, P., & Connor, M. (2021). Were higher education institutions communication strategies well suited for the COVID-19 pandemic? *Journal of Education and Learning*, 10(4), 1927–5269.

Carbonell, K. B., Dailey-Hebert, A., & Gijselaers, W. (2013). Unleashing the creative potential of faculty to create blended learning. *The Internet and Higher Education*, 18(1), 29–37.

Clyde & Co. (2020). *COVID-19 education: Ongoing issues affecting the education sector across the GCC*.

Cohen, J. (1988). *Statistical power analysis for the behavioral sciences* (2nd ed.). Lawrence Erlbaum Associates.

Chesser, A., Drassen, H. A., & Keene, W. N. (2020). Assessment of COVID-19 knowledge among university students: Implications for future risk communication strategies. *Health Education & Behavior*, 47(4), 540–543.

Chin, W. W. (1998). The partial least squares approach to structural equation modeling. *Modern Methods for Business Research*, 295, 295–336.

Coombs, W. T. (1999). *Ongoing crisis communication: planning, managing, and responding*, Sage Publications.

Coombs, W. T. (2007). Attribution theory as a guide for post-crisis communication research. *Public Relations Review*, 33(2), 135–139.

Coombs, W. T. (2015). The value of communication during a crisis: Insights from strategic communication research. *Business Horizons*, 58(2), 141–148.

Coombs, W. T., & Holladay, S. J. (2002). Helping crisis managers protect reputational assets: Initial tests of the situational crisis communication theory. *Management Communication Quarterly*, 16(2), 165–186.

Diamantopoulos, A., & Siguaw, J. A. (2006). Formative versus reflective indicators in organizational measure development: A comparison and empirical illustration. *British Journal of Management*, 17(4), 263–282.

Dakduk, S., Santalla-Banderali, Z., & van der Woude, D. (2018). Acceptance of blended learning in executive education. *SAGE Open*, 8(3), 1–16.

Doucet, A., Netolicky, D., Timmers, K., & Tuscano, F. J. (2020). *Thinking about pedagogy in an unfolding pandemic: An independent report on approaches to distance learning during COVID19 school closures, Version 2.0*. Education International and UNESCO.

Eisenberger, R., Fasolo, P., & Davis-LaMastro, V. (1990). Perceived organizational support and employee diligence, commitment, and innovation. *Journal of Applied Psychology*, 75(1), 51.

Fedynich, L., Bradley, K. S., & Bradley, J. (2015). Graduate students' perceptions of online learning. *Research in Higher Education Journal*, 27(1), 1–13.

Ferdig, R. E., Baumgartner, E., Hartshorne, R., Kaplan-Rakowski, R., & Mouza, C. (2020). *Teaching, technology, and teacher education during the COVID-19 pandemic: Stories from the field*. Association for the Advancement of Computing in Education. https://www.learntechlib.org/p/216903/

Frandsen, F., & Johansen, W. (2011). The study of internal crisis communication: Towards an integrative framework. *Corporate Communications: An International Journal*, 16(4), 347–361.

Graham, C. R., Woodfield, W., & Harrison, J. B. (2013). A framework for institutional adoption and implementation of blended learning in higher education. *The Internet and Higher Education*, 18(1), 4–14.

Gurley, L. E. (2018). Educators' preparation to teach, perceived teaching presence, and perceived teaching presence behaviours in blended and online learning environments. *Online Learning*, 22(2), 179–220. https://doi.org/10.24059/olj.v22i2.1255

172 Ridwan Adetunji Raji and Bahtiar Mohamad

Hair, J. F., Black, W. C., Babin, B. J., & Anderson, R. E. (2010). *Multivariate data analysis* (7th ed.). Pearson.

Hair, J. F., Hult, G. T. M., Ringle, C. M., & Sarstedt, M. (2017). *A primer on partial least squares structural equation modeling (PLS-SEM)* (2nd ed.), Sage Publications Inc.

Heide, M., & Simonsson, C. (2015). Struggling with internal crisis communication: A balancing act between paradoxical tensions. *Public Relations Inquiry*, *4*(2), 223–255.

Heide, M., & Simonsson, C. (2019). *Internal crisis communication: Crisis awareness, leadership and coworkership*. Routledge.

Henseler, J., Ringle, C. M. & Sinkovics, R. R. (2009). The use of partial least squares path modeling in international marketing. *New Challenges to International Marketing (Advances in International Marketing)*, *20*, 277–319.

Hillman, V., Martins, J. P., & Ogu, E. C. (2021). Debates about EdTech in a time of pandemics should include youth's voices. *Postdigital Science and Education*. https://doi.org/10.1007/s42438-021-00230-y

Holdsworth, E., Bowen, E., Brown, S., & Howat, D. (2014). Offender engagement in group programs and associations with offender characteristics and treatment factors: A review. *Aggression and Violent Behavior*, *19*(2), 102–121.

Howard, S. K., Tondeur, J., Siddiq, F., & Scherer, R. (2020). Ready, set, go! Profiling teachers' readiness for online teaching in secondary education. *Technology, Pedagogy and Education*, *30*(1), 141–158. https://doi.org/10.1080/1475939X.2020.1839543

Huang, Y., & DiStaso, M. (2020). Responding to a health crisis on facebook: The effects of response timing and message appeal. *Public Relations Review*, *14*, 101909.

Jin, Y., & Pang, A. (2010). Future directions of crisis communication research: Emotions in crisis—the next frontier. In *Handbook of crisis communication* (pp. 677–682). https://ink.library.smu.edu.sg/lkcsb_research/6037

Johansen, W., Aggerholm, H. K., & Frandsen, F. (2012). Entering new territory: A study of internal crisis management and crisis communication in organizations. *Public Relations Review*, *38*(2), 270–279.

Kim, J. N., & Grunig, J. E. (2011). Problem solving and communicative action: A situational theory of problem solving. *Journal of Communication*, *61*(1), 120–149.

Kim, Y. (2018). Enhancing employee communication behaviors for sensemaking and sensegiving in crisis situations: Strategic management approach for effective internal crisis communication. *Journal of Communication Management*, *22*(4), 451–475.

Kim, Y., Kang, M., Lee, E., & Yang, S. U. (2019). Exploring crisis communication in the internal context of an organization: Examining moderated and mediated effects of employee-organization relationships on crisis outcomes. *Public Relations Review*, *45*(3), 101777.

Korn, C., & Einwiller, S. (2013). Media coverage about organisations in critical situations. *Corporate Communications: An International Journal*, *18*(4), 451–468.

Liang, L., & Jiang, M. (2017). Crisis Management of Group Events in Chinese Universities Under the Background of Internet: A Literature Review. *Higher Education of Social Science*, *13*(2), 23–28.

Lovell, D., Dolamore, S., & Collins, H. (2022). Examining public organization communication misalignments during COVID-19 through the lens of higher education. *Administration & Society*, *54*(2), 212–247.

Mazzei, A., Kim, J. N., & Dell'Oro, C. (2012). Strategic value of employee relationships and communicative actions: Overcoming corporate crisis with quality internal communication. *International Journal of Strategic Communication*, 6(1), 31–44.

Mazzei, A., & Ravazzani, S. (2011). Manager-employee communication during a crisis: The missing link. *Corporate Communications: An International Journal*, 16(3), 243–254.

Mazzei, A., & Ravazzani, S. (2015). Internal crisis communication strategies to protect trust relationships: A study of Italian companies. *International Journal of Business Communication*, 52(3), 319–337.

Meyer, J. P., & Allen, N. J. (1991). A three-component conceptualization of organizational commitment. *Human Resource Management Review*, 1(1), 61–89.

Meyer, J. P., Becker, T. E., & Vandenberghe, C. (2004). Employee commitment and motivation: A conceptual analysis and integrative model. *Journal of Applied Psychology*, 89(6), 991.

Meyer, J. P., Becker, T. E., & Van Dick, R. (2006). Social identities and commitments at work: Toward an integrative model. *Journal of Organizational Behavior*, 27(5), 665–683.

Mohamad, B., Adamu, A. A., & Akanmu, M. D. (2022). Structural model for the antecedents and consequences of internal crisis communication (ICC) in Malaysia oil and gas high risk industry. *Sage Open*, 12(1), 1–18.

Nunnally, J. C. & Bernstein, I. H. (1994). The assessment of reliability. *Psychometric Theory*, 3, 248–292.

Oxford Business Group. (2020). Has COVID-19 changed GCC education forever? https://oxfordbusinessgroup.com/news/has-covid-19-changed-gcc-education-forever.

Penrose, J. M. (2000). The role of perception in crisis planning. *Public Relations Review*, 26(2), 155–171.

Quiroz Flores, A., Liza, F., Quteineh, H., & Czarnecka, B. (2021). Variation in the timing of Covid-19 communication across universities in the UK. *PLoS ONE*, 16(2), e0246391. https://doi.org/10.1371/journal.pone.0246391

Sanders, K., Nguyen, P. T., Bouckenooghe, D., Rafferty, A., & Schwarz, G. (2020). Unraveling the what and how of organizational communication to employees during COVID-19 pandemic: Adopting an attributional lens. *The Journal of Applied Behavioral Science*, 56(3), 289–293. https://doi.org/10.1177/0021886320937026

Scully, D., Lehane, P., & Scully, C. (2021). It is no longer scary: Digital learning before and during the COVID-19 pandemic in Irish secondary schools. *Technology, Pedagogy and Education*, 30(1), 159–181. https://doi.org/10.1080/1475939X.2020.1854844

Shmueli, G., Sarstedt, M., Hair, J. F., Cheah, J.-H., Ting, H., Vaithilingam, S. & Ringle, C. M. (2019). Predictive model assessment in PLS-SEM: guidelines for using PLSpredict. *European Journal of Marketing*, 53(11), 2322–2347. https://doi.org/10.1108/EJM-02-2019-0189

Solinger, O. N., Van Olffen, W., & Roe, R. A. (2008). Beyond the three-component model of organizational commitment. *Journal of Applied Psychology*, 93(1), 70.

12 Impact of Job-related Stress on Professional and Personal Life During Coronavirus Pandemic

Vishal Jain, Amitabh Mishra, and Mohit Kukreti

Introduction

Employees are recognised as an asset to the company as they bring new and innovative ideas for growth and development. The workforce plays an essential role in increasing organisational productivity and performance, however, it has posed many workplace issues (Bedeian et al., 1981). One of these issues is growing job-related stress and its impact on both professional and personal life. Workplace stress has emerged as one of the challenging tasks at all levels of management in the organisation.

When employees adapt their lives to the ever-changing working environment, stress is felt. Usually, stress is argued in a negative perspective, but it also has a positive significance. Stress sometimes gives a valuable chance when it offers prospective achievement. Therefore, stress should not consider always in the negative sense. In this way, stress will 'help or hinder' individuals depending on how they react to it (Adams, 1999). Stress has both physical and emotional effects on humans and can create either positive or negative feelings.

During the pandemic period, coronavirus contributed to "multifaceted severe consequences for people's lives and their health. Governments mandated hard measures of social distancing, quarantine, and lockdowns, and businesses shut down, highlighting the inevitable long-term" impact on job-related stress (Vinkers et al., 2020). The most common sources of stress for workers are fear of the virus, lack of information, and increased workloads (Billings et al., 2021). Employers are asking their workers to do more with fewer resources, on the other hand, employees are struggling with guilt over not being able to work or care for their loved ones. The constant worry about the health of oneself and loved ones, combined with the fear of job loss, can be overwhelming.

Job-related stress is an interdisciplinary topic having endless scope for research over time. In this small piece of work, an attempt has been made to assess the types of stress an employee is facing in the higher education institutions (HEIs) during the pandemic. How they match their lifestyle at work and at home to reduce stress and contribute their best in improving the productivity.

This chapter explores the relationship between job-related stress and both positive and negative outcomes among higher education employees during the

DOI: 10.4324/9781003457299-15

Impact of Job-related Stress on Professional and Personal Life 175

coronavirus pandemic. The main objective of the study is to explore several factors of stress, its symptoms, potential sources, varied reasons, and strategies for reducing the employees' stress caused during the coronavirus pandemic. An attempt is also made to investigate various demography that control job-related stress and help to balance between work and home life. To achieve the overall purpose, the chapter to analyse the following specific objectives:

- Assess job-related stresses among higher education employees during the Coronavirus pandemic.
- Examine whether there are differences in job-related stresses among the higher education staff during the Coronavirus pandemic according to their demographic characteristics.
- Identify dimensions associated with job-related stresses among the higher education staff during the Coronavirus pandemic.
- Find out the impact of job-related stress experienced in the three dimensions [Work Interference with Personal Life (WIPL), Personal Life Interference with Work (PLIW), and Work/Personal Life Enhancement (WPLE)] of Work-Life Balance (WLB) during the Coronavirus pandemic.

On Stress

The introductory concept of stress in behavioural sciences was first postulated by Selye Hans in 1936. It was derived from the Latin word *stringere*, it meant the experience of physical hardship, starvation, torture, and pain. Selye (1976) defined stress as "the non-specific response of the body to any demand placed upon it." According to Robbins (2001), "Stress is a dynamic condition in which an individual is confronted with an opportunity, constraint or demand related to what he/she desires and for which the outcome is perceived to be both uncertain and important."

Every individual is constantly adapting its environment, both physically and behaviourally. These external forces disturb the internal metabolism and generate stress (Meharunisa, 2019). Therefore, stress must be appropriately addressed and perfectly balanced for maintaining the external-internal equilibrium. Stress is an all-top common part of life today, something that only few individuals can avoid. Stress influences each of us in diverse ways, which can be managed by identifying several factors and their symptoms (Ornek & Sevim, 2018). There are many factors that contribute to develop the stress, such as environmental, organisational, and individual factors (Christiana, 2017).

Classically, stress relates to restrictions and anxieties, the former stops you from doing what you desire, whereas the latter refers the loss of something desired. Growing evidence suggests that high-level of stress adversely affect physical health, psychological well-being, and many aspects of task performance (Deb et al., 2008). "Two conditions are necessary for potential stress to become actual stress. There must be uncertainty over the outcome and the outcome must be important" (Deb & Biswas, 2011). Consequently, the strength

176 *Vishal Jain, Amitabh Mishra, and Mohit Kukreti*

Table 12.1 Factors and symptoms of stress

Factors		Symptoms	
Environmental factors	Economic uncertainty Political uncertainties Technological uncertainty Ecological uncertainty	Physiological symptoms	Ulcers Digestive problems Headaches Metabolic disorders
Organisational factors	Task Demands Role Demands Interpersonal Demands Organisational structure Organisational Leadership Organisation's life stage	Psychological symptoms	High blood pressure Sleep disruption Emotional instability Moodiness Nervousness and tension Chronic worry
Individual factors	Family problems Economic problems Personality	Behavioural symptoms	Anxiety and Depression Burnout Excessive smoking Abuse of alcohol or drugs Absenteeism Safety problems Productivity / Performance problems

Note:
Adapted from Christiana (2017)

of the stress depends on the level of uncertainty and importance (Makhbul et al., 2011). The higher perceived uncertainty and outcome importance will generate a higher level of stress among individuals (Pathak, 2010).

The present-day fast-moving life is accumulating stress levels and creating a myth that stress has only negative effects. However, previous studies show that the impact of stress can be neutral, negative, or positive (Singh, 2012). Therefore, all stress is not bad; however, the identification of stress responses is highly recommended. This will determine the impact that these experiences have on one's life. "To properly perform a job function, a certain amount of stress is required. These beneficial stressors are motivation, energy, alertness, and a positive attitude" (Ingram & Pilla, 2007). Hence, an efficient management of causes of stress may lead to a beneficial outcome.

On Job-related Stress

Job-related stress, also termed as workplace, organisational, or occupational stress, is one of the most common complaints that employees have. It takes time, energy, and focus away from our personal lives (Cox & Rial-González, 2000). Work is an integral part of a person's life. When one's job takes place in a high-stress environment, it becomes particularly challenging to maintain a productive and satisfying WLB (Alemu, 2013; Dolai, 2015).

According to the American Psychological Association (Abramson, 2022), job-related stress is one of the leading causes of health problems. When employees

Impact of Job-related Stress on Professional and Personal Life   177

are highly stressed, they are not productive, which can lead to decreased productivity, increased absenteeism, and even higher rates of employee turnover (Fisher-McAuley et al., 2003). Therefore, it is important for both employees and employers to be aware of the signs of job-related stress and take steps to manage it.

Job-related Stress during Coronavirus Pandemic

A pandemic can refer to an outbreak of any infectious disease but usually refers to influenza. The pandemic has everyone on edge and feeling stressed. One of the biggest sources of stress is the fear of the unknown. Not knowing what will happen next or how the situation will develop can be very unsettling (Bell et al., 2012). The World Health Organisation has declared the stress caused by the pandemic a global health emergency (Kennedy, 2020).

Recently, the coronavirus (COVID-19) pandemic has caused a great deal of stress for people who are employed. The coronavirus pandemic has created a situation of unprecedented stress, which is producing a long-lasting impact at workplace (International Labour Organization, 2020). World-wide known as the pandemic of the century, COVID-19 virus has created a massive catastrophe and added the job-related stress. A large fraction of the population has lost their jobs and homes or seen reduced revenues in their businesses.

Impact of Job-related Stress on Professional and Personal Life

Everyone, more or less, is under stress in their professional and personal lives (work-life conflict) to produce, abide by rules and exist compatible on the job and with others (Carlson et al., 2000). Therefore, the absence of work-life conflict will create the balance between professional and personal life (Suganya, 2019). There is a limited scholarly literature that investigates workplace stress to balance work and personal life and overcome work-life conflict (Bell et al., 2012). The two topics of job-related stress and WLB are often intertwined. It can be difficult to maintain a healthy WLB when you are feeling stressed out by your job. And if you are not careful, job-related stress can quickly take over your life.

The balance between work and family is becoming a challenging task for every individual in all facets of life. Its heightened stress level has both personal as well as job effects (Miller et al., 2018). Especially at the workplace, employees at every level experience several stressful situations that must be dealt with to maintain our WLB (Meharunisa, 2019). In the late 1970s, the concept of WLB was first introduced to understand the balance between an individual's work and personal life. Several researchers (Fisher, 2001; Hayman, 2005) conclude that WLB is comprised of three dimensions: WIPL, PLIW, and WPLE. The WIPL dimension includes the negative influence of work on personal life, whereas the PLIW dimension describes the negative influence of personal life on work. The WPLE dimension covers both WPLE as well as personal life to work enhancement items. Empirical evidence based on previous studies confirms the relationship between job-related stress and WLB (Baker et al., 2019).

Pandemic and Higher Education Institutes

In recent years, there have been several outbreaks on university campuses, causing schools to close and students to be quarantined (UNESCO, 2020). With large populations of people coming together from all over the world, HEIs are particularly vulnerable to the threat of pandemics (International Labour Organization, 2020). The pandemic has forced HEIs to close, however, it is also providing a unique opportunity for learning.

Prior to the pandemic traditional lecture methods, in which mostly face-to-face teaching-learning, dominate the classrooms. During the pandemic, HEIs gained many new ways to the nature of active learning, through wearing face masks and physical distancing (Kaplan et al., 2020). The concept of remote learning (online learning) was used extensively during the COVID-19 situation (Ionescu et al., 2020). Remote learning can take many forms, from sending work packets home to assigning video lessons on YouTube. Teachers can also record themselves lecturing and post them online for students to watch later (Cavus et al., 2021). Several Internet of Things-based learning management systems have been utilised to continue the process of teaching-learning even from home (Jain & Jain, 2022).

Conceptual Model and Analytical Frame

In line with the extensive empirical literature on Job-related Stress, Coronavirus Pandemic, Health Conditions, HEIs, and WLB, a few hypotheses are developed (Figure 12.1).

The association of demographics and health conditions with job stress is comprehensively presented in the previous studies (Midorikawa et al., 2021). It is sufficiently evident from the scholarly articles that the stress levels are observed significantly different in relation to the demography of the respondents (Bonanno et al., 2007; Persaud & Persaud, 2015). Additionally, demographics have the potential to influence WLB (Keeton et al., 2007; Kumar & Rao, 2020). Researchers found statistical relationships between WLB and demographic factors (Joseph & Sebastian, 2017; Soni & Bakhru, 2019; Warrier, 2013).

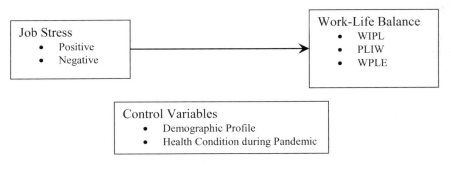

Figure 12.1 Conceptual model.

Impact of Job-related Stress on Professional and Personal Life 179

Moreover, the involvement of the employees' health is crucial for WLB (Gragnano et al., 2020; Khoury, 2021). Therefore, it can be hypothesised that:

Hypothesis 1: Both negative and positive job-related stressors (NEST, POST) and three dimensions of WLB (WIPL, PLIW, and WPLE) are significantly different from the respondent's demographic profile (including health condition) during pandemic in HEIs.

Hypothesis 1 consists of nine sub-hypotheses:

H1a: Both negative and positive job-related stressors (NEST, POST) and three dimensions of WLB (WIPL, PLIW, and WPLE) are significantly different to the respondent's gender during the pandemic in HEIs.

H1b: Both negative and positive job-related stressors (NEST, POST) and three dimensions of WLB (WIPL, PLIW, and WPLE) are significantly different to the respondent's age during the pandemic in HEIs.

H1c: Both negative and positive job-related stressors (NEST, POST) and three dimensions of WLB (WIPL, PLIW, and WPLE) are significantly different to the respondent's nationality during the pandemic in HEIs.

H1d: Both negative and positive job-related stressors (NEST, POST) and three dimensions of WLB (WIPL, PLIW, and WPLE) are significantly different to the respondent's marital status during the pandemic in HEIs.

H1e: Both negative and positive job-related stressors (NEST, POST) and three dimensions of WLB (WIPL, PLIW, and WPLE) are significantly different to the respondent's education level during the pandemic in HEIs.

H1f: Both negative and positive job-related stressors (NEST, POST) and three dimensions of WLB (WIPL, PLIW, and WPLE) are significantly different to the respondent's salary during the pandemic in HEIs.

H1g: Both negative and positive job-related stressors (NEST, POST) and three dimensions of WLB (WIPL, PLIW, and WPLE) are significantly different to the respondent's job type during the pandemic in HEIs.

H1h: Both negative and positive job-related stressors (NEST, POST) and three dimensions of WLB (WIPL, PLIW, and WPLE) are significantly different to the respondent's job duration during the pandemic in HEIs.

H1i: Both negative and positive job-related stressors (NEST, POST) and three dimensions of WLB (WIPL, PLIW, and WPLE) are significantly different to the respondent's health condition during the pandemic in HEIs.

Job stress and WLB are closely related, as job-related stress can significantly affect an individual's ability to maintain a healthy WLB (Bell et al., 2012). When a person experiences high levels of job stress, they may feel overwhelmed, anxious, and exhausted, which can lead to a lack of balance between their professional and personal life (Kelly et al., 2020). On the other hand, when an employee is better able to manage their job stress, (s)he has a good WLB. Employees can have time and energy to engage in self-care activities and spend time with loved ones. This can help them feel more refreshed and

180 *Vishal Jain, Amitabh Mishra, and Mohit Kukreti*

motivated when they return to work (Ross & Vasantha, 2014). Overall, better management of job stress can help individuals in achieving a healthy WLB, while excessive job stress can make it challenging to maintain a healthy balance between work and personal life (Saeed & Farooqi, 2014). Hence, it suggests:

Hypothesis 2: Both negative and positive job-related stressors (NEST, POST) are significantly related to the three dimensions of WLB (WIPL, PLIW, and WPLE) during the pandemic in HEIs.

Hypothesis 2 includes six sub-hypotheses:

H2a: Negative job-related stressors (NEST) are significantly related to the WIPL during the pandemic in HEIs.
H2b: Positive job-related stressors (POST) are significantly related to the WIPL during the pandemic in HEIs.
H2c: Negative job-related stressors (NEST) are significantly related to the PLIW during the pandemic in HEIs.
H2d: Positive job-related stressors (POST) are significantly related to the PLIW during the pandemic in HEIs.
H2e: Negative job-related stressors (NEST) are significantly related to the WPLE during the pandemic in HEIs.
H2f: Positive job-related stressors (POST) are significantly related to the WPLE during the pandemic in HEIs.

The present study makes up a quantitative approach to the descriptive research design requires both secondary and primary data. The sources of secondary data are scholarly articles and published reports. The primary data is obtained by administering an online questionnaire to the respondents under study. The instrument was designed to assess the impact of job stress on professional and family life. A structured questionnaire was constructed and pretested to ensure adequate and authentic collection of relevant data, entry, and analysis.

The anonymous survey is separated into several sections. The first section of the questionnaire consists of the demographic profile of the respondents. While the second section examines stress in the workplace during a pandemic using the eight items of the 5-point Workplace Stress Scale™ (The Marlin Company & American Institute of Stress, 2001). Finally, the third section measures the respondents' beliefs about having a balance between work and family life related to the feelings of stress in the current job during the pandemic. For this purpose, a 13-item WLB 7-point scale is adapted, originally developed, and validated by (Fisher-McAuley et al., 2003). The WLB measurement assesses three distinct dimensions: WIPL, PLIW, and WPLE. The WPLE items are worded positively to indicate higher levels of perceived WLB. Conversely, the WIPL and PLIW items are worded negatively, which specifies higher levels of work-life conflict.

This study is conducted among the employees working in the different HEIs in the Sultanate of Oman by using a sample survey method. In the sample, Google form-based questionnaires were distributed among respondents.

Impact of Job-related Stress on Professional and Personal Life 181

The respondents were requested to fill out the questionnaires and send them back to the researcher. With two follow-ups, 100 completed questionnaires were returned. The collected information has been systematically arranged, tabulated, and analysed to draw appropriate conclusions.

The collected data is analysed using frequency, percentage, mean, and standard deviation. After descriptive and factor analysis, the bivariate correlations between the study variables are presented. Finally, structural equation modelling and analysis of variance (ANOVA) analysis resulted in the test of the hypotheses under study.

Several ethical issues are under consideration during the whole research. The present research is ethically approved by the University. Participation in the study is optional and confidentiality is assured. Subsequently, the statistical methods of analysis are free from any prejudice, hence expected results are more precise.

Demographics and Analytical Frame

In the sample under consideration, 61% of the respondents were male, 76% expat, and 76% married. Majority of respondents were in teaching profession (93%), between 41–50 years old (46%) and holding PhD degree (49%). Mostly, the monthly salary of the respondents was between OMR 1001–1500 (40%) and present job duration was 1–5 years (33%).

Respondents were asked to indicate the self-rated health (SRH) condition (Woo et al., 2020) with which they have felt during the Coronavirus pandemic period using a five-point time-related scale. "The reliability of self-rated health is as good as or even better than that of most of the more specific questions" (Lundberg & Manderbacka, 1996). In the survey, the respondents revealed

Table 12.2 Demographic profile

Gender	Male	Female			
	61	39			
Nationality	Expat	Omani			
	76	24			
Marital Status	Married	Single	Other		
	76	17	7		
Job Type	Teaching	Non-teaching			
	93	7			
Age	21–30	31–40	41–50	51–60	
	4	27	46	23	
Education Level	Graduate	Postgraduate	PhD		
	7	44	49		
Monthly Salary (OMR)	1–500	501–1000	1001–1500	1501–2000	2000+
	1	9	40	31	19
Present Job Duration (years)	1–5	6–10	11–15	16–20	21+
	33	25	28	9	5

Note:
Sample Size n = 100

182 *Vishal Jain, Amitabh Mishra, and Mohit Kukreti*

Table 12.3 Health condition affected during Coronavirus pandemic

Negligibly	Slightly	Moderately	Extremely	Severely	Total
23	24	33	18	2	100

that their health was affected negligibly 23%, slightly 24%, moderately 33%, extremely 18%, and severely 2% during the coronavirus pandemic (Table 12.3).

Using IBM SPSS Statistics 26 and IBM SPSS Amos 21, five factors have been extracted (Table 12.4). The Kaiser-Meyer-Olkin (KMO) Measure of sampling adequacy is 0.881 at 0.000 level of significance. The factor loading indices are sufficiently high for all items. The factor analysis of the items generated the two components of stress, also confirmed the three dimensions of the work/life balance scale.

After applying Principal Component Analysis and Varimax rotation method (Table 12.5), Negative Stressors (NEST) with 5 items resulted in 7.012 eigenvalues and 33.393% of variance. Positive Stressors (POST) with 3 items resulted in 2.954 eigenvalues and 14.065% of variance. WIPL with 5 items resulted in 2.824 eigenvalues and 13.449% of variance. PLIW with 4 items resulted in 1.937 eigenvalues and 9.224% of variance. WPLE with 4 items resulted in 1.918 eigenvalues and 9.135% of variance.

Reliability refers to the precision of an instrument and is often assessed by calculating Cronbach's alpha (α) for each construct. As shown in Table 12.6,

Table 12.4 Factor loading and descriptive statistics

Factors	Items	Mean	SD	NEST	POST	WIPL	PLIW	WPLE
Negative	NEST1	2.65	1.058	0.594				
Stressors	NEST2	2.79	1.282	0.767				
(NEST)	NEST3	3.15	1.167	0.862				
	NEST4	2.88	1.328	0.739				
	NEST5	2.99	1.275	0.883				
Positive	POST1	3.28	1.036		0.484			
Stressors	POST2	2.59	1.083		0.639			
(POST)	POST3	3.33	1.083		0.836			
Work	WIPL1	3.26	1.813			0.943		
Interference	WIPL2	3.26	1.878			0.955		
with Personal	WIPL3	3.45	1.904			0.938		
Life (WIPL)	WIPL4	3.57	1.887			0.924		
	WIPL5	3.57	1.865			0.917		
Personal Life	PLIW1	3.14	1.954				0.868	
Interference	PLIW2	2.80	1.758				0.924	
with Work	PLIW3	2.04	1.435				0.713	
(PLIW)	PLIW4	1.98	1.263				0.623	
Work-Personal	WPLE1	4.65	1.817					0.754
Life	WPLE2	3.64	1.967					0.861
Enhancement	WPLE3	4.61	1.869					0.770
(WPLE)	WPLE4	4.07	1.860					0.816

Note:
Kaiser-Meyer-Olkin (KMO) = 0.881 (0.000).

Impact of Job-related Stress on Professional and Personal Life 183

Table 12.5 Total variance explained

Component	Extraction sums of squared loadings			Rotation sums of squared loadings		
	Total	% of Variance	Cumulative %	Total	% of Variance	Cumulative %
NEST	9.258	44.087	44.087	7.012	33.393	33.393
POST	3.261	15.530	59.617	2.954	14.065	47.458
WIPL	1.613	7.679	67.296	2.824	13.449	60.907
PLIW	1.521	7.244	74.541	1.937	9.224	70.131
WPLE	0.992	4.725	79.265	1.918	9.135	79.265

Notes:
Extraction method: Principal component analysis. Rotation method: Varimax with Kaiser normalisation.

the alpha values were 0.896 for the negative stressors, and 0.674 for positive stressors. Alpha values for the three dimensions of WLB were 0.972 for WIPL, 0.876 for PLIW, and 0.879 for WPLE. Hence, all reliabilities (α) were reasonably above the minimum required value of 0.67 (Taber, 2018).

The bivariate correlations determine an insignificant relationship between the negative and positive stressors. However, there are significant correlations between the three dimensions of WLB.

Previous literature proposes various demographic-related variables that may differentiate stress and WLB. These variables include Gender, Age, Nationality, Marital Status, Education Level, Salary, Job Type, Job Duration, and Health Condition. To evaluate the Hypothesis 1, mean score comparisons by One-way ANOVA with accompanying mean comparison tests were undertaken for the two directions of stress (NEST, POST) and three dimensions of WLB (WIPL, PLIW, and WPLE). Result of the F values (Table 12.7) show that only the health condition (H1i supported) is significantly different for all variables under study. However, there are significant differences between nationality and PLIW (H1c partially supported), as well as marital status and WPLE (H1d partially supported). Rest of the hypotheses (H1a, H1b, H1e, H1f, H1g, and H1h) are not supported in this study.

Following the recommendations of Hair et al., (2010) to report multiple fit indices of the structural model (Figure 12.2), the study includes the chi-square

Table 12.6 Descriptive statistics, reliability coefficients, and inter-construct correlations

	Mean	SD	NEST	POST	WIPL	PLIW	WPLE
NEST	2.892	0.190	**0.896**				
POST	3.067	0.413	−0.140	**0.674**			
WIPL	3.422	0.155	0.897***	−0.130	**0.972**		
PLIW	2.490	0.572	0.782***	−0.177*	0.702***	**0.876**	
WPLE	4.243	0.481	−0.244**	0.513***	−0.221*	−0.224*	**0.879**

Notes:
Bivariate correlations values at ***p < 0.001, **p < 0.01, *p < 0.05 significance levels.
Coefficients in bold denote Cronbac(α) alpha values.

Table 12.7 One-way ANOVA for demographics and health condition differences

	NEST	POST	WIPL	PLIW	WPLE	Result
Gender	1.682	0.568	1.260	0.715	0.421	H1a not supported
Age	0.801	0.339	1.543	2.560	0.756	H1b not supported
Nationality	2.303	0.518	1.845	4.043*	1.311	H1c partially supported
Marital Status	0.392	1.535	0.448	0.750	4.104*	H1d partially supported
Education Level	0.187	1.603	0.534	0.695	2.958	H1e not supported
Salary	0.551	0.517	1.049	1.692	1.691	H1f not supported
Job Type	2.580	0.681	3.165	1.576	1.115	H1g not supported
Job Duration	1.000	0.099	0.657	1.225	0.387	H1h not supported
Health Condition	4.777**	3.214*	5.425**	3.288*	3.188*	H1i supported

Notes:
F values at ***$p < 0.001$, **$p < 0.01$, *$p < 0.05$ significance levels.

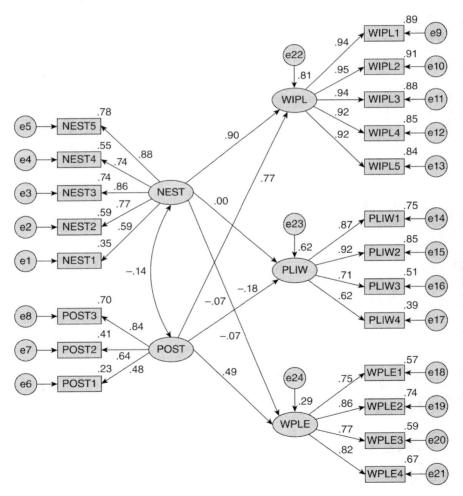

Figure 12.2 Structural model.

Impact of Job-related Stress on Professional and Personal Life   185

Table 12.8 Standardised regression weights

Predictors	DV	Estimate	S.E.	C.R.	P	R^2	Result
NEST	WIPL	0.897	0.391	6.239	***	0.805	H2a supported
POST	WIPL	−0.004	0.233	−0.063	0.950		H2b not supported
NEST	PLIW	0.772	0.383	5.451	***	0.616	H2c supported
POST	PLIW	−0.068	0.306	−0.754	0.451		H2d not supported
NEST	WPLE	−0.176	0.233	−1.645	0.100	0.293	H2e not supported
POST	WPLE	0.488	0.434	3.070	0.002		H2f supported

fit test (CMIN/DF = 2.426), comparative fit index (CFI = 0.860), standardised root mean square residual (SRMR = 0.091), and root mean square error of approximation (RMSEA = 0.077). All model fit indices are within the acceptable range except CFI (Hu & Bentler, 1999). One of the reasons for low CFI may be the sample size (Iacobucci, 2010; Kim, 2005). However, in the presence of satisfactory RMSEA and other fit indices, overall proposed model may be accepted (Kim et al., 2016; Taasoobshirazi & Wang, 2016).

The results of the regression analysis for Hypothesis 2 are presented in Table 12.8. These results indicate that negative stressors (NEST) significantly relate to the WIPL (β = 0.897, p < 0.001) and PLIW (β = 0.772, p < 0.001) dimensions of the WLB. On the other hand, positive stressors (POST) significantly relate to the WPLE (β = .488, p < .05) dimension of the WLB. Further, results show that the rest of the three relationships between POST and WIPL (β = −0.004, p > 0.05), between POST and PLIW (β = −0.068, p > 0.05), between NEST and WPLE (β = −0.176, p > 0.05) are statistically insignificant.

Discussion

The present study explores how job-related stress can affect WLB. It is also important to be aware of the health risks associated with job-related stress. The article looks at how different health conditions and employee demographics can influence stress and WLB during the pandemic. The results of the study show that the demographic profile of the respondent mostly does not significantly influence job-related stress and WLB. However, the sample under study suggests that the nationality of the respondent influences PLIW, whereas the marital status affects the WPLE. Mainly the health conditions significantly relate with both directions of stress and three dimensions of WLB of the respondent.

The study further identifies there is no correlation between negative and positive stress. Both negative and positive stressors can independently activate the dimensions of WLB. WLB refers to the balance between work-related activities and other aspects of one's life, such as family and personal interests. There are mainly three dimensions of WLB, WIPL, PLIW, and WPLE. Out of the three, WIPL and PLIW dimensions refer to the negative side, whereas WPLE denotes the positive side of the WLB.

Negative stressors, such as work overload, job insecurity, and interpersonal conflict at work, can disrupt the balance between work and other aspects of life, leading to the negative consequences of work on one's personal life, namely WIPL. Moreover, decreased satisfaction and increased strain can deteriorate the personal life that obstructs the work, called as PLIW. On the other hand, positive stressors, such as job autonomy, social support, and challenging tasks, can enhance the balance between work and other aspects of life, leading to the positive outcomes of work on one's personal life, known as WPLE.

The significance of the study is to postulate three "Golden Rules" that address workplace stress and its impact on WLB.

1 The employee's demographic profile is usually immaterial to manage job-related stress and WLB. Only one thing is most important, i.e., the health condition.
2 The negative and positive are two independent job-related stressors. Every employee must work on these two stressors separately to achieve a healthy WLB.
3 The negative stressors trigger the negative dimensions (WIPL and PLIW) of WLB. Whereas positive stressors enhance the positive dimension (WPLE) of WLB.

Conclusion

Job-related stress and WLB are two of the biggest challenges that employees face. Managing the demands of the job with the needs of personal life can be difficult, but it is not impossible. American Psychological Association declares job-related stress as the number one health concern among workers. WLB has become a hot-button issue in recent years during the Coronavirus pandemic, with people increasingly vocalizing the importance of having time for both work and personal pursuits. Though it can be difficult to achieve, maintaining a healthy balance is crucial for overall happiness and well-being. Most employees know that job-related stress can take a toll on one's mental and physical health, but what many do not know is how to manage that stress.

The effects of the COVID-19 pandemic on HEIs in the Gulf region have had a major impact. As worldwide quarantine measures were implemented, educational institutions had to adapt in a short amount of time and become virtual to keep courses running. There are both short and long-term implications of the pandemic on HEI employees. The pandemic has resulted in a transformation of the work-life of HEI employees. The number of hours worked and divided between one's own needs and family responsibilities has shifted. As a result, there is an urgent need to investigate the psychological and physiological effects of the pandemic on their work-related stress and WLB. The HEIs employees were assigned new tasks and had to adapt to a new work environment and new tools. This caused a great deal of stress as well as changes in their personal life as they had to balance family and work.

Impact of Job-related Stress on Professional and Personal Life 187

In conclusion, the present research with a limited sample size discusses job-related stress, WLB, and health conditions during pandemics as they are assumed to be related to employee demography. It is also noted that job-related stress is a growing distress, particularly among young workers. WLB is also a concern, with many employees feeling that they are unable to balance the demands of work with their personal lives. The pandemic is also a worry, as the recent outbreak of coronavirus has shown. Finally, promoting employee health can lead to a more productive and engaged workforce, which can help employees achieve a better balance between work and life.

References

Abramson, A. (2022). Burnout and stress are everywhere. *Monitor on Psychology, 53*(1), 72.

Adams, E. (1999). Vocational teacher stress and internal characteristics. *Journal of Vocational and Technical Education, 16*(1), 1–13.

Alemu, M. A. (2013). An assessment on job satisfaction of academic employees: A survey on Ethiopian private Institutions of higher learning. *International Journal of Research in Commerce & Management, 4*(12), 138–144.

Baker, R., Jaaffar, A. H., Sallehuddin, H., Mohd Saudi, N., & Hassan, S. (2019). The relationship between emotional intelligence, depression, anxiety, stress and work-life balance: An examination among Malaysian army personnel. *Asia Proceedings of Social Sciences, 4*(2), 27–30. https://doi.org/10.31580/apss.v4i2.707

Bedeian, A. G., Armenakis, A. A., & Curran, S. M. (1981). The relationship between role stress and job-related, interpersonal, and organizational climate factors. *Journal of Social Psychology, 113*(2), 247–260. https://doi.org/10.1080/00224545.1981.9924377

Bell, A. S., Rajendran, D., & Theiler, S. (2012). Job stress, wellbeing, work-life balance and work-life conflict among Australian academics. *E-Journal of Applied Psychology, 8*(1), 25–37. https://doi.org/10.7790/ejap.v8i1.320

Billings, J., Ching, B. C. F., Gkofa, V., Greene, T., & Bloomfield, M. (2021). Experiences of frontline healthcare workers and their views about support during COVID-19 and previous pandemics: A systematic review and qualitative meta-synthesis. *BMC Health Services Research, 21*(1), 923. https://doi.org/10.1186/s12913-021-06917-z

Bonanno, G. A., Galea, S., Bucciarelli, A., & Vlahov, D. (2007). What predicts psychological resilience after disaster? The role of demographics, resources, and life stress. *Journal of Consulting and Clinical Psychology, 75*(5), 671–682. https://doi.org/10.1037/0022-006X.75.5.671

Carlson, D. S., Kacmar, K. M., & Williams, L. J. (2000). Construction and initial validation of a multidimensional measure of work-family conflict. *Journal of Vocational Behavior, 56*(2), 249–276. https://doi.org/10.1006/jvbe.1999.1713

Cavus, N., Sani, A. S., Haruna, Y., & Lawan, A. A. (2021). Efficacy of social networking sites for sustainable education in the era of COVID-19: A systematic review. *Sustainability (Switzerland), 13*(2), 1–18. https://doi.org/10.3390/su13020808

Christiana, M. B. V. (2017). *Strategic stress management of gold collars.* Educreation Publishing.

Cox, T., & Rial-González, A. G. E. (2000). *Research on work-related stress.* European Agency for Safety and Health at Work.

188 Vishal Jain, Amitabh Mishra, and Mohit Kukreti

Deb, B. C., & Biswas, S. K. (2011). Stress management: A critical view. *European Journal of Business and Management*, *3*(4), 205–213.

Deb, S., Chakraborty, T., Chatterjee, P., & Srivastava, N. (2008). Job-related stress, causal factors and coping strategies of traffic constables. *Journal of the Indian Academy of Applied Psychology*, *34*(1), 19–28.

Dolai, D. (2015). Measuring work life balance among the employees of the insurance industry in India. *International Journal of Advanced Research in Management and Social Sciences*, *4*(5), 140–151.

Fisher-McAuley, G., Stanton, J. M., Jolton, J. A., & Gavin, J. (2003). Modeling the relationship between work/life balance and organizational outcomes. In *Annual Conference of the Society for Industrial-Organizational Psychology Orlando* (Vol. 1, p. 26).

Fisher, G. G. (2001). *Work-personal life balance: A construct development study*. Bowling Green State University.

Gragnano, A., Simbula, S., & Miglioretti, M. (2020). Work–life balance: Weighing the importance of work–family and work–health balance. *International Journal of Environmental Research and Public Health*, *17*(3), 907. https://doi.org/10.3390/ijerph17030907

Hair, J., William, C., Babin, B., & Anderson, R. (2010). *Multivariate data analysis* (7th ed.). Pearson Prentice Hall.

Hayman, J. (2005). Psychometric assessment of an instrument designed to measure work life balance. *Research and Practice in Human Resource Management*, *13*(1), 85–91.

Hu, L., & Bentler, P. M. (1999). Cutoff criteria for fit indexes in covariance structure analysis: Conventional criteria versus new alternatives. *Structural Equation Modeling: A Multidisciplinary Journal*, *6*(1), 1–55. https://doi.org/10.1080/10705519909540118

Iacobucci, D. (2010). Structural equations modeling: Fit indices, sample size, and advanced topics. *Journal of Consumer Psychology*, *20*(1), 90–98. https://doi.org/10.1016/j.jcps.2009.09.003

Ingram, J. S., & Pilla, S. D. (2007). Stress in the workplace, global risk control services, occupational health and safety, Research White Paper, ESIS, Inc.

International Labour Organization. (2020). *The impact of the COVID-19 pandemic on jobs and incomes in G20 economies* (pp. 1–46).

Ionescu, C. A., Paschia, L., Nicolau, N. L. G., Stanescu, S. G., Stancescu, V. M. N., Coman, M. D., & Uzlau, M. C. (2020). Sustainability analysis of the e-learning education system during pandemic period—Covid-19 in Romania. *Sustainability (Switzerland)*, *12*(21), 1–22. https://doi.org/10.3390/su12219030

Jain, V., & Jain, P. (2022). From industry 4.0 to education 4.0: Acceptance and use of videoconferencing applications in higher education of Oman. *Journal of Applied Research in Higher Education*, *14*(3), 1079–1098. https://doi.org/10.1108/JARHE-10-2020-0378

Joseph, J., & Sebastian, D. J. (2017). Do the demographics have the potential to influence work-life conflict. *International Journal of Research Culture Society*, *1*(6), 166–171.

Kaplan, G., Moll, B., & Violante, G. (2020). *The great lockdown and the big stimulus: Tracing the pandemic possibility frontier for the U.S. SSRN Electronic Journal*, 119. https://doi.org/10.2139/ssrn.3685207

Keeton, K., Fenner, D., Johnson, T., & Hayward, R. (2007). Predictors of physician career satisfaction, work–life balance, and burnout. *Obstetrics and Gynecology*, *109*(4), 949–955.

Impact of Job-related Stress on Professional and Personal Life   189

Kelly, M., Soles, R., Garcia, E., & Kundu, I. (2020). Job stress, burnout, work-life balance, well-being, and job satisfaction among pathology residents and fellows. *American Journal of Clinical Pathology*, *153*(4), 449–469. https://doi.org/10.1093/ajcp/aqaa013

Kennedy, M. (2020). WHO declares coronavirus outbreak a global health emergency. The Coronavirus Crises. https://www.npr.org/sections/goatsandsoda/2020/01/30/798894428/who-declares-coronavirus-outbreak-a-global-health-emergency

Khoury, M. M. (2021). Work-life balance constructs and job satisfaction: Evidence from the Palestinian investment sector. *International Business Research*, *14*(2), 13. https://doi.org/10.5539/ibr.v14n2p13

Kim, H., Ku, B., Kim, J. Y., Park, Y.-J., & Park, Y.-B. (2016). Confirmatory and exploratory factor analysis for validating the phlegm pattern questionnaire for healthy subjects, *Evidence-Based Complementary and Alternative Medicine*, *2016*, 1–8, https://doi.org/10.1155/2016/2696019

Kim, K. H. (2005). The relation among fit indexes, power, and sample size in structural equation modeling. *Structural Equation Modeling: A Multidisciplinary Journal*, *12*(3), 368–390. https://doi.org/10.1207/s15328007sem1203_2

Kumar, B., & Rao, T. (2020). Effect of demographics on work life balance of women employees in it industry-an analytical study. *International Journal of Advanced Research in Management and Social Sciences*, *9*(10), 91–105.

Lundberg, O., & Manderbacka, K. (1996). Assessing reliability of a measure of self-rated health. *Scandinavian Journal of Social Medicine*, *24*(3), 218–224. https://doi.org/10.1177/140349489602400314

Makhbul, Z. M., Alam, S. S., Azmi, S. M., & Talib, N. A. (2011). Ergonomics and work stress issues in banking sector. *Australian Journal of Basic and Applied Sciences*, *5*(9), 1301–1309.

Meharunisa, S. (2019). Work-life balance and job stress among female faculties in India's higher education institutions. *International Journal of Recent Technology and Engineering*, *8*(2S11), 846–852. https://doi.org/10.35940/ijrte.B1139.0982S1119

Midorikawa, H., Tachikawa, H., Taguchi, T., Shiratori, Y., Takahashi, A., Takahashi, S., Nemoto, K., & Arai, T. (2021). Demographics associated with stress, severe mental distress, and anxiety symptoms during the COVID-19 pandemic in Japan: Nationwide cross-sectional web-based survey. *JMIR Public Health and Surveillance*, *7*(11), e29970. https://doi.org/10.2196/29970

Miller, M. K., Edwards, C. P., Reichert, J., & Bornstein, B. H. (2018). An examination of outcomes predicted by the model of judicial stress. *Judicature*, *102*(3), 50–61.

Ornek, O. K., & Sevim, E. (2018). Work-related stress and coping profiles among workers in outer garment sector. *COJ Nursing & Healthcare*, *3*(February), 1–7. https://doi.org/10.20944/preprints201802.0061.v1

Pathak, M. (2010). Managing organizational conflict. *Oeconomics of Knowledge*, *2*(4), 2–12.

Persaud, N., & Persaud, I. (2015). The relationship between socio-demographics and stress levels, stressors, and coping mechanisms among undergraduate students at a university in Barbados. *International Journal of Higher Education*, *5*(1), 11–27. https://doi.org/10.5430/ijhe.v5n1p11

Robbins, S. P. (2001). *Organizational behavior* (9th ed.). Prentice-Hall.

Ross, D., & Vasantha, S. (2014). A study on impact of stress on work-life balance. *Sai Om Journal of Commerce & Management*, *1*(2), 61–65.

Saeed, K., & Farooqi, Y. A. (2014). Examining the relationship between work life balance, job stress and job satisfaction among university teachers. *International Journal of Multidisciplinary Sciences and Engineering*, 5(6), 9–15.

Selye, H. (1976). Stress without distress. In G. Serban (Ed.), *Psychopathology of Human Adaptation* (pp. 137–146). Springer. https://doi.org/10.1007/978-1-4684-2238-2_9

Singh, D. P. (2012). Control of workplace stress : A study. *International Journal of Education and Applied Research*, 2(2), 165–172.

Soni, P., & Bakhru, K. M. (2019). A review on teachers eudaemonic well-being and innovative behaviour: Exploring the importance of personality, work-life balance, self-efficacy and demographic variables. *International Journal of Learning and Change*, 11(2), 169–189. https://doi.org/10.1504/IJLC.2019.101661

Suganya, K. (2019). The factors affecting work life balance among post graduate students in Eastern province, Sri Lanka. *Asian Journal of Economics, Business and Accounting*, 11(1), 1–9. https://doi.org/10.9734/ajeba/2019/v11i130118

Taasoobshirazi, G., & Wang, S. (2016). The performance of the SRMR, RMSEA, CFI, and TLI: An examination of sample size, path size, and degrees of freedom. *Journal of Applied Quantitative Methods*, 11(3), 31–39.

Taber, K. S. (2018). The use of Cronbach's alpha when developing and reporting research instruments in science education. *Research in Science Education*, 48(6), 1273–1296. https://doi.org/10.1007/s11165-016-9602-2

The Marlin Company, & American Institute of Stress. (2001). The workplace stress scale. *The Seventh Annual Labor Day Survey*, 20, 1–11.

UNESCO. (2020). *UNITWIN/UNESCO chair holders institutional responses to COVID-19.*

Vinkers, C. H., van Amelsvoort, T., Bisson, J. I., Branchi, I., Cryan, J. F., Domschke, K., Howes, O. D., Manchia, M., Pinto, L., de Quervain, D., Schmidt, M. V., & van der Wee, N. J. A. (2020). Stress resilience during the coronavirus pandemic, *European Neuropsychopharmacology*, 35, 12–16, https://doi.org/10.1016/j.euroneuro.2020.05.003

Warrier, U. (2013). A study on work-life balance as a function of demographic variables at an IT company in Bangalore. *Journal of Organisation and Human Behaviour*, 2(4), 40–47.

Woo, D., Lee, Y., & Park, S. (2020). Associations among working hours, sleep duration, self-rated health, and health-related quality of life in Korean men. *Health and Quality of Life Outcomes*, 18(1), 287. https://doi.org/10.1186/s12955-020-01538-2

13 COVID-19 and the New Normal

Re-imagining the Future of Higher Education

Khuram Shahzad, Muhammad Rehan Shaukat, and Syeeda Shafiya

Introduction

The lingering impact of COVID-19 posed a monumental challenge for all the segments across the globe and changed human interactions dramatically with the lockdown and adoption of physical distancing guidelines. Turnbull et al. (2021) accentuated that prior to pandemic, simple tasks required little thought. However, the anxiety and uncertainty caused by the COVID-19 impacted the social interactions and collective efficacy of societies all around the world. The in-person correspondence was replicated with the digital meetings and this measure turned around the routine operations of the higher education institutions (HEIs) globally. The havoc generated due to COVID-19 stressed worldwide educational institutions to adopt digital learning (Mseleku, 2020). There was precariousness among various stakeholders in the higher education sector on the transition from traditional classroom teaching to an online mode due to the potential impact on the students' learning opportunities. However, they had to adapt the digital learning to mitigate the impact of this unprecedented challenge.

Higher education was severely impacted by the COVID-19 pandemic, with educational institutes closing their doors and the governments closing their borders in reaction to the lockdown regulations. The HEIs were compelled to substitute face-to-face teaching with online learning and this changeover impacted the educational process and wellbeing of the learners, particularly of the overseas students. The institutions attempted to employ technology and opt online learning methods as an alternative to ensure the continuity of education despite the lockdown and other challenges. Contrarily, several HEIs struggled to adopt the alternate ways during the pandemic apparently due to the lack the experience and time required to devise the new methods of delivering teaching and the lesson plans (Schleicher, 2020). To counter the damage done by the COVID-19, some measures to foster the resilience needs to be taken. The current research identifies the issues faced by the learners during the pandemic and analyses their potential impact on the learning process.

Due to the unprecedent challenges posed during the pandemic, students and the teaching staff entered a new era of remote learning through the virtual

DOI: 10.4324/9781003457299-16

classrooms (Neuwirth et al., 2021). Teachers and students faced various challenges as they went through the transition from the traditional method of delivery to the online mode. Though most of the HEIs across the globe have adopted the new normal, however, the lingering impact of those challenges needs to be dealt with to overcome the learning losses and mitigate the socio-emotional stress on the key stakeholders like the students and teachers. Healthy collaboration among the teachers and the learners is essential, and a number of studies reveal that the association was influenced negatively during the era of pandemic. For the students with difficulties in learning, several resource persons undertook an additional outreach and contact opportunities during the pandemic to check on their academic progress and facilitate their learning. Higher education institutes need to reimagine their learning environments with the widening of digitalisation and enhance the virtual interaction with the stakeholders.

According to Tesar (2020), many of the conjectures of COVID-19 have been dispelled. The current academic year in most of the countries is ending on a high note with the return of in-person teaching, high vaccination rates, and the physical access to resources at HEIs. However, the COVID-19 wreaked havoc on the education system globally during the last couple of years. The impact of the pandemic is mitigated and it is believed that it won't necessarily be developed further in a linear fashion. Thus, it is widely acknowledged that a protracted change is on the horizon of the academic sector and leading it towards the 'new normal' with blended learning and flexible work settings. Experts believe that the new normal will gradually evolve into more technology-driven and offer new opportunities and challenges with the accelerated use of digital platforms. This study is an attempt to capture the lived experiences of the students in HEIs of Oman and explores the dilemmatic context which the COVID-19 pandemic developed in the country's higher education society's fabric.

The Proposition of HEIs during the Pandemic

Since 11 March 2020, when the COVID-19 was declared a pandemic by the World Health Organisation, speculations about the catastrophic effects of the virus and its impact on the education system have been widespread. Several researchers investigated the impact of temporary measures opted by the HEIs on the process of teaching and learning and the unique space the students and teaching staff found themselves in during the pandemic. The literature review analyses the current state of knowledge and discuss some methodological issues arose due to the COVID-19.

The pandemic had a worldwide impact on the teaching and learning operations of HEIs. The COVID-19 outbreak drastically altered the way HEIs operate globally (Turnbull et al., 2021). With the closure of on-campus activities, HEIs across the world hastened their transition to online learning, which had major implications for both students and teachers. This transformation is facilitated by the incorporation of digital learning systems, broadly categorised as asynchronous and synchronous, with an aim to opt an online delivery system. Asynchronous learning systems are based on communication platforms that eliminate the need for time-sensitive interactions between educational stakeholders. Moodle and Blackboard are two well-known learning management systems that are intended to promote stakeholder interactions using a 'request-response' paradigm. Synchronous online learning, on the other hand, is often accomplished with the use of video conferencing platforms such as Zoom, Skype, or Microsoft Teams. These applications are proven critical to the attempts of various HEIs to reproduce face-to-face classroom settings online (Kohnke & Moorhouse, 2022).

The conventional face-to-face pedagogical techniques were accommodated with remote teaching to continue the learning process in disruptive situations. The literature identifies five critical barriers to effective online transition: integrating synchronous and asynchronous tools into seamless online delivery, overcoming technological access barriers, improving online competencies for learners and faculty, addressing academic dishonesty issues in online assessment, and maintaining privacy and confidentiality. The HEIs locally and globally adopted various techniques to maximise online learning opportunities for students. The high visibility of the educational institutions' revised frameworks was crucial to materialise the technological support and the updated instructional resources for the staff and students. Similarly, the ability of students to overcome anxiety and close engagement with remote teaching was strengthened to enhance the effectiveness of the online learning management system (Turnbull et al., 2021). In line with the expectation of HEIs administration, the teaching staff made an extra effort to optimise the online learning of the students and concurrently learned the new digital platforms. To help their students get through the challenging circumstances during COVID-19, teachers regarded themselves as actual second-line responders.

Context of Oman

The chaos of the pandemic brought several restrictions like the closure of educational establishments, lockdowns, social distancing measures, and extra-level hygiene which disrupted the teaching and learning process locally and globally (Pokhrel & Chhetri, 2021). A vast majority of HEIs in Oman had no prior experience in delivering online programmes and hence they transitioned to online learning with tentative planning considering the guidelines issued by the Ministry of Higher Education Oman (Malik & Javed, 2021). HEIs in Oman continued the online teaching and learning system with all possible means for more than a year even when the institutes were opened for the teaching staff. Students gradually adjusted with the new normal as a result of several alternative and innovative ways adopted to support their learning. Students enrolled during the pandemic faced several constraints like weak orientation, social isolation, home confinement, and lack of peer-to-peer support.

Many other students faced issues to adopt the online learning like poor access to the adequate devices or the internet particularly in some rural areas, lack of an appropriate space in their homes to study online and less familiarity with digital technologies. The mental health of students is greatly impacted by their home bubbles and institutional support. The HEIs in Oman extended their flexibility in terms of technical and academic support to all the students during the implementation of online learning. However, the challenges posed due to the frequent lockdowns, anxiety of unknown, and lack of perceived support affected their overall learning capabilities. Numerous studies have shown that when communities face public health emergencies, their mental health suffers significantly, and higher education students are no exception. The COVID-19 outbreak has been more devasting than any other public health disaster in recent history. For over a year, university students have been removed from the physical campuses, and the programmes are delivered online for all that period (Malik & Javed, 2021).

HEIs in Oman switched to online teaching and learning from the traditional face-to-face mode when on 15 March 2020, the Sultanate of Oman's Supreme Committee decided to suspend in-person classes. As a result of this transition to the online education, HEIs altered their assessment methods and revised strategies to utilise their IT investments. It enabled HEIs to advance with the delivery of their academic programmes while collaborating with all key stakeholders. A constraint to the online education can be posed due to learning difficulties, lack of consciousness from the academic staff, job burn-out, and limited access to the digital technology and tools of learning which can hamper the students' focus and result in the learning losses (Al-Maskari et al., 2021). Some students from rural and distant areas in Oman faced the challenge of accessing the necessary digital technologies when the Ministry of Higher Education mandated all HEIs to employ online teaching methods for the continuity of the academic year. However, the situation was well addressed with the flexibility in the processes and the support extended by the academic institutions towards their students. Microsoft Teams was widely adopted by the HEIs in Oman to continue the delivery of online teaching. Accordingly, the German University of Technology in Oman made experimental e-learning classes and coursework for Bachelor of Computer Science students and that will be incorporated for other programmes (Bensaid & Brahimi, 2020).

Impact of COVID-19 Pandemic on Gulf Cooperation Council

The ripple effects of the pandemic were handled through different measures across the Gulf Cooperation Council (GCC) states. In the aftermath of the COVID-19 pandemic, the UAE seemed quite successful in containing the spread of the virus by implementing several precautionary measures. Closure of all schools and universities, cancellation of public events, suspension of entry into the country, precautionary measures by food outlets, flight restrictions, country-wide disinfection, and the adoption of working from home for

COVID-19 and the New Normal 195

employees were among the core measures (Crawford et al., 2020). In response to the COVID-19, all UAE universities were responsive to shifting their teaching to an online mode. As a result of this global shift, many UAE universities have been thrown into a new world of digital delivery and online classes. In a survey conducted in the United Arab Emirates, Almuraqab (2020) discovered that more than 58% of the respondents felt that the online method offered confined learning opportunities and impacted the collaborative learning process by reducing their capacity to learn and engage with their peers and teachers. According to Gillis and Krull (2020), learners encountered difficulties in studying online, either due to interruptions, technological glitches, loss of enthusiasm, or greater uneasiness. The universities implemented online educational systems by adopting digital platforms such as Big Blue Button, MS Teams, and BlackBoard Connect to facilitate the students and academic staff in terms of the continuity of their learning process (Visvizi et al., 2021). This increase is attributable in part to the government funding for the quick adoption of new online learning methods, including those that were already in place before the epidemic. In the United Arab Emirates, for example, the MBRSLP collaborated with the Ministry of Education and the UAE's Telecommunications Regulatory Authority to quickly deploy virtual classrooms for all students across the country in partnership with Microsoft (Eslick & Abdeljaber, 2020).

Several universities in the Kingdom of Saudi Arabia (KSA) organised workshops in preparation for the virtual courses and established specific methods for the final exams (Visvizi et al., 2021). The Saudi Innovation and Technology Network and The Integrated Telecom Company experimented in the KSA to succeed in creating an online digital platform specialised in transmitting materials to instructors, parents, and students to provide an excellent digital learning system and learning platform (Bensaid & Brahimi, 2020). Similarly, The American University of Kuwait launched an e-learning site allowing students to examine course content and communicate with university lecturers regarding the course curriculums, rather than holding examinations. During the pandemic, the University of Kuwait used Blackboard connect to develop the teaching and learning process (Visvizi et al., 2021).

Numerous digital programmes are employed by educational institutions in Bahrain, including ClassDojo, Microsoft Teams, and Zoom. In addition, online learning applications such as Moodle, Blackboard, and others are available in HEIs. The shift to online learning was seamless at all Bahraini universities because the Higher Education Council and Bahrain's Education and Training Quality Authority (BQA) explored and made appropriate recommendations to most of the companies. It further emphasises that all such universities had clear policies, methodologies, adequate infrastructure, learning resources, e-learning platforms, and many other services and amenities (Al-Rawi et al., 2021). According to UNESCO data, COVID-19 has affected 12,085,898 learners in the GCC nations, out of a total population of 58,664,098, as illustrated in Table 13.1.

Table 13.1 Number of affected male and female learners in GCC

Number of affected learners	Bahrain	Kuwait	Oman	Qatar	KSA	UAE	Total-GCC
Male	144,535	376,419	445,430	168,540	4,304,758	712,370	6,152,052
Female	147,894	400,750	454,723	174,984	4,105,506	649,989	5,933,846
Total	292,429	777,169	900,153	343,524	8,410,264	1,362,359	12,085,898

The COVID-19 Education Response of the International Association of Universities and UNESCO created a list of activities, resources, and tools for HEIs throughout the world to ensure the smooth continuation of teaching and learning during the COVID-19 pandemic. UNESCO also facilitated several measures focusing on readiness, privacy protection, programme integration, psycho-social challenges, assistance for teachers and parents, the ease of digital learning platforms, and monitoring the students' learning process to ensure the effectiveness of online education during the pandemic (Bensaid & Brahimi, 2020).

Several HEIs across the GCC extended their e-library services to assist students and faculty members with their learning approaches. Various technology projects since the pandemic are being expanded and diversified significantly to enhance the efficacy of the virtual learning environment, and to collaborate actively at all levels to strengthen the remote educational resources. The earlier stage of digital transformation systems in smart education, like the 'Classroom of the Future,' included online learning platforms and information and communication technology (ICT) material, which contributed significantly to facilitate the transition from traditional face-to-face learning to remote learning. Digital transformation represents the process of enhancement using information, communication, and connection while considering increasing needs into account (Al Fadhel et al., 2022). The transition in the education system of HEIs in the GCC during the pandemic was largely reinforced by the governing bodies. The Ministries of Education in the GCC states aided the provision of technological platforms required to encourage remote learning while maintaining internet penetration rates of over 90%. Many research projects and government grants on COVID-19 have been established by GCC HEIs, together with educational health programmes and training sessions, as well as an application system to track the impact of the pandemic (Bensaid & Brahimi, 2020).

The analysis of existing literature indicates relatively less emphasis paid on training the teaching staff during the pandemic whereas personal and professional development is considered mandatory for the instructors (Allam, 2020). The training of the teaching staff and addressing their dissonance can benefit their utilisation of the digital education mechanisms and optimise their scholarship of the different online learning management systems.

This eventually can aid their adaptation to the new normal (Vlachopoulos, 2020). An online evaluation system made it easier for teachers to monitor the students' abilities based on their knowledge rather than their recollection. With the progressive elaboration of digital learning platforms, students were not able to not only continue their education, but they mastered the most recent online applications that unquestionably increased their technical abilities. Additionally, the use of flipped classrooms has consequently increased the potential for faculty to teach courses via recorded lectures. As a result, they were able to spend more time on the effective implementation of the delivered knowledge, which in turn generates adjudicates (Chick et al., 2020). The use of recorded lectures and online one-to-one support sessions facilitated the students' learning and promoted the student engagement (Muthuprasad et al., 2021). The rapid expansion of higher education in the Gulf region is supported by public funds and private investors who contributed to meet the cost of higher education. In Qatar, the digital transformation partnership of Ooredoo and the Ministry of Education and Higher Education is an excellent example of the government working with a private business enterprise to facilitate digital learning. Meanwhile in Oman, Ooredoo has improved the quality of the internet subscriptions of the educational institutions in order to support the online education.

Reimaging the Scholarship Parameters

According to Pellegrini et al. (2020), opportunities for learners need to be offered on equal grounds. Basic research funding will need to be reconsidered as well, since it has taken a heavy hit in recent years but will be able to generate in the future if it is permitted to fulfil its function of predicting knowledge and making that information accessible in general, but particularly in times of crisis. The scholarship or financial assistance was crucial during the pandemic due to the uncertainty and financial slump most of the HEIs were facing across the globe (Aristovnik et al., 2020). For this reason, it is essential that the state supplements fund for the issuance of student grants be sustained in the post-pandemic phase to avoid the occurrence of 'beneficiaries without grants' and so comply with art. There will be a significant amount of work to be done in order to guarantee that educational and research demands are satisfied satisfactorily utilising virtual instruments in light of the tremendous disruption created by the epidemic. The incubators in the education establishments are also working on novel therapies and vaccinations, as well as new ways to produce respirators and face protection. Universities have shown their dynamism and adaptability by meeting the challenge with competence in virology, epidemiology, or sociology and aiding society in so many ways. A visible number of staff and students across HEIs worldwide still need to improve their digital literacy to take advantage of the new learning settings. Higher education's future is definitely in need of adjustment in a variety of ways. HEIs, governments,

198   *Khuram Shahzad, Muhammad Rehan Shaukat, and Syeeda Shafiya*

communities, and other stakeholders are in dire need to collaborate more globally and multilaterally.

Objectives of the Chapter

This chapter aims to predict and explicate the phenomena of interest (Williams, 2007) in order to investigate the impact of COVID-19 on students' learning and identify the challenges they faced in adopting online education. The quantitative orientation allows to target a large sample of respondents who, in this chapter, are students enrolled in public and private HEIs in Oman. To conduct this quantitative study, a survey method is employed which has a widespread use in collecting data, particularly for exploratory and descriptive studies (Gürbüz, 2017). The surveys are conducted in various ways like online, telephonic, interview, and through post (Henn et al., 2006). In this approach, the sample respondents are engaged to collect data through an online questionnaire and the findings are drawn based on their responses.

The target population for this study were the students studying in the HEIs of Oman. As per the Ministry of Higher Education Research and Innovation (MOHERI) website, there are 42 HEIs (both public and private) in Oman. This number does not include the vocational training institutes. During the COVID-19, students aiming to complete their academic degrees suffered a great deal of learning losses due to the jeopardising of the academic calendars. Therefore, considering them as the key recipients, the current study emphasised collecting data from the students investigating their personal experiences during the pandemic.

An online questionnaire, with a self-completion method, was designed to collect the data from the students. A questionnaire refers to a set of statements developed with the aim of recording the specific responses of the participants of the study. The first part of the questionnaire briefed the respondents about the nature and purpose of this research, and they were ensured on the confidentiality of their responses. The emails of the authors were provided to address any queries or ambiguities of the participants. The participation rate in the beginning was good; however, it slowed down after a couple of weeks and we had to send reminders to follow up with the students and requested the teaching staff of the respective HEIs to encourage the students to participate in the survey. The blend of efforts resulted in a positive outcome, and we were able to receive responses from 214 students.

The decision on sample size is a significant contributor to the study and a small or very large sample size can add to the complexity of the research (Martínez-Mesa et al., 2014). The study has deployed non-probability sampling to induce the sample respondents. Within the frame of non-probability sampling, the convenience sampling technique was used to select the respondents. The convenience sampling is often preferred due to its ease of accessibility (Rahi, 2017) and offers flexibility in the data collection process.

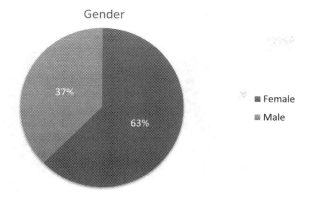

Figure 13.1 Gender distribution of participants

Learning Experiences during COVID-19 Pandemic

The majority (63%) of the respondents are females. The enrolment of female students in higher education institutes in Oman has been on the rise in recent years as compared to male students. As per the statistics of the Higher Education Admission Centre (HEAC) Oman, the number of new students enrolled in the academic year of 2019–20 was 24,445 and out of which 57.3% were females.

Similarly, the HEAC reported that the students enrolled in the academic year of 2020–21 were 25,316 with a 56.4% enrolment of female students.

A large number of students (70%) from the private higher education institutes across Oman participated in the survey whereas the representation from the public sector HEIs was 30%. The government higher education institutes, as per the MOHERI Oman, largely include Sultan Qaboos University,

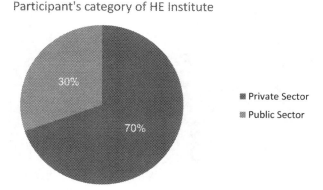

Figure 13.2 HEI sector of participants

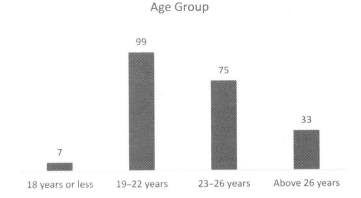

Figure 13.3 Age categories of participants

13 colleges under the umbrella of the University of Technology and Applied Sciences, and the College of Shariah Science whereas there are 27 private colleges and universities in the Sultanate.

The respondents from the different age groups shared their learning experiences during the pandemic. As Figure 13.3 demonstrates, the majority of the participants (99, 46%) of the study belong to the age group of 19–22 years, whereas only 7 students (3%) of age 18 years or less volunteered to take part in the survey.

Figure 13.4 exhibits that the respondents with a range of education levels participated in the study. Out of the 214, the majority (128, 60%) are enrolled in the Bachelors programme while 14 students (7%) from the Master degree contributed to the survey. 51 (24%) of the participants are enrolled in a Diploma whereas the representation from a Foundation programme is 21 (9%).

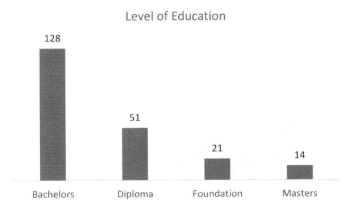

Figure 13.4 Educational level of participants

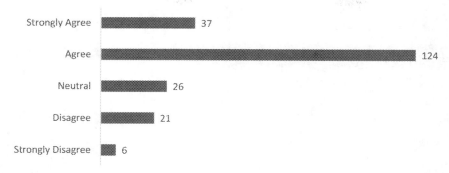

Figure 13.5 The teaching staff was able to tailor the academic activities into an online mode.

Thus a representative sample from a range of programmes offered at the HEIs in the Sultanate participated in this survey.

The majority of the respondents of this study (75%) believe that the teaching staff effectively transformed the academic activities into an online mode which reflects a reasoned effort from the academic staff to ensure the continuity of the module delivery during the academic calendar.

The drastic impact of COVID-19 and the unprecedented transition from traditional classroom teaching to an online delivery resulted in learning losses for the students as evident in Figure 13.6. As much as 69% of the participating students feel that their learning ability was negatively impacted due to this transition.

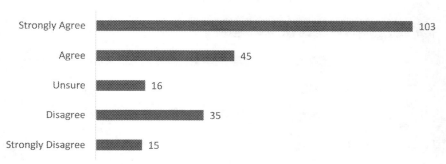

Figure 13.6 The transition from the traditional to online education reduced my learning efficacy.

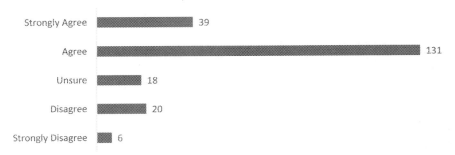

Figure 13.7 My college/university opted effective measures to convert the educational process in an online mode during COVID-19.

A significant number of the participants (79%) reflected their satisfaction with the measures taken by their colleges/universities to switch the educational process to an online mode due to the lockdowns in COVID-19. This high satisfaction rate among the students indicates the timely and effective decision-making of the higher education institutes across the country to ensure undisrupted studies.

As Figure 13.8 illustrates, 75% of the participants confirmed that they were able to access the necessary equipment to continue their education in an online mode. According to the World Bank data, the GDP per Capita of Oman in 2021 was USD 16,439.3 signifying the country is reasonably supplying the inhabitants with what they require. However, around 25% of the respondents of this study faced challenges in acquiring the needed material to support their studies.

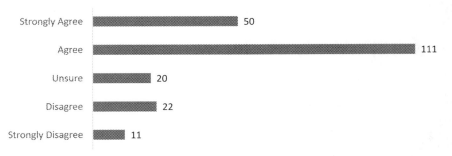

Figure 13.8 I was able to access the essential equipment or tools (like laptop, desktop, internet connection) for continuing education through online.

COVID-19 and the New Normal 203

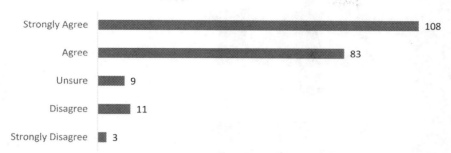

Figure 13.9 The stress due to COVID-19 concerns impacted my learning ability.

A vast majority of the research participants (89%) reflected that the COVID-19-related stress had an impact on their learning ability. The temporal closure of the HEIs disrupted the physical learning mode of the students and led to some psychological and mental health concerns as well. The International Council for Open and Distance Education revealed that the emergency responses to opt the remote learning were less effective in some cases due to the inadequate support services for the students.

Figure 13.10 depicts a high satisfaction rate (72%) among the participants for the IT resources their colleges/universities provided for remote learning during COVID-19. On the other hand, 19% of respondents were not satisfied with the IT facilities offered to support their online learning whereas 9% students didn't reflect their satisfaction. To sum up, it can be inferred that most

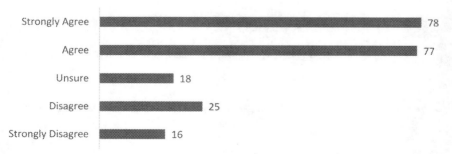

Figure 13.10 I am satisfied with the digital (IT) resources my HEI provided during the COVID-19.

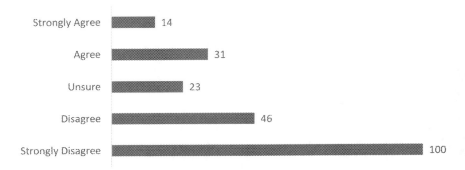

Figure 13.11 I found it easier to study individually in an online mode as compared to the face-to-face classroom teaching.

of the colleges and universities in Oman developed their ICT resources and expanded their use in the learning process.

The current study reveals that 68% of students didn't find that easier to study individually in an online mode means majority of the students faced some challenges in continuing their studies at home, while 21% of the participants found online education easier over the traditional classroom teaching. Among the participants, 11% could not determine which mode of study was easier to opt.

In the phase of providing online education during the COVID-19, a large number of the participants (47%) of this study couldn't connect with their teachers for additional support as they could do in the traditional mode of delivery. On the other hand, 41% of the respondents expressed their satisfaction

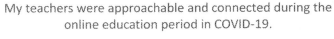

Figure 13.12 The teaching staff was approachable and connected in the virtual learning settings during COVID-19 pandemic.

COVID-19 and the New Normal 205

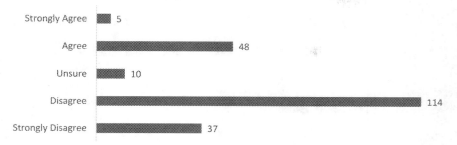

Figure 13.13 I was able to arrange a quiet place at home to attend the lectures online.

in terms of approaching their teachers to seek any additional support required during remote teaching.

Another big challenge the students encountered during the online teaching was to arrange a quiet place at home where they could attend the online lectures. As evident in above Figure 13.13, a majority of the respondents (71%) of this study informed that they suffered from managing a tranquil place to concentrate on the sessions delivered online.

In the post-COVID scenario, 139 out of 214 participants (65%) preferred the physical or traditional mode of learning at their colleges or universities whereas 48 (22%) responded in favour of the hybrid mode of learning. Only 27 (13%) students voted in favour of online education.

In the 'new normal' with the resumption of traditional classroom teaching, the majority of the participants (76%) informed that they are able to concentrate on their studies which is an extremely favourable aspect. However, 14%

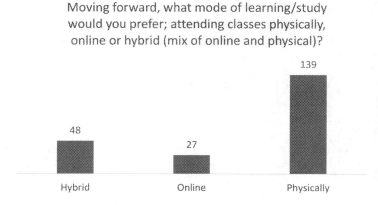

Figure 13.14 Moving forward, what mode of study would you prefer; attending classes physically, online or hybrid (mix of physical and online)?

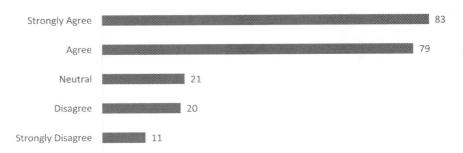

Figure 13.15 After the resumption of on-campus education, I feel more comfortable to concentrate on my studies.

respondents in the study are still struggling to regain the level of concentration required to continue their education, whereas 10% of the participants didn't reflected on their feeling of resuming their studies in normal mode.

Conclusion and Recommendations

Students agonised a drastic impact of the COVID-19 pandemic not only on their studies but their personal lives as well. The containment measures taken by the government and HEIs posed unique challenges for the learners and constricted their opportunities for personal and professional growth. With the resumption of campus-based learning systems, the imperative should ensure the rigorous implementation of evidence-based initiatives to reimagine the education system in the longer run. The following are some of the proposed recommendations informed by the analysis presented in this chapter:

1 **Introducing learning recovery programmes**
   The HEIs in Oman are opened for the students after a temporal closure and resumed campus-based teaching. Through this research, a large number of students revealed that their learning abilities were negatively impacted due to the stressors of COVID-19 and they struggled to study individually in an online mode. Therefore, at this stage, identifying the students who faced psychological distress during the unprecedented situation of the pandemic and offering them remedial education and socio-emotional support to recover their unfinished learning and instill a sense of epidemiological safety. Higher education institutes can formulate well-being teams for this purpose to support such emerging needs of both staff and the students.
2 **Blended learning or flexi-working**
   The emergency remote modality resulted due to COVID-19 necessitated online teaching universally for the continuity of the academic year(s).

COVID-19 and the New Normal 207

Higher education institutes can opt a hybrid learning mode pertinent to the nature of the modules/programmes engaging students in an effective learning environment. The blended learning can be layered with synchronous and asynchronous platforms to yield maximum learning output. Further, agile or flexible working can support the teaching staff to maintain a good work-life balance.

3 **Groundwork for the future events**

The decision-makers of the higher education institutes can contemplate preparing for the future as their core agenda in policymaking as the policy-level intervention is crucial at this stage. The appointments of dedicated resource persons and the updated risk registers can help to avoid or mitigate similar potential threats in the future.

4 **New normal for the future learning**

In the post-pandemic era, equipping HEIs with the necessary resources, procedures and training seems integral. For an effective utilisation of the digital learning platforms, professional development programmes can be offered to enhance the digital skills of the teachers. Similarly, some innovative pedagogical practices can be opted to facilitate the learning of the students in the new normal.

References

Al Fadhel, H., Aljalahma, A., Almuhanadi, M., Asad, M., & Sheikh, U. (2022). Management of higher education institutions in the GCC countries during the emergence of COVID-19: A review of opportunities, challenges, and a way forward. *International Journal of Learning in Higher Education, 29* (1), 83–97.

Allam, Z. (2020). Demystifying the aspect of quality in higher education: Insights from Saudi Arabia. *SAGE Open*, 10 (1), 215824401989905.

Al-Maskari, A., Al-Riyami, T., & Kunjumuhammed, S. K. (2021). Students academic and social concerns during COVID-19 pandemic. *Education and Information Technologies, 27*, 1–21.

Almuraqab, N. A. (2020). Shall universities at the UAE continue distance learning after the covid-19 pandemic? Revealing students' perspective. *International Journal of Advanced Research in Engineering and Technology, 11*(5), 226–233.

Al-Rawi, Y. M., Subhi Al-Dayyeni, W., & Reda, I. (2021). COVID-19 impact on education and work in the Kingdom of Bahrain: Survey study. *Information Sciences Letters, 10*(3), 5

Aristovnik, A., Keržič, D., Ravšelj, D., Tomaževič, N., & Umek, L. (2020). Impacts of the COVID-19 pandemic on life of higher education students: A global perspective. *Sustainability, 12*(20), 8438.

Bensaid, B., & Brahimi, T. (2020). Coping with COVID-19: Higher education in the GCC countries. *The International Research & Innovation Forum*, 137–153. https://link.springer.com/chapter/10.1007/978-3-030-62066-0_12#citeas

Chick, R. C., Clifton, G. T., Peace, K. M., Propper, B. W., Hale, D. F., Alseidi, A. A., & Vreeland, T. J. (2020). Using technology to maintain the education of residents during the COVID-19 pandemic. *Journal of Surgical Education, 77*(4), 729–732.

Crawford, J., Butler-Henderson, K., Rudolph, J., Malkawi, B., Glowatz, M., Burton, R., & Lam, S. (2020). COVID-19: 20 countries' higher education intra-period digital pedagogy responses. *Journal of Applied Learning & Teaching, 3*(1), 1–20.

Eslick, A., & Abdeljaber, J. (2020). *A report card for distance education in the UAE. Reed-Smith.* https://www.reedsmith.com/en/perspectives/2020/11/a-report-card-for-distance-education-in-the-uae

Gillis, A., & Krull, L. M. (2020). COVID-19 remote learning transition in spring 2020: Class structures, student perceptions, and inequality in college courses. *Teaching Sociology, 48*(4), 283–299.

Gürbüz, S. (2017). Survey as a quantitative research method. *Research Methods and Techniques in Public Relations and Advertising, 2017,* 141–162.

Henn, M., Weinstein, M., & Foard, N. (2006). *A short introduction to social research.* Sage.

Kohnke, L., & Moorhouse, B. L. (2022). Facilitating synchronous online language learning through Zoom. *RELC Journal, 53*(1), 296–301

Malik, M., & Javed, S. (2021). Perceived stress among university students in Oman during COVID-19-induced e-learning. *Middle East Current Psychiatry, 28*(1), 1–8

Martínez-Mesa, J., González-Chica, D. A., Bastos, J. L., Bonamigo, R. R., & Duquia, R. P. (2014). Sample size: How many participants do I need in my research?. *Anais Brasileiros de Dermatologia, 89*(4), 609–615.

Mseleku, Z. (2020). A literature review of e-learning and e-teaching in the era of Covid-19 pandemic. *SAGE, 57*(52), 6.

Muthuprasad, T., Aiswarya, S., Aditya, K. S., & Jha, G. K. (2021). Students' perception and preference for online education in India during COVID-19 pandemic. *Social Sciences & Humanities Open, 3*(1), 100101.

Neuwirth, L. S., Jović, S., & Mukherji, B. R. (2021). Reimagining higher education during and post-COVID-19: Challenges and opportunities. *Journal of Adult and Continuing Education, 27*(2), 141–156.

Pellegrini, M., Uskov, V., & Casalino, N. (2020). Reimagining and re-designing the post-COVID-19 higher education organizations to address new challenges and responses for safe and effective teaching activities. *Law and Economics Yearly Review Journal-LEYR, Queen Mary University, London, UK, 9*(part 1), 219–248.

Pokhrel, S., & Chhetri, R. (2021). A literature review on impact of COVID-19 pandemic on teaching and learning. *Higher Education Future, 8*(1), 133–141.

Rahi, S. (2017). Research design and methods: A systematic review of research paradigms, sampling issues and instruments development. *International Journal of Economics & Management Sciences, 6*(2), 1000403.

Schleicher, A. (2020). *The impact of COVID-19 on education: Insights from education at a glance 2020.* OECD.

Tesar, M. (2020). Towards a post-Covid-19 'new normality?': Physical and social distancing, the move to online and higher education. *Policy Futures in Education, 18*(5), 556–559.

Turnbull, D., Chugh, R., & Luck, J. (2021). Transitioning to E-learning during the COVID-19 pandemic: How have higher education Institutions responded to the challenge? *Education and Information Technologies, 26*(5), 6401–6419.

Visvizi, A., Lytras, M. D., & Aljohani, N. R. (2021). *Research and innovation forum 2020: Disruptive technologies in times of change.* Springer.

Vlachopoulos, D. (2020). COVID-19: Threat or opportunity for online education?. *Higher Learning Research Communications, 10*(1), 16–19.

Williams, C. (2007). Research methods. *Journal of Business & Economics Research (JBER), 5*(3), 65–72.

14 Gulf Higher Education Reforms vis-à-vis the Pandemic

Conclusion

Reynaldo Gacho Segumpan and John McAlaney

Higher education institutions (HEIs) in the Gulf need to grapple with the ramifications of the COVID-19 pandemic. One of the strategic options is to institute reforms that (re)build strengths and fortify weaknesses of HEIs from macro and micro perspectives. In *An Empirical Analysis of Oman's Public and Private HEI Students' Behavioural Intention (BI) in Using E-learning during COVID-19*, the authors explored the potentials of e-learning in shaping learners' behaviours in the teaching-learning processes. Using the Technology Acceptance Model, the authors unpacked the importance of creating a conducive atmosphere for e-learning as well as the critical roles of perceived usefulness, self-efficacy, perceived ease of use, environment readiness, and behavioural intention. Without a doubt, the landscape of higher education (HE) in the global scenario has been altered by COVID-19 and although e-learning has been in place prior to the pandemic, HEIs need to catalyse their e-learning initiatives, policies, and programmes in order to prepare the academic community for any similar waves of disruption in HE in the future.

At the individual level, COVID-19 has also impacted academics from a socio-psychological perspectives. One of the authors of *Transforming Online Teaching of a First-year Business Course: An Autoethnographic Reflection of Managing Teaching and Learning amidst the Pandemic in the Gulf Region* shared the challenges brought about by the pandemic. The narratives of educators and students echo the classroom realities that were reshaped by the impact of the pandemic. Foremost of them was on social interaction and then the anxiety of uncertain future. The concerned lecturer, who made a qualitative enquiry on how to transform online teaching, recommends that the class environment be given attention in order to sustain motivation among learners. In a nutshell, academics must create a positive teaching-learning environment that will sustain learners' interest and scaffold understanding of concepts not only in a business class but also in other subject areas.

As a case in point, the authors of *University of Buraimi in Oman: Pandemic Lessons and Initiatives for Education Reform from Instructors' Perspectives* explored the issues and challenges faced by academics during COVID-19

DOI: 10.4324/9781003457299-17

210 *Reynaldo Gacho Segumpan and John McAlaney*

and the measures that could be instituted in order to cushion the impact of the pandemic on HE. Using primary and secondary data, the chapter authors succinctly recommend some reforms that need to be implemented in HEIs in Oman, in particular, and the Gulf, in general, such as "enhancing the competencies of faculty members in HE to foster the advancement of the education system, measuring and facilitating student growth in evolving circumstances, and implementing a variety of strategies to transform the educational process and promote the integration of digital technologies". In other words, educational reforms during the pandemic should substantially focus on elevating HE faculty members' job-related knowledge and skills. With the shift to online learning during COVID-19, it is also imperative that HEIs should (re)consider technological reforms in order to keep up with the demands of e-learning even after the pandemic is over. Such reforms should be continuous, realistic, situation-tailored, and supported by key decision-makers.

Another aspect of educational reforms for consideration is communication and communication dissemination. Without a doubt, communication play a critical role during a crisis, such as the COVID-19 pandemic. In *The Role of Internal Crisis Communication on Faculty Members' Implementation of Blended Learning Practices in the Gulf,* the importance of internal crisis communication was emphasised in the context of blended learning (BL). The authors of the chapter explored how certain conditions such as faculty members' crisis perception, perceived technological support, university administrative support, and affective commitment would facilitate the implementation of BL during COVID-19. As supported in their research, the authors reaffirm the necessity for these conditions for HE reforms to be communicated effectively. Communication shall, at all times, establish open networks and cultivate positive climate in order to complement ground realities.

The authors of *Impact of Job-related Stress on Professional and Personal Life during Coronavirus Pandemic* highlight how the pandemic has aggravated stress levels among academics as well as its negative implications on their work-life (im)balance. Their study calls for institutional reforms that will help higher educators in the Gulf, in particular, deal with stress more efficaciously and frame better outlooks in striking a balance between the demands of work and the fear of the pandemic. Mental health promotion and related programmes need to be sustained in HEIs not only in Oman but also in the Gulf as a whole. Apparently, this requires top management endorsement and commitment.

The tasks ahead seem to be Herculean but as mentioned in the beginning of this chapter, HEIs cannot be complacent in their approaches and strategies in dealing with the issues and challenges of COVID-19. In *COVID-19 and the New Normal: Re-imagining the Future of Higher Education,* the authors recommend the implementation of a learning recovery programme for those who were psychologically distressed during the pandemic, and

Gulf Higher Education Reforms vis-à-vis the Pandemic 211

intensifying policy formulation and clarifying policy directions. They also highlight the need for "going digital" as the "new normal" for the HE landscape in the Gulf.

In a nutshell, reforms in HEIs in the Gulf are not optional anymore; they are the needs of the times. The chapters in this section have demonstrated that these HEIs must evolve with the current ecosystem and be steadfast in their institutional efforts, educational programmes, and strategic policies in order to withstand any recurrence of any pandemic or any disruptions that may stifle creativity and HE developments.

We both agree to disagree that change is not constant.

Index

Note: *Italicized* and **bold** page numbers refer to figures and tables.

Aasland, K. E. 45
Abushammala, M. 138
access to education 19, 70; online classes and 61–62
accreditation 14, 17, 18, 20, 23, 47, 52, 55, 65, 74
Adamu, A. A. 161, 162, 165
adhocracy 63
Adobe Connect 9
Agrawal, J. 43–44
Ahmad, W. 79
Al-Adwan, A. 108
Al-Amri, A. S. 43
Aldulaimi, S. H. 78
Al-Fadhel, H. 77
Al Khalili, S. 138–139
Al-Mamari, K. 30
Al-Maskari, A. 138
Almuraqab, N. A. 195
Al-Rahmi, W. M. 110
Al-Saidi, A. 138
Al Shamsi, I. 139
Al-Zaabi, H. K. 138
American Psychological Association 176
American University of Kuwait 195; mitigation plans for HEIs 94
ANOVA analysis 77
Anthony, B. 165
artificial intelligence 2, 91
Ashour, S. 160
Ayoub, A. E. A. H. 9–10

Bahrain 86; *BeAware Bahrain* 91; COVID-19 pandemic 89, 91, **196**; Education and Training Quality Authority (BQA) 195; faculties challenges to using ICT during COVID-19 80, **80–82**; Higher Education Council 195; ICT-based higher education 76, 79; mitigation plans for HEIs 94; *SkipLino* 91; students challenges to using ICT during COVID-19 **84**
Bahrain University: mitigation plans for HEIs 94
Bangladesh: post-pandemic crisis of education system 44; post-pandemic digitalisation 49
Barro cross-sectional endogenous growth model 67
BBNDL *see* broadband penetration for middle- and low-income countries (BBNDL)
behavioural intentions (BIs), of using e-Learning 107–120; environmental readiness 110; findings 113–115, **114**, **115**; future implications 119–120; KMO and Bartlett's test 115–116, **115**, **116**; limitations 119–120; measurements 112–113, **112**; methods and analytical frame 111–112; model reliability and fit measures 116–117, **116**, *117*; perceived ease of use 110; perceived self-efficacy 110; perceived usefulness 109–110; recommendations 118–119; standardised regression weights 117–118, **117**
Bensaid, B. 10
Big Blue Button 94, 195
Biggs, J. 2, 126, 134

Index 213

BIs *see* behavioural intentions (BIs), of using e-Learning
BL *see* blended learning (BL)
Blackboard 79, 93, 107, 127, 131, 193; Blackboard Connect 94, 195; Blackboard Learn 36
blended learning (BL) 10, 42, 78–79, 150, 154, 155, 157–170, 192, 206–207, 210; internal crisis communication on faculty members implementation of 157–170; during pandemic in GCC, implementation of 159–160
Bloom, B. S. 126, 134
Bolman, L. G. 78
bracketing 130
Brahimi, T. 10
broadband benefits, for development of countries 66–67
broadband penetration for middle- and low-income countries (BBNDL) 67
Brown, S. 43
bureaucracy: organisational structures of 63
business sustainability plans 96
Bystrov, I. 157

CAFU Model 49, 55, *55*
Calonge, D. S. 162
Campbell's Law 65
Canvas 127
Carbonell, K. B. 157
Carnegie Mellon University 60
"CIPP" evaluation model 138
ClassDojo 195
coercive isomorphism 65, 67
Cohen, J. 167
College of Shariah Science 200
comprehensive theory of adaptation 64
constructive alignment, theory of 134
continuous professional development 15
Coombs, W. T. 162
Cornell University 60
counterbalancing 65
Coursera 41
COVID-19 Education Response of the International Association of Universities 196
COVID-19 pandemic 1, 2, 7; and higher education *see* higher education; impact on Gulf education 90–93;

influence on e-Learning *see* e-Learning, COVID-19 influence on; learning experiences during 199–206, *199–206*; ramifications of 8–10
critical analysis of Gulf higher education 60–65; access to education, online classes and 61–62; quality of education, online classes and 62–64; validity of credentials, online classes and 64–65
critical thinking 15
culture shock 127, 128, 135
cybercrime 36

Deal, T. E. 78
decentralisation 63–64; horizontal 63; vertical 63
deep learning 126, 134
Delphi Protocol 11–17, 47, 101; emphathising 12–17, *13*; results, thematic analysis of 16–17, **16**
designing stage of design thinking model 17, **17**
design thinking (DT) model 101; defining stage 17, **17**; empathising stage 11–17, *13*, **16**; ideating stage 18–19, *18*; prototyping stage 19–22, *19–21*; stages of 11–20; testing stage 22–23
DingTalk 107
distance education: Oman 145–147, *145–147*; University of Buraimi 141–145, **142**
divisionalised form of bureaucracy 63
DT *see* design thinking (DT) model
Duponchel, L. 112
dynamic model of quality assessment, for online instruction 67–70

Education City, Doha 60, 71
effective online assessments tasks 131–133
EFQM *see* European Foundation for Quality Management (EFQM) excellence model
Einwiller, S. 161
e-Learning 8–10, 14, 17, 18, 27, 28, 108; behavioural intentions of using 107–120; COVID-19 influence on *see* e-Learning,

214 *Index*

COVID-19 influence on; tools, for higher education 31–32
e-Learning, COVID-19 influence on 30–31; challenges 32–33, 78; implications 34–35; opportunities 33–34, 78; recommendations 35–36
e-library services 9, 93, 196
El Said, G. R. 41
emergency contingency plans 96
Emergency Remote Education 9
Emergency Response Team 96
empathising stage of design thinking model 11–17, *13*, **16**
entrepreneurship 2, 62, 78, 98
environment readiness (ER) 108–111, 113, 118
e-portfolio 132
ER *see* environment readiness (ER)
European Foundation for Quality Management (EFQM) excellence model 45–46

face-to-face interaction 75, 79
face-to-face learning 8, 14, 15, 29, 41, 75, 98, 108, 126, 129, 196
faculty: challenges to using ICT during COVID-19 79–83, **80–83**; members implementation of blended learning, internal crisis communication on 157–170
feedback 11, 12, 20, 23, 42, 43, 45, 46, 48–51, 54–56, *55*, 67, 75, 94, 119, 131, 132, 135, 139, 141, 149, 150, 163
FGD *see* Focused Group Discussions (FGD)
Firefox 33
first-year business course, transforming online teaching of 124–135; appropriateness of task and timing 134; empirical research outcomes 124–125; learning shock 128–130; meaningful assessments 133; outcome 134; pandemic anxiety 126–127; pedagogical practice 125–126; takeaway 134–135; teaching shock 127–128; transformation process 130–133
First Year Higher Education (FYHE) 124, 125, 130, 132
five-layered Generalised Quality Assurance (GQA) model 42, 43, 46, 49

5-point Workplace Stress Scale™ 180
flexi-working 206–207
'flipped classroom' approach 131
Focused Group Discussions (FGD) 47, 57
focus group sessions 15
FOM Model 49, 52, *52*
4D Model 49, 56, *56*
4IR *see* fourth Industrial Revolution (4IR)
fourth Industrial Revolution (4IR) 77
FYHE *see* First Year Higher Education (FYHE)

Gandhi, A. 44
GCC *see* Gulf Cooperation Council (GCC)
Georgetown University 60
Ghavifekr, S. 76
Gillis, A. 195
GN University: e-Learning tools 32
Google 79, 111, 143, 180; Google Chrome 33; Google Classroom 9, 36; Google Hangouts Meet 107
GQA *see* five-layered Generalised Quality Assurance (GQA) model
Grade Point Average 93
grading systems 9, 14–15, 93
Griffiths, D. S. 128
Grunig, J. E. 165
Gulf Cooperation Council (GCC): countries, ICT-based perspective for 74–87; COVID-19 pandemic, impact of 194–197, **196**; higher education post COVID-19, potential reforms in 7–23; Ministries of Education 196

Hamdan Bin Mohammed Smart University: online teaching 93
Hans, S. 174
Hashim, S. 10
HE *see* higher education (HE)
HEIs *see* higher education institutions (HEIs)
Heriot-Watt University Dubai: Vision learning 93
higher education (HE): COVID-19 pandemic and 28–30, 60–72; directions in 101–103; future of 191–207; ICT-based 74–87; reforms 26–37, 209–211; *see also individual entries*

Index

higher education institutions (HEIs) 27, 28, 90, 92–93, 138, 158, 174, 191, 197–198, 206, 209–211; during COVID-19, proposition of 192–193; COVID-19 pandemic, impact of 36–37, 178; dynamic model of quality assessment 67–70; face-to-face lab facilities 35; future of 97–98; mitigation plans risk for 93–97; quality assurance 43; quality of education 64; self-sustainable higher education quality assurance system 41–58; staff, voices from 47–49; validity of credentials 65; virtual environment 32; *see also individual entries*

higher-order thinking skills taxonomy 134

high stakes 65–66

HMW (How Might We Solve the Problem) Model 11, 17, **17**

hybrid learning 8, 10–15, 30, 101, 207

ICT *see* information and communication technology (ICT)

ideating stage of design thinking model 18–19, *18*

Impact/Cost matrix 11

Impact/Effort model 18–19, *18*

India: post-pandemic digitalisation 49

information and communication technology (ICT) 10, 41, 44, 66, 74–87, 102–103, 150, 196, 204; challenges faced by faculty 79–83, **80–83**; challenges faced by students 83–86, **84–86**; definition of 75; on teaching and learning, impact of 77–79

Inoue, M. 45

institutional isomorphism 65, 67

instructor-led courses 30

Integrated Telecom Company, The 94, 195

interactive instrumentalism 64

internal crisis communication on faculty members implementation of blended learning 157–170; affective commitment 162–164; crisis perception 161, 163; demographic profile of respondents 164; hypotheses development 160–164; instrumentation 165; measurement 165; measurement model assessment 165–166, **166**; structural model assessment 166–168, **167**, **168**; technological support 162–164; theoretical framework 160–164, *160*; university administrative support 161–163

International Council for Open and Distance Education 203

Internet 31, 93

Internet World Stats 93

iPad intuitive 78

ISIL 33

Javed, S. 138

Jenga model 46

job-related stress 174–187; analytical frame 178–185; conceptual model 178–181, *178*; during COVID-19 pandemic 177; demographics of 181–185, **181–185**, *184*; Golden Rules of 186; impact on professional and personal life 177

Johansen, W. 158

Joshi, H. D. 110

KAUST *see* King Abdullah University of Science and Technology (KAUST)

Khalifa University: online teaching 93, 95

Khan, M. A. 78, 112

Kift, S. 130

Kim, J. N. 154

Kim, Y. 158, 162

King Abdullah University of Science and Technology (KAUST) 94, 95

Knowledge Village, Duba 60, 71

Korn, C. 161

Krull, L. M. 195

Kumar, S. 46

Kuwait 86; COVID-19 pandemic 89, 90, 92, **196**; faculties challenges to using ICT during COVID-19 **80–82**, 81; ICT-based higher education 76; Kuwait Foundation for the Advancement of Sciences 159; mitigation plans for HEIs 94; Risk Mitigation and Recovery Plan under COVID-19 (RMRP) 94; students challenges to using ICT during COVID-19 **84**

216 *Index*

Leader-Laggard Model 68–69, **69**
learning management systems (LMSs)
9, 19, 30, 43, 79, 93, 127, 149,
150, 162, 178, 193, 196
learning recovery programmes 206
learning shock 128–130
Lego Set model 46
Liguori, E. 108
Likert scale 12, 77
LinkedIn 41
LMSs *see* learning management systems
(LMSs)
lockdown 12, **16**, 41, 61, 62, 64, 70,
78, 79, 107, 108, 174, 191, 193,
194, 202
Lodgaard, E. 45
Lovell, D. 164
Luxton, A. 45

machine bureaucracy 63
Mahfoodh, H. 10
Major Emergency Management
Committee 96
makerspace 91
Malik, A. 79
Maruyama, T. 45
Massive Online Open Courses (MOOC)
41, 91
Materu, P. N. 43
MBRSLP 195
Meyer, J. P. 164
Microsoft Teams 94, 107, 111, 193,
194, 195
mimetic isomorphism 64
Mintzberg, H. 62–63
M-learning 79, 91
mobile telephony on economic growth,
impact of 67
Mohamad, B. 161, 162, 165
Mohamed, A. H. H. M. 107, 138
Mohammadi, H. 110
Mohmmed, A. O. 138, 139
MOOC *see* Massive Online Open
Courses (MOOC)
Moodle 193
Mseleku, Z. 108
Mustafa, M. M. 138

Namey, E. 28
National Health Commission of China
89
Nelson, K. 124
new normal 191–207
New York University (NYU) 60

NFCFFE Model 42, 49–58, *57*; CAFU
Model 55, *55*; FOM Model 52,
52; 4D Model 56, *56*; limitation
of 57; OTR Model 53–54, *53*;
PCPGDR Model 49–51, *51*; RII
Model 54, *54*
Northwestern University 60
nternet of Things-based learning
management systems 178
NYU *see* New York University (NYU)

Oberg, K. 135
Odhiambo, G. O. 43
Oman 86; *Akeed* 91; College of Shariah
Science 200; COVID-19
pandemic 89–91, **196**;
COVID-19 pandemic on higher
education, impact of 153–155;
distance education 145–147,
145–147; faculties challenges to
using ICT during COVID-19
80, **80–82**; German University
of Technology 194; Higher
Education Admission Centre
(HEAC) 199; higher education
institutions 193–194; ICT-based
higher education 76, 78; Ministry
of Higher Education 94, 193;
Ministry of Higher Education
Research and Innovation
(MOHERI) 198, 199; mitigation
plans for HEIs 94; National
Strategy for Education 148;
post-pandemic digitalisation
49; public and private HEIs
student's BI in using e-Learning
during COVID-19 107–120;
students challenges to using
ICT during COVID-19 **84**;
"Sultanate of Oman Preparedness
and Response to COVID-19
Pandemic" 138; Sultan Qaboos
University 94, 137, 199; *Talabat*
91; University of Buraimi
137–155; University of
Technology and Applied Sciences
200
Omanuna 138
online engagement, enhancement of
130–131
online learning *see* e-Learning
open-test exams 15
Organisational Diffusion Model 68,
69, **69**

Index 217

organisational isomorphism 64
Orr, D. 46
Osman, M. E. 137
OTR Model 49, 53–54, *53*

pandemic anxiety 126–127
pandemic challenges of higher education
60–72; broadband benefits, for
development of countries 66–67;
critical analysis 60–65; dynamic
model of quality assessment, for
online instruction 67–70; high
stakes 65–66
Parasuraman, A. 113
PCPGDR Model 49–51, *51*
PDCA cycle 45, 49, 50
Pellegrini, M. 197
PEOU *see* perceived ease of use (PEOU)
perceived ease of use (PEOU) 108, 110,
111, 113, 118
perceived self-efficacy (PSE) 108, 110,
111, 113, 118
perceived usefulness (PU) 108–111,
113, 118
personal connections to learning
130–131
Personal Life Interference with Work
(PLIW) 175, 177, 179, 180,
182–186, **182–184**
Plan-Implement-Evaluate-Act model 45
PLIW *see* Personal Life Interference with
Work (PLIW)
privacy 28, 36, 193, 196
professional bureaucracy 62–64
prototyping stage of design thinking
model 19–20, *19–21*
PSE *see* perceived self-efficacy (PSE)
PU *see* perceived usefulness (PU)

QA *see* quality assurance (QA)
Qatar 86; COVID-19 pandemic 89, 90,
92, **196**; faculties challenges to
using ICT during COVID-19
80, **80–82**; ICT-based higher
education 76; Ooredoo–
Ministry of Education–Higher
Education partnership 198;
Qatar Foundation for Education,
Science and Community 159;
Qatar University (QU) 92;
students challenges to using ICT
during COVID-19 **84**
QIA *see* quality improvement and
assurance (QIA)

quality assurance (QA) 98, 102,
141; bodies 15; policies 14;
programmes 74; self-sustainable
higher education 41–58
quality improvement and assurance
(QIA) 42–44, 49–58, 102;
NFCFFE Model for 42, 49–58,
57
quality of education 36, 60, 65, 72, 75,
86, 102, 103, 152, 171; online
classes and 62–64

Ramírez-Correa, P. E. 110
Ramsden's model of student learning
126
Rani, K. 44
Regional Diffusion Model 68
remote education 7–9, 13, 15, 17–19,
21, 23, 101, 196
'request-response' paradigm 193
RII Model 49, 54, *54*
risk management, by universities 89–99
risk transfer mechanisms 97–98
Robbins, S. P. 175
Rodriguez, M. B. 44
Roy, S. 43

Sabherwal, R. 109–110
Sarkar, S. S. 44
SARS 90
Saudi Arabia 86; 2030Vision 77; blended
learning 78–79, 159–160;
"Community COVID-19
Innovation Challenge" 95;
COVID-19 pandemic 89–92,
196; faculties challenges to
using ICT during COVID-19
80, **80–82**; higher education
77; ICT-based higher education
76–79; Ministry of Education
89; mitigation plans risk for
HEIs 93, 95; Saudi Research and
Innovation Network, The 94,
195; "Shaheen-II" 95; students
challenges to using ICT during
COVID-19 **84**; Supercomputer
Core Laboratory (KSL) 95;
Umm Al-Qura University 95
scholarship 197–198
self-paced courses 30
self-sustainable higher education
quality assurance system
41–58; CAFU Model 55, *55*;
European Foundation for Quality

218 *Index*

Management excellence model 45–46; five-layered Generalised Quality Assurance model 46; FOM Model 52, *52*; 4D Model 56, *56*; future higher education models 46; OTR Model 53–54, *53*; PCPGDR Model 49–51, *51*; PDCA cycle 45, 49; Plan-Implement-Evaluate-Act model 45; post-pandemic 43–44; pre-pandemic 42–43; RII Model 54, *54*; voices from HEI staff 47–49
Selye, H. 174
sense of belonging 130–131, 135
Shannaq, B. 139
Sharjah Private Education Authority 159
Sharma, R. K. 43, 46, 49, 55
Sharma, S. C. 43
Situational Crisis Communication Theory 160
Skype 107, 193
SMART framework 22, 23
Smart Linking 32
social isolation 92–93, 120, 193
Solinger, O. N. 164
Sporn, B. 62–64
stress 174–175; definition of 175; factors and symptoms of **176**; job-related 174–187
structural model assessment 166–168, **167**, **168**
students: challenges to using ICT during COVID-19 83–86, **84–86**; engagement 19, 20, 22, 32–34, 36, 113, 135, 151, 154, 197; retention 36; and teachers, interaction between 32, 34
Sukendro, S. 110
Sultan Qaboos University 94, 137, 199
summative assessments 132–133
sustainable development 10, 137
Sustainable Development Goals 10

TAER-Project 154–155
TAM *see* Technology Acceptance Model (TAM)
Tamagotchi model 46
Tang, C. 2
Taylor, J. A. 131, 132
teachers: and students, interaction between 32, 34; training 15, 126
TEACHINGENGLISH 62
teaching shock 127–128

teaching shock 130, 135
Technology Acceptance Model (TAM) 108–110, *111*, 113, 118, 209
Teo, T. 110
Tesar, M. 192
testing stage of design thinking model 22–23
Texas A&M University 60
Thakkar, S. R. 110
Trahar, S. 125
Transformer model 46
Transition Pedagogy 124
Turkey 108
Turnbull, D. 191

UAE *see* United Arab Emirates (UAE)
UDL *see* Universal Design for Teaching and Learning (UDL)
UGC 42
Ultra Collaborative 36
Umm Al-Qura University 94
UN *see* United Nations (UN)
UNCT *see* United Nations Country Team (UNCT)
UNESCO 92, 195, 196; Global Convention on the Recognition of Qualifications Concerning Higher Education 43
UNICEF 108
United Arab Emirates (UAE) 86; American University of Kuwait 94, 195; blended learning 159; COVID-19 pandemic 89–91, 194–195, **196**; faculties challenges to using ICT during COVID-19 **80–82**; ICT-based higher education 76; Ministry of Education (MOE) 91, 195; students challenges to using ICT during COVID-19 **84**; Telecommunications Regulatory Authority 195
United Arab Emirates University: Blackboard systems 93
United Nations (UN): Sustainable Development Goals 10
United Nations Country Team (UNCT) 94
Universal Design for Teaching and Learning (UDL) 7, 12; multiple means of action and expression 20–21, *21*; multiple means of engagement 21–22, *21*; multiple

means of representation 20, *20*; prototyping 19–20, *19*; testing 22–23

University City, Sharjah 60, 71

University of Buraimi 137–155; distance education 141–145, **142**; initiatives to support instructors' development in new conditions 147–153, *152, 153*; instructor support 150–151; methodological shortage 149; Qedex project 147, 148; research tool, reliability and consistency of 144, **144**; research tools 143–144, **144**; secondary data 142, *142, 143*; Staff Professional Development Committee 147; technical and technological shortages 149–150; unpreparedness/rejection to use new technologies 148–149, *148*

University of Edinburgh: e-Learning 31

University of Kuwait: Blackboard Collaborate 94

University of Sharjah: Blackboard systems 93

University of Technology and Applied Sciences 200

university ranking criteria 70–71

validity of credentials, online classes and 64–65

Vertical Influence Model 68, **69**

virtual education 35, 77, 94

virtual environment 32, 150

virtual learning 8, 35, 78, 79, 159, 196, *204*

virtual reality (VR) 34–35

VR *see* virtual reality (VR)

Waverman, L. 67

WebEx 79

WeChat Work for Chinese 107

Weick, K. E. 63–64

WFH *see* work from home (WFH)

WhatsApp 107, 111

Wi-Fi 36, 44, 114

Winkler, C. 108

WIPL *see* Work Interference with Personal Life (WIPL)

WLB *see* Work-Life Balance (WLB)

work from home (WFH) 91, 96

Work Interference with Personal Life (WIPL) 175, 177, 179, 180, 182–186, **182–184**

Work-Life Balance (WLB) 175–177, 179, 180, 183, 185–187

Work/Personal Life Enhancement (WPLE) 175, 177, 179, 180, 182–187, **182–184**

World Bank 202

World Bank Group: Development Economics Data Group 66; Global Information and Communication Technologies Department 66

World Bank report 2020 44

World Bank report 2022 44

World Health Organization 89, 126, 177, 192

WPLE *see* Work/Personal Life Enhancement (WPLE)

Yilmaz, R. 110

YouTube: e-Learning 33

Zayed University: Adobe Connect 93

Zimmerman, J. 8

Zoom 9, 36, 79, 107, 193, 195